Prehistory at Sumburgh, Shetland

Excavations at Sumburgh Airport 1967–74

Jane Downes and Raymond Lamb

with contributions by
Christopher Barrowman, Ann Clarke, Bill Finlayson,
(the late) Tom Henderson, Sian Rees, Paul Sharman
and Clare Yarrington

Oxbow Books
2000

Published by
Oxbow Books, Park End Place, Oxford OX1 1HN

© Oxbow Books and the individual authors 2000

ISBN 1 84217 003 1

This book is available direct from
Oxbow Books, Park End Place, Oxford OX1 1HN
(Phone: 01865–241249; Fax: 01865–794449)

and

The David Brown Book Company
PO Box 511, Oakville, CT 06779, USA
(Phone: 860–945–9329; Fax: 860–945–9468)

and

via our website
www.oxbowbooks.com

*This volume has been published with the aid of a grant
from Historic Scotland*

Printed in Great Britain at
Short Run Press
Exeter

CONTENTS

ACKNOWLEDGEMENTS vi
SYNOPSIS vii
LIST OF CONTRIBUTORS viii

1 HISTORY OF EXCAVATIONS AND SITE CONTEXT 1
THE REPORT BY J. DOWNES 1
HISTORY OF THE EXCAVATIONS BY T. HENDERSON AND R. LAMB 2
EXCAVATION METHODOLOGY BY J. DOWNES, T. HENDERSON AND R. LAMB 2
    Recording and archive 4
SITE LOCATION AND TOPOGRAPHY BY J. DOWNES AND R. LAMB 5
GEOLOGY AND CONDITIONS OF PRESERVATION BY R. LAMB 7

2 EXCAVATIONS BY J. DOWNES AND R. LAMB 8
NORTH HOUSE 8
    Features underlying the North House: later Neolithic and earlier Bronze Age 8
    North House: later Bronze Age 11
    North House: early Iron Age 16
CORRIDOR BETWEEN THE NORTH AND SOUTH HOUSES 22
SOUTH HOUSE 24
    Features antedating the South House: later Neolithic and earlier Bronze Age 24
    South House: later Bronze Age 25
    South House: early Iron Age 30
POST-ABANDONMENT ACTIVITY 32
SUMMARY ACCOUNT OF THE SEQUENCE OF ACTIVITIES BY J. DOWNES 34

3 SITE SEQUENCE AND CHRONOLOGY BY J. DOWNES 35
THE POTTERY AS A CHRONOLOGICAL INDICATOR 35
    Aims of the analysis 37
    Methods of analysis by J. Downes and C. Yarrington 37
    Fabric groups by C. Yarrington 38
    Vessel forms by J. Downes 39
    Bases by C. Yarrington 52

Decorative techniques by J. Downes and C. Yarrington 52
THE CERAMIC SEQUENCE BY J. DOWNES 60
   Bronze Age phases 61
   Early Iron Age phases 63
   Post-abandonment phase and ploughing 64
   Summary of the ceramic sequence 64
STEATITE AND OTHER FINE STONE OBJECTS AS CHRONOLOGICAL INDICATORS
BY P. SHARMAN 65
COARSE STONE TOOLS AS CHRONOLOGICAL INDICATORS BY A. CLARKE 69
   Methods of analysis 70
   Summary of contexts and phasing 70
   Inter-site comparison 73
SUMMARY OF THE ARTEFACTS AS CHRONOLOGICAL INDICATORS BY J. DOWNES 75

4 THE MANUFACTURE, USE AND DEPOSITION OF ARTEFACTS
BY J. DOWNES 77
THE POTTERY 77
   Sources of materials used; method and location of manufacture by C. Yarrington 77
   Range and use of pottery vessels by J. Downes 78
   Context of the pottery vessels 79
STEATITE AND OTHER FINE STONE OBJECTS BY P. SHARMAN 82
   Sources of steatite and other fine stone 82
   Method and location of manufacture 84
   The range and use of steatite and other fine stone artefacts 85
   Context of the steatite and other fine-stone artefacts 87
COARSE STONE ASSEMBLAGE 87
   Sources of coarse stone by R. Lamb 87
   Range and use of coarse-stone artefacts and the method and location of
      manufacture by A. Clarke, with S. Rees on the ard points 88
   Context of the coarse-stone artefacts 101
CHIPPED STONE ASSEMBLAGE BY B. FINLAYSON 104
   Sources of the materials used 104
   Method and location of manufacture 105
   Context of the chipped stone artefacts 109
PUMICE 109
   Source of the material by C. Barrowman 109
   Use of pumice by C. Barrowman 109
   Context of pumice artefacts by J. Downes 111
ORIGINS OF MATERIALS AND ARTEFACTS BY J. DOWNES 112
ARTEFACT CONTEXT AND DISTRIBUTION BY J. DOWNES 112

5 ARCHITECTURE, SPATIAL ORGANISATION AND MATERIAL CULTURE
BY J. DOWNES 117
INTRODUCTION 117
THE USE OF SPACE IN THE SUMBURGH AIRPORT HOUSES 117

THE SHETLAND HOUSE: TERMINOLOGY AND CHRONOLOGY	119
CHARACTERISTICS OF THE SHETLAND HOUSE	123
Recesses	123
Heel shaped facades	124
Building with midden	125
Ard points and mattocks	126
SPATIAL ORGANISATION AND ORIENTATION	126
BIBLIOGRAPHY	129

ACKNOWLEDGEMENTS

Raymond Lamb and Jane Downes extend thanks to Olwyn Owen of Historic Scotland for her help in bringing the report to completion, to Historic Scotland for providing a grant for publication, and to Historic Scotland and Shetland Amenity Trust for financing the post-excavation analysis. We are grateful to the contributors to this report who remained very patient, in some cases for a long time.

Jane Downes would like to thank Tommy Watt and Ian Tate of Shetland Museums Service for their kind help during post-excavation work. Thanks are due to John Barrett for guidance with the pottery vessel series and to Olivia Lelong for assistance with the context database andpottery sequence. Danny Hind provided invaluable assistance with the report preparation and prepared tables 1, 5 and 6. John Barrett, Colin Richards and Jo Brück provided helpful comments on text. Thanks also go to Jerry O'Sullivan for useful editorial comments, and to Michael Lane for excellent copy editing. Anna Badcock gave unfailing support during the near-final touches. Olwyn Owen and Simon Buteux kindly provided unpublished information on Kebister, Shetland and Skaill, Orkney respectively.

Paul Sharman would like to thank Dr Alison Sheridan of the Archaeology Department in the National Museum of Scotland for the generous amount of help she gave in identifying the battle-axe and providing comments, parallels, dates and further references about such items, Dr Alex Livingston of the Geology Department in the Royal Museum of Scotland for his readiness to identify the type of stone used for the non-steatitic artefacts and the staff of the National Museums of Scotland library in Queen Street for their help.

Clare Yarrington acknowledges the late Mr Tom Henderson, who had previously studied the pre-1974 pottery and kindly allowed her to use his information, and Mr A. Williamson of Shetland Museum, who supplied photographs of relevant charts and pots.

Illustrations were drawn for publication by Jill Sievewright (Figs 3, 4, 5, 6, 7, 11, 13, 29, 36, 37, 38, and 39), Anna Badcock (Fig 12), Clare Yarrington (Figs 15–27), Jo Mincher (Figs 30 and 40), Sian Rees (Fig 31) and Raymond Lamb (Figs 32–35).

SYNOPSIS

Development at Sumburgh Airport revealed later prehistoric remains which proved to comprise two stone-built houses linked by a passage. The stone-built houses date to the later Bronze Age and were rebuilt in the early Iron Age.

The northernmost house of the two was built upon the remains of an early Bronze Age timber structure, which in turn was built on ground that had been previously cultivated. During the later Bronze Age the north house comprised an inner, recessed compartment and an outer, circular structure with narrow stone-built walls. Toward the centre of the outer area was a tank. The south house was added on to the north house and comprised a stone-built wall surrounding a large hearth.

The form of both these houses was substantially modified simultaneously at the beginning of the Iron Age. Repaving covered over the large hearth in the south house, and hearths were situated in the newly constructed cubicles of the north house.

Excavation revealed complex stratification, which, combined with redeposition of artefacts, makes interpretation of the site sequence and formation processes problematic. Post-excavation analysis of the contexts and finds, however, shows the two stone-built houses to have functioned as a single unit of domestic space within which the location of activities changed through time.

Inter-site comparison of house forms show the two-house unit to be a feature of the later Bronze Age in Shetland, in contrast to the earlier Bronze Age oval house, and the early Iron Age circular house divided by radial piers. Later prehistoric settlement can also be characterised by longevity of occupation on a single site, where, as at Sumburgh Airport, these three house forms can be seen to have suceeded one another.

The site was excavated by the Shetland Archaeological and Natural History Society from 1967–71, and by Raymond Lamb for Historic Scotland's predecessor department in 1974.

LIST OF CONTRIBUTORS

Chris Barrowman
Dept of Archaeoloy
Gregory Building
University of Glasgow
Glasgow G12 8QQ

Ann Clarke
Rockville Lodge
By Kingston
North Berwick
East Lothian

Jane Downes
Orkney College
University of the Highlands
and Islands Project
Kirkwall
Orkney KW15 1LX

Bill Finlayson
CFA
Old High School
12 Infirmary Street
Edinburgh EH1 1LT

Raymond Lamb
Highland College
University of the Highlands
and Islands Project
Ormalie Road
Thurso
Caithness KW14 7EE

Sian Rees
CADW
Crown Building
Cathays Park
Cardiff CF1 3NQ

Paul Sharman
3 Cornwallis Terrace
Edinburgh EH3 6NG

Clare Yarrington
Cloak House
Lumphanan
Aberdeenshire AB31 4PS

1. HISTORY OF EXCAVATIONS AND SITE CONTEXT

The Report by J. Downes

The purpose of this report is to synthesise the stratigraphic information and artefact analysis from the two excavations and various post-excavation stages in such a way as to present a readable and continuous site history. The structure of the report does reflect the manner in which post-excavation analysis took place, and the order in which the interpretation of the site was undertaken. The report contains an interpretative account of the activities that took place in and around the houses and the relationship between these activities and the architectural form and development of the houses. Throughout we endeavour to maintain a level of detail which both interests us, and which represents the material conditions in which people once dwelt.

The site stratigraphy is described in the second section of the report, firstly in terms of the North House and secondly the South House. The relationship between the two houses and the period to be assigned to the structures and phases were unknown until the contexts were closely scrutinised against the artefact assemblages. In the third section of the report the type and form of the artefacts are described. Parallels to other assemblages are identified, and through this the artefact sequence is developed, which is set against the site stratigraphy. Through this analysis it was possible to ascertain the chronological relationship of the structural phases.

The history of human occupation is set within the structural development of the building in the fourth section of the report. In this section the analysis of the material culture is centred around the nature and organisation of activities inside and immediately outside the houses, and the changes that occur in the use of space. All categories of artefacts are considered, firstly in terms of their manufacture, then in their use, and lastly in the context of their deposition.

The fifth and final section of the report contains a description of the way the houses were occupied and places this occupation and the architecture in the context of other Shetland houses. The architecture and material culture is also considered with relation to theoretical frameworks concerned with the use of space and orientation of houses.

History of the Excavations by T. Henderson and R. Lamb

During the 1930s Sumburgh Airport was developed as the main airfield for Lerwick, and regular commercial flights were run by Highland Airways Ltd. In 1940 substantial improvements were made by the RAF, during which the blown sand was removed from the site. After the war the airport was further developed, during which time the site described by this report lay concealed within a grassy knoll between the flying control tower and one of the runways. This was perceived as a hazard to flying safety as it was large enough to obscure view from the tower of individuals crossing the runway. It had been the intention of the Air Field to remove this obstruction, and when the prolonged snowfall during the winter of 1966/67 depleted stocks of sand, the Roads Department was permitted to remove sand from the mound.

Work commenced on the eastern end of the mound, and the cement floor of the wartime buildings was used as the level at which machining would proceed. The machine moved sterile sand for some way into the mound, when a firmly fixed stone upright together with a layer of red peat ash and a dark layer containing pottery made the excavators realise that prehistoric structures were being damaged. It was agreed with the Royal Commission for Ancient and Historic Monuments and with the then Ministry of Public Buildings and Works that sand removal would not continue until the site had been investigated by the newly formed Shetland Archaeological and Natural History Society (hereafter referred to as SANHS).

Archaeological investigation commenced at the site in July 1967 and continued to take place each summer until 1970. During these four seasons the interior of two interconnected later prehistoric houses was excavated. During the excavations a significant assemblage of pottery and a substantial amount of stone tools were recovered. The pottery was later classified by the late Tom Henderson, then curator of Shetland Museum, who also directed excavations.

The use of the airport increased dramatically due to the North Sea exploitation, with the result that it was necessary to lengthen the east-west runway. The levelling of the ground on either side of the runway for a safety margin involved the total removal of the archaeological remains. Historic Scotland's predecessor department funded a rescue excavation before this development, which took place in 1974 under the direction of Raymond Lamb.

Excavation Methodology by J. Downes, T. Henderson and R. Lamb

The area where the stone structures were located was cleared of sterile sand by machine during 1967, leaving a smooth and fairly level surface just at the top level of stones across which levels were taken (Fig 1). The site was surveyed and located on a map of the area, and a metre grid was established, which was adhered to during the course of the SANHS excavations. The excavations commenced in 1967 with the opening of four pits, each 2 m² located between the two houses (on the 55 and 58 N lines), followed by the excavation of further small areas to the north,

Figure 1: The start of the SANHS excavations (Copyright Shetland Museum).

allowing the east-west passage between the houses and part of the northern structure (North House) to be investigated. These squares were extended until the passage running east-west between the houses was exposed. The excavated area was extended further still, exposing the interior of the North House, excepting the south-west cubicle (which was not discovered until the 1974 excavations) and the northern cubicle. Material was removed down to the latest phase of paved floor of the structure and passage way, although this was not recorded stratigraphically (see Recording below).

During 1968 the majority of the interior of the southern building (South House) was cleared of debris, and during 1969 excavations of the extension of the southern part of the building took place. Unlike the excavation of the North House, the later phase paving in the South House was removed apart from a sample section of the secondary paving left standing in the west of the building close to the hearth. It would appear that very little excavation was carried out in 1970; there are no records of any finds from this year, and one from 1971.

The investigations carried out by the SANHS concerned only the internal parts of the buildings. They did not involve the removal of the walls or the investigation of areas outside the buildings.

Figure 2: 1974 excavation, looking down the length of the South House to the North House (R. Lamb).

In 1974 the area was extended to take in the whole of both houses and some of the surrounding area (Fig 2). As excavation proceeded, the stone structures were systematically demolished to reveal earlier phases of their construction. The enormous thickness of the house walls proved to have grown through successive modifications; it was necessary to dismantle the masonry features in the reverse order of their building, while maintaining their relationship to the surrounding deposits which were excavated according to the normal principles of stratigraphy.

In the interior of the buildings the later phase of flooring in the North House was removed revealing an earlier phase of paving, and the south-west cubicle that had not been discovered in the previous investigations was excavated. The interior of the South House was cleaned, the portion of later paving that had been left was excavated, as were the layers within the hearth.

Recording and archive

Site records for the SANHS excavations comprise intermittent site diaries from 1967 and 1968 and a finds list. Although no contextual record was made, some contextual information was attached to artefact information within the finds list.

The quality of this information varied from one year to another – there was no site diary for 1969 or 1970 and the contextual information within the finds list was more limited for these years. During the 1974 excavations the site was subdivided into areas according to the shape of the structures, and layers within these areas described and given context numbers.

In order to reconcile the differences in excavation techniques and variation in standards of recording between the SANHS excavations and those of Raymond Lamb in 1974, a context database has been produced. This involved the extraction of contextual information from the SANHS finds list and the creation of context records from this information. These records were then set alongside the 1974 contexts to assess whether there were any correlations. The contexts thus established were given a running sequence of numbers, which was then used by the finds specialists during the final phases of post-excavation analysis.

It should be noted that although a geophysical survey was carried out in advance of the 1974 excavation by the Department of Environment Ancient Monument Laboratory, the results of this survey were mislaid before Raymond Lamb was able to analyse them. It should also be noted that all black-and-white photographic negatives from the 1974 excavation were lost in circumstances beyond the director's control.

The excavations at Sumburgh Airport resulted in the recovery of an exceptional quantity of artefacts. Concordances of artefacts by context and phase are summarised within this report, but catalogues remain in the archive which is held by Shetland Museums Service.

Site Location and Topography by J. Downes and R. Lamb

The site at Sumburgh Airport, Dunrossness, were situated at NGR HU 3921 1078, at a height of 4 m OD on the isthmus of Sumburgh, between West Voe and the Pool of Virkie (Fig 3). Sumburgh Head constitutes the southernmost point of Shetland. Shetland forms a land barrier extending nearly sixty nautical miles from north to south, and the rush of tides around the sheer cliff promontory of Sumburgh Head creates streams of great complexity and, at times, of exceptional violence. The Norse named the area Dunrossness or Dynrostarnes, the Ness of the Roaring Tide Race. West Voe and the Pool of Virkie (now filled with sand) were, however, two of several sheltered anchorages around this tip.

In historical times settlement in Shetland has been confined to the lower land, mainly on the coastal fringes and at the heads of voes. Most of Shetland, in contrast with Orkney, is hill country, largely peat covered, with very steep slopes up from the fjord-like voes. The wealth of prehistoric remains in the vicinity of the Sumburgh Airport houses is evidence of the attractiveness of the area as a place to settle; although subject to sandblows throughout prehistoric and historic times, the parish of Dunrossness was, until the 18th century, very fertile and cultivable.

Earlier Neolithic activity at Sumburgh Airport was ascribed after the discovery, also through development of the airfield, of a multiple burial (Hedges and Parry

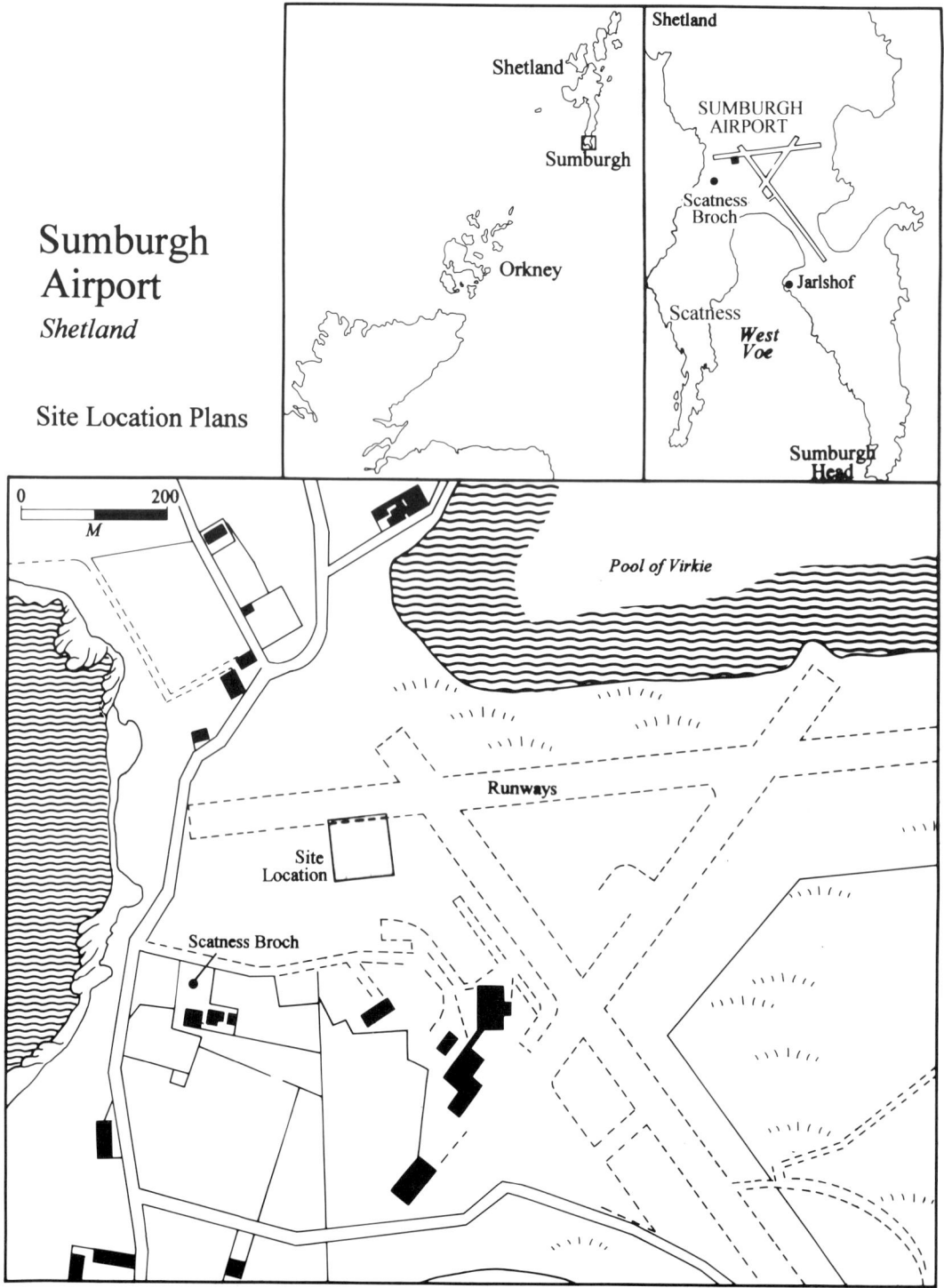

Figure 3: Sumburgh Airport, Shetland: site location plans.

1980). The multiperiod site of Jarlshof lies on the bay of the West Voe, 1.3 km to the south-west of Sumburgh Airport. Some of the occupation in this complex is contemporary with that at Sumburgh Airport. There were also two promontory forts on Scatness and another on Sumburgh Head, and three brochs – one at Jarlshof, one on the north-east shore of the Pool of Virkie, and a third, Scatness (Fig 3), which lies only 250 m to the south-west of the houses at Sumburgh Airport. This broch was discovered during the building of an airport access road early in 1975, and a programme of several years of excavation by Shetland Amenity Trust and the University of Bradford commenced in 1995 (Nicholson and Dockrill 1998).

Geology and Conditions of Preservation by R. Lamb

The isthmus of Sumburgh consists of Old Red Sandstone beds overlying a core of metamorphosed rocks. It is only on this southernmost tip and the western part of mainland Shetland that Old Red Sandstone beds are present; the rest of the island consists of metamorphosed rocks with igneous intrusions.

The study of the site within its surrounding landscape was undertaken by Dr S. Limbrey, who proposed the existence of a two-metre raised beach composed of the natural marine sand on which the settlement is founded. This raised beach must date from a post-glacial period, and on it, before the arrival of settlers, an immature soil had developed. It was this soil which was cultivated with the ard, such cultivation being the earliest human activity detected by the excavation. Sandblows occurring during the occupation of the houses at Sumburgh Airport are detailed below. The site was essentially preserved by post-Medieval sandblow.

The instability of such landscapes was demonstrated during the 17th century when historical sources make reference to the prosperity of the area. However, by the time of the visit of George Low in 1774 the area was completely devastated by a cover of deep, shifting sand, resulting in the Sumburgh Airport houses being covered with (and protected by) two to three metres of blown sand.

The reasons for this catastrophic sandblow are unclear, as the geomorphological history of the coast has not been studied in detail. It may be that natural processes were the cause, perhaps linked to a change in the tidal pattern. It is likely, however, that thousands of years of human activity played a part in shaping the beach patterns. Overgrazing of grass-stabilised dunes is the most likely progenitor of the sandblow episodes visible in the prehistoric stratigraphic record. The introduction of the rabbit may have done much to aggravate the 17th-century situation, by preventing the regrowth of turf on denuded areas. The most difficult question to answer is that regarding the source of the vast amounts of sand that were blown inland. No information exists about the shape of this coast before the 17th century, and it is possible that there were large stabilised dunes along the coastal edge, similar to those still existing in the Outer Hebrides and at Tres Ness in Sanday, Orkney. The history of the area within which Sumburgh Airport is situated, and the mobility and changeability of such an environment must be borne in mind when considering the topography and surrounding landscape of the site.

2. EXCAVATIONS

J. Downes and R. Lamb

This section comprises a descriptive and interpretative account of the contexts beginning with the earliest deposits. The North and South Houses are described separately. During the post-excavation analysis a site phasing was devised and the stratigraphic and artefact analysis set against this (Table 1). Through this analysis it was possible to assign periods to the structural elements, and this process is detailed in section 3, where the history of the settlement and site sequence are described and the contemporaneity of the two buildings is assessed.

North House

Features underlying the North House: later Neolithic and earlier Bronze Age
Ard marks
Ard marks were the earliest traces of activity on the site of the North House. These cut the natural marine sand and appear to have covered almost the whole of the excavated area, but had been almost completely removed under the floor of the house through disturbance accompanying its construction (Fig 4). Covering the ard marks was a thin layer of contaminated brown soil.

Postholes and stakeholes
Beneath the stone-built North House a great many dark patches were observed, which on excavation proved to be holes and slots of various shapes (Fig 4). These features cut through the ard marks and in turn were cut by drains (Fig 4, see discussion below), which underlay and were associated with the stone building. Many of these features, from their shape and filling, had the appearance of postholes. Others were the holes in which the upright slabs from the upper levels were set, yet some of these appeared on excavation to be enlargements of older holes which may have held timbers. Some large shapeless holes near the drain running north-north-east proved to be shallow depressions containing groups of small stakeholes. In the north-west corner of the excavation a series of parallel slots occurred, running

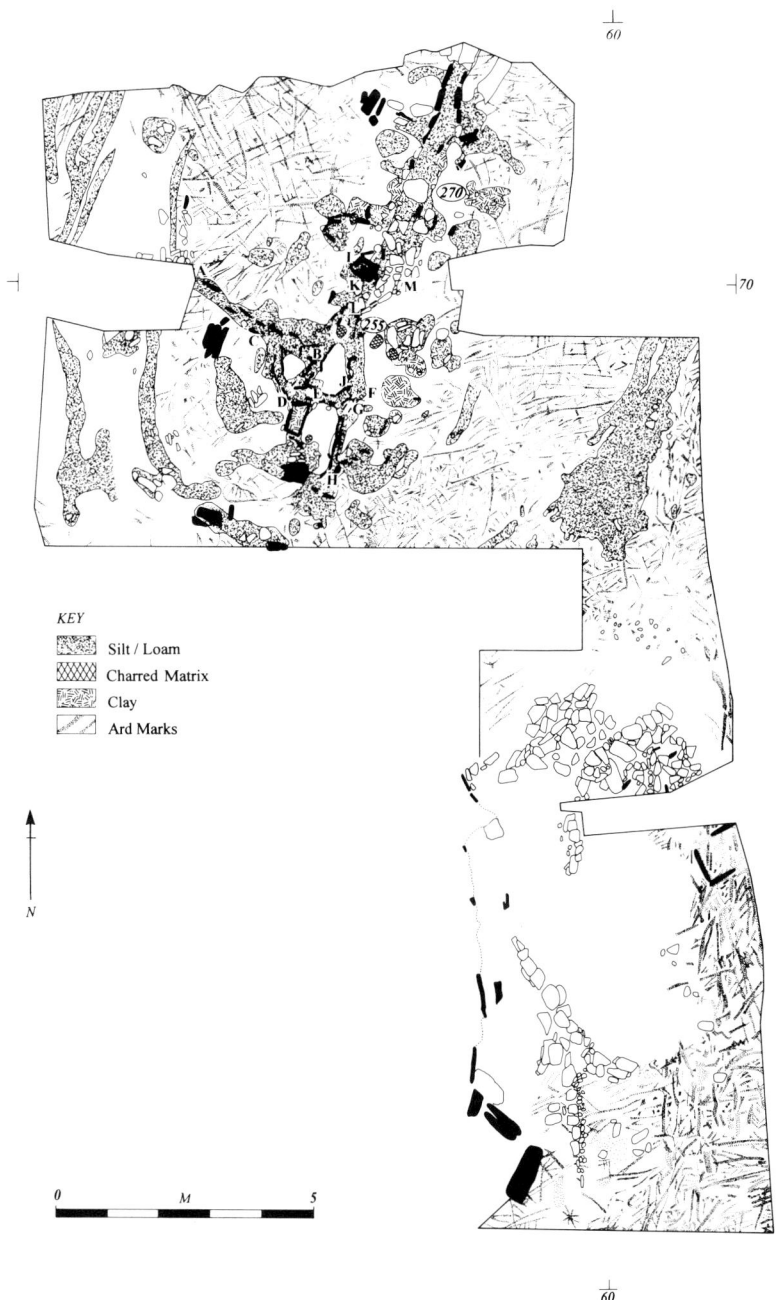

Figure 4: Site plan: late Neolithic and early Bronze Age (Phases 1 and 2), also showing later Bronze Age drains (Phase 4).

approximately south-west to north-east; one of these had a groove in the bottom, as if to contain a light barrier such as stakes or wickerwork.

It is evident that the surviving depth of the postholes represented only the bottom of these features, and that no associated floor levels survived. These must have lain higher up (probably on the former ploughsoil) and were removed along with most of this ploughsoil when the drain system and paved floor of the first phase of the stone building were laid down. No stratigraphic relationship existed among the postholes, which may represent several different timber structures lasting an unknown length of time. It is possible that the surviving postholes were only the deepest ones belonging to structures, most of whose posts were set wholly in the ploughsoil. These factors should discourage us from attempting to reconstruct these early timber structures, although those with the eye of faith may see a sub-oval building among the postholes depicted in Figure 4.

On analysis, the organic material from some of the postholes proved to comprise assorted debris, including pine charcoal, twigs of ericaceous plants, and pieces of charred heather rope. This is the sort of debris which would have been lying around on a living area, and it is suggested that the posts were pulled out of their holes while the occupation of the area continued, and that this rubbish was then swept into the holes. Figure 4 shows the postholes and stakeholes as they appeared after excavation of all the features. It therefore represents a period of timber building(s) constructed after the use of the area as a ploughed field and before that of the stone house with its drain system.

Radiocarbon dates

The charred material from two of these features (255 and 270, Fig 4), was dated by radiocarbon methods. Feature 255 comprised a shallow pit 0.08 m deep which contained much carbonised wood and lumps of hardened clay. The wood lay for the most part around the sides and base of the feature. The radiocarbon date was obtained from a piece of carbonised rope. The calibrated age range is 2290–1510 BC to two sigma (Sample 960, GU1015–3535±153 bp). Feature 270 was an irregularly shaped feature measuring 0.55 m north-south and 0.79 m east-west, much of the base of which was covered by a large stone, underneath which lay a lump of charred wood, the material from which the radiocarbon date was obtained. Stones around the rim of this feature were reddened and fire cracked, and the fill was red peat ash. The feature possibly represents the remains of a hearth or cooking pit. The radiocarbon date obtained from this feature calibrates to 2140–1790 BC to two sigma (Sample 1069, GU1006–3629±53 bp).

Overlap therefore exists between these two dates. The calibrated median dates for 255 lie between 1880–1829 BC, while the middle range date for 270 is 1972 BC. It appears that some, if not all, of the occupation activity represented by the negative features dates to the early Bronze Age. A ploughsoil then developed over these occupation remains.

North House: later Bronze Age

The drains

Within the North House, beneath the paving slabs floor (Fig 4), the cover-slabs of the drain running north-north-east and the stonework forming the inner wall-faces of the earliest structural phase were uncovered. As already noted, most of the ploughsoil had been removed and the paving stones had been laid on an introduced foundation of soft, vivid lemon-yellow sand, which formed a saucer-shaped area corresponding to the paving above, 0.10 m deep at the centre and thinning towards the edges. The tops of several drains were seen protruding through this sand, the paving slabs above having been their cover. Below the slabs was a thin layer of earth in which was set a complex pattern of slab-formed drains, which were cut into the natural sand beneath (Fig 4).

As a piece of hydraulic engineering, the function of the drain system is not immediately obvious. Drains came into or left the central area under the paved floor, at three points on its circumference. In the middle of the area was a complicated intersection. Some of the drains had perceptible inclinations, but in others the direction of flow could not be determined. A very neat box or tank, made of thin slabs sealed with clay, adjoined one of the drains, and appeared to form part of the system. This tank was central to the house and lay south of centre of the paved floor (Fig 5).

The drains appeared originally to have been slab-formed throughout; the slabs were set at an angle giving a V-shaped section; very occasionally the section was a U-shaped section. There was no evidence of any attempt to seal the bottoms of the drains either with slabs or with clay, although they were cut into porous sand. Some of the drains were blocked here and there with transverse slabs.

Drain AB (Fig 4), averaging 0.15 m deep, ran from the end of the section baulk to the middle of the floor; its flow was toward the centre of the house, as it followed a slope in the natural sand surface. Drain CD branched off it and had a fall south-eastwards toward the slab tank. The tank, 0.84 m x 0.34 m x 0.42 m deep, was made of closely fitted stones well sealed with clay. When found the tank was entirely filled with clay as part of the reflooring of the house in a later phase, when the feature fell into disuse. The tank was set in a hole just big enough for it, except that it had to be dug 0.17 m too long because the base slab exceeded the dimension of the tank by this amount. The sides were four slabs 0.03–0.04 m thick; two small square stones were placed high up beside the north-east and south-west corners. The south-eastward flow in CD met a westward flow in EF, which began as a shallow groove at F, and became a 0.15 m deep U-sectioned, slab-sided drain toward the west.

GH was a very narrow drain, 0.19 m deep, running north from the hole in which the later doorway threshold was set to the slab forming the side of drain EF; it is uncertain whether there was any communication with EF, which at this that was much shallower. The direction of flow was not apparent. Further northward ran JK, a very broken drain, for the most part a U-shaped groove 0.10 m deep. At its north end it ran alongside BK, or was amalgamated to it, which in its southern part had

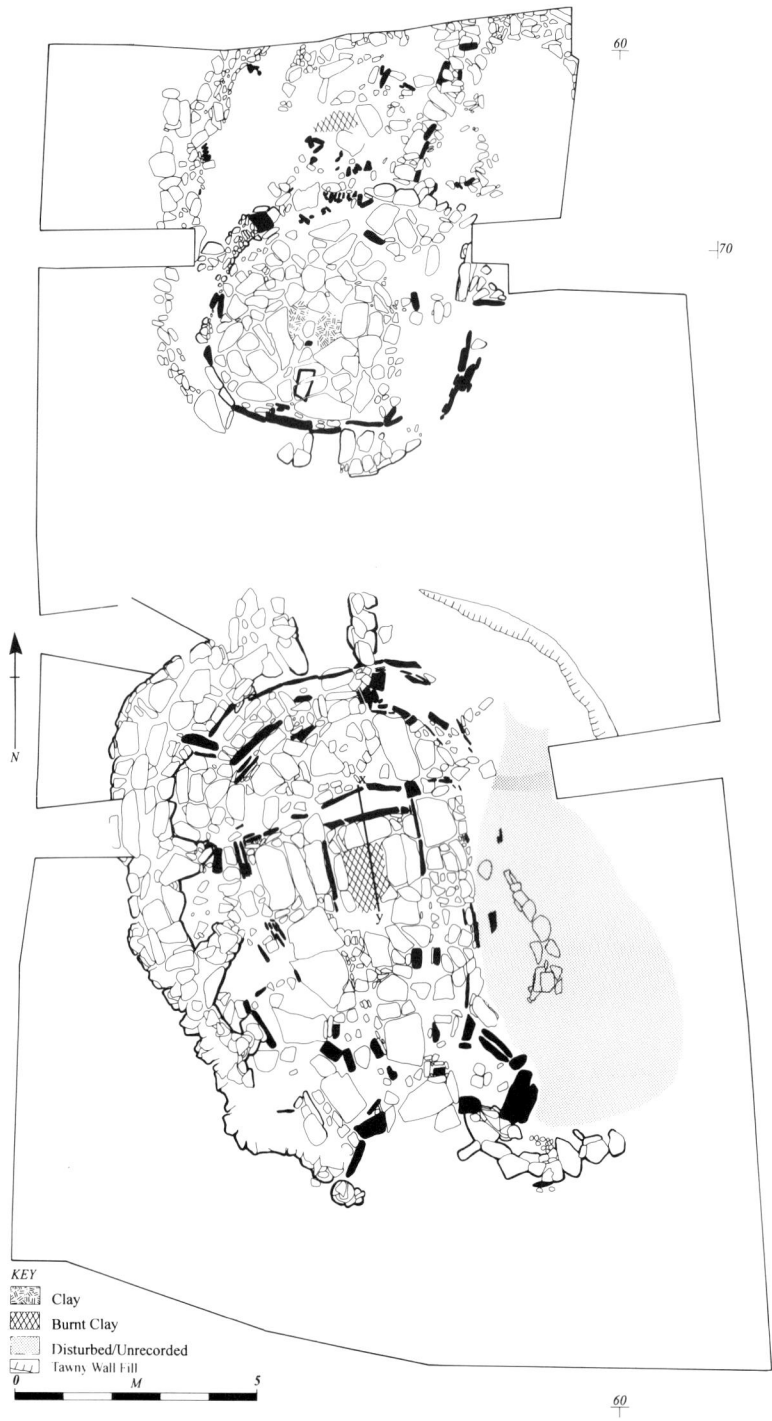

Figure 5: Site plan: later Bronze Age (Phases 4–7).

a slab-lined, V-shape section and further north was a U-shaped groove 0.10 m deep. Both these drains were blocked at K by the deep-set upright slab and its packing stones, which projected well above the paving level and was interpreted as part of the circuit of the wall-face of the later Bronze Age house. The branch LM was a much more substantial feature, increasing north-eastward to a maximum depth of 0.28 m. Its course around the blocking stones at K was not certain, but it appeared to have linked to the main drain flowing north-north-east which ran beneath a spread of red clay. It may have been a by-pass drain to get around the blockage at K, although it is far from certain that the drain system was in use at the time that stone was inserted. The drain running north-north-east was V-sectioned and slab-lined, although many of the lining stones had slumped out of position; its maximum depth was 0.28 m. In the central area, BD was a small and enigmatic channel, blocked by slabs at both ends, with a maximum depth of 0.11 m; perhaps it was intended to lead water from CD and EF into BK and thence to the main drain running north-north-east away from the settlement.

The interior
The well-set circular paved floor overlying the drains was set close against the inner wall-face. Northwards, the paving gave way to hard, burnt red clay which rested for the most part directly upon the undisturbed marine sand subsoil. In places under the red clay, and on the subsoil where there was no clay, there was a thin layer of dirty grey-brown sandy soil. Eastwards also there was yellow clay merging into red, which in the south east sector sloped sharply upwards.

There was an amorphous, vaguely rectangular spread of the clay north-north-east of the circular paved floor (Fig 5). The clay was uniformly burnt, and the occasional flat stones set flush with its surface were reddened and shattered by fire. It is suggested that this clay represents the truncated remains of the burnt floor surface of an inner chamber to which access was gained from the north of the circular paved floor. The large, square, upright pillar which is situated in the north west part of the wall (Figs 5 and 12, ba) may be the remains of the entrance to this chamber. The inner chamber appears to have gone out of use during the later Bronze Age phases.

Near the east side of the north-east clay area, a drain ran from under the central paved floor north-north-east to disappear into the north side of the trench (Figs 4 and 5). This drain, which was cut through the red clay into the natural sand, was covered by slabs set flush with, or slightly above, the clay surface. On the cover slabs, but separated from them by 0.01 m of earth, was a small, complete trough quern.

The paving of the house was overlain by a thick covering of yellow clay (Fig 6), which formed a floor surface inside the house. This was a secondary floor surface to the paved floor, and it was the laying of this clay which filled the tank in (see above). It is possible that this secondary floor coincided with the modification of the building when the wall was extended eastwards (see below).

Covering the clay and paved floor surfaces associated with the later Bronze Age phases of occupation within the North House was a layer of rubble and earth

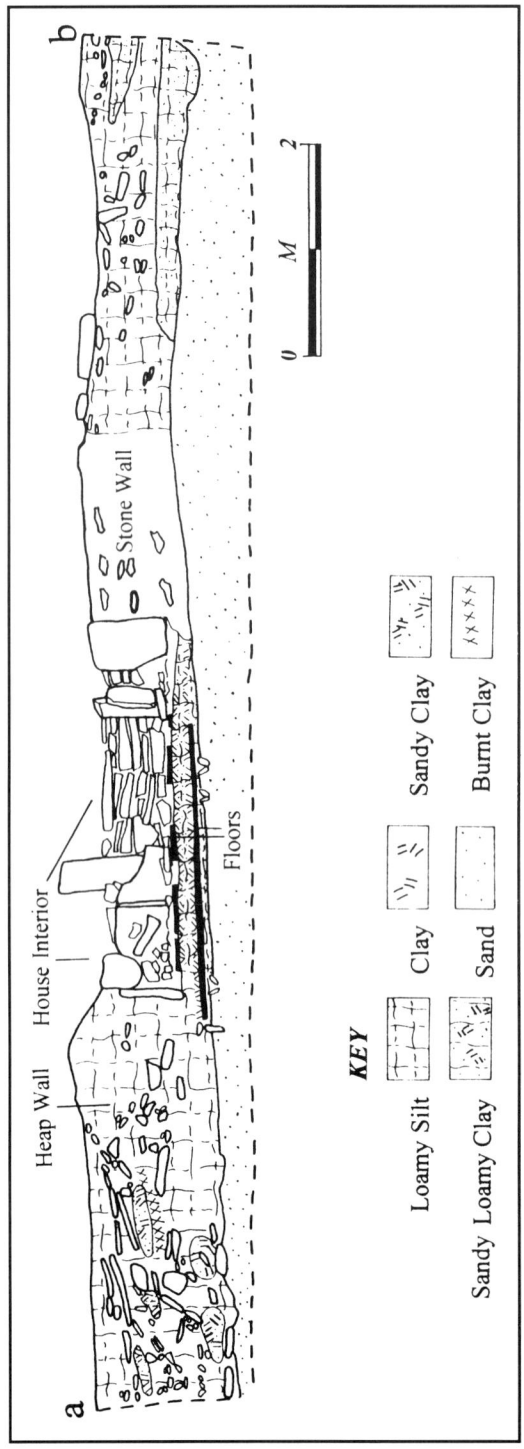

Figure 6: South-facing section through North House (indicated on Fig. 5). Centre of section shows view of house interior.

corresponding to that which also spread across the South House. This is interpreted as material which was used to level the surfaces before the rebuilding of the connecting passages and the remodelling of the walls and interior of the house. The rubble layer appears to have comprised in part *in situ* debris, and in part material which may have derived from the walls or have been introduced.

The walls
The earliest stone walling of the North House was faced on both inner and outer surfaces (Fig 5); during the later Bronze Age occupation material accrued against the outer face causing the walls to increase in thickness. The wall-face, which only in the north-west sector survived more than 0.2 m above the paving level, consisted of orthostats with occasional lengths of coursed masonry consisting of quite small stones. In the north-west sector such a masonry length adjoined a square-sectioned monolithic pillar set flush with the wall-face. This pillar (Figs 5 and 12, ba), set in packing stones which projected above floor level, stood 1.05 m above the paving and had been completely concealed within the material of the later phases. North-east of the pillar, the wall-face was interrupted and the wall coursing was not traceable on the east side of the house.

The later Bronze Age entrance was overlain by the early Iron Age entrance passage which used the foundations of the earlier entrance. The even curve of the west sector of the interior of the wall ran into two large orthostatic slabs (Fig 5), immediately west of the entrance, which fulfilled the same function in the later wall. The entrance passage into the later Bronze Age North House had been shorter than that of the early Iron Age one because the wall was narrower.

To the east of the earlier passage the well-preserved outer wall-face (Fig 5), consisting of three or four courses of stonework, was found buried within the later wall thickness. The start of a similar outer face was found on the west side of the passage. Westwards, however, this face became lost in a confusion of earth and rubble; on the east side, it continued only 1.7 m from the entrance passage before vanishing there too.

The red clay of the floor in the east of the North House was piled against a setting of erect slabs (Figs 5 and 12, bj). These were not on the line of the inner wall-face; they did, however, continue the curve of the section of outer wall-face east of the entrance passage. On excavation of the clay, no trace of the inner wall-face was found beneath it. At two points just to the north-east of the perimeter of the paving there were, however, single deep-set erect slabs (Fig 5). One of these had projected through the rubble-and-earth layer above, into the hearth of the cubicle floor above it, so that its top had been reddened and shattered by heat. The other slab was set north-north-east of the paved area; it was set against an enigmatic block of stonework resting upon the clay. Immediately in front of the end of the section baulk was a massive rectangular monolith also lying on the clay; on top of it was another stone nearly as large. Running east from the south-east corner of the rectangular monolith was an erect slab set radially from the curve of the wall (Fig 5).

In the profusion of erect slabs and short lines of curved wall various possible wall lines can be seen. The circular paved area is a well defined shape, but the hard red or yellow clay in which the stones are set spreads out both east and north in a shapeless form (Fig 5). An inner wall-face is clear only on the west and south sides, and only on the south-west sector does this relate sensibly to the paving. In the north-west sector, the curve of the wall-face diverges from the curve of the paving edge. On the south side, immediately east of the doorway, again there is a divergence; and what happened to the wall east and north of the paved area is not obvious.

A probable sequence of events is that this part of the house had been extended eastwards at the same level. This involved the demolition of the eastern wall. The inner wall-face was removed, leaving just three erect slabs which were set too deep for easy removal – the single slabs standing north-north-east and east of the paved area, and the northern of the two in V-formation east of the doorway (Fig 5). The outer wall-face of the original wall became the inner wall-face of the new wall, and the clay was piled up against this from the inside. Except in this south-east quadrant and immediately west of the entrance, the North House seems to have lacked an outer wall-face on most of its perimeter. As with the later Bronze Age phases of the South House, the walls were of heap construction, and were given an outer masonry face only in the early Iron Age.

Where the hard red clay of the floor extended northwards and was later covered by a blocking wall there was a curious pattern of stone features. Within the rubble and earth behind the blocking wall, but lower than the level at which the early Iron Age house wall was founded, was a intermittent line of stones forming a curve on the same arc as the wall of the house (Fig 7). These stones, however, were entirely within the rubble and earth, and their setting may have been fortuitous. Set within the underlying red clay, below the floor of the rear cubicle, was a line of stones set on edge, side-to-side with narrow gaps between, in a line running east-west (Fig 12, bc).

The confusion of clay and stones in the northern sector is difficult to interpret. The walling at this end of the house was much altered, and it is likely that these features relate at least in part to the possible earlier inner chamber discussed above.

North House: early Iron Age

The interior

Both the North and South houses were remodelled in the early Iron Age. The North House in its final form had a roughly circular interior, asymmetrical at the south end, measuring at maximum diameter 4.8 m north-south by 4.6 m east-west. It was divided by short radial piers forming mural cubicles which were inserted after the remodelling of the building (Fig 7). Four of these cubicles had been cleared during the SANHS excavations, the fifth was discovered and excavated in 1974. The house was entered from the south through a passage 1.3 m long (i.e. the thickness of the wall at this point), its width narrowing from 0.64 m at the outside to 0.54 m at the inner threshold. The walls were standing up to one metre above the cleared floor level. The central cubicles on the east and west sides were approximately

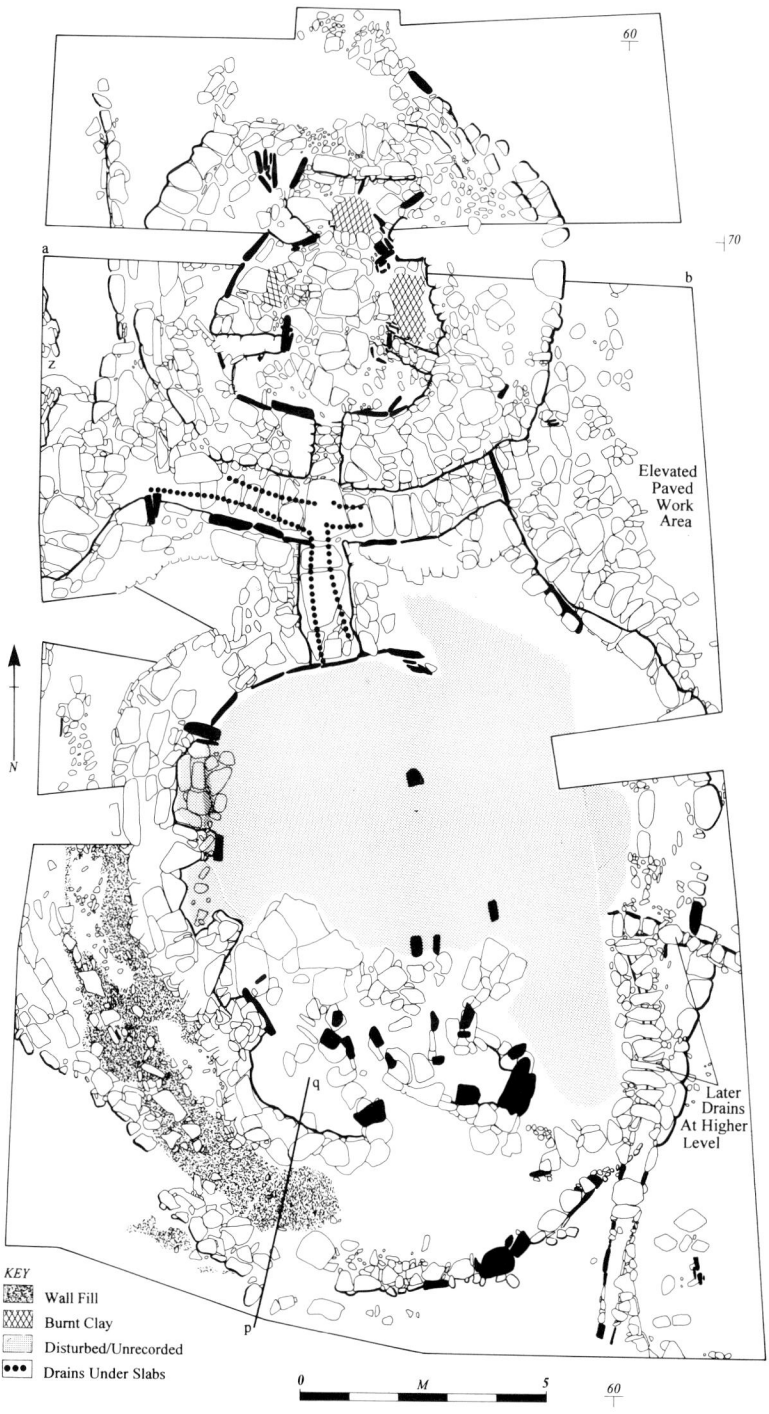

Figure 7: Site plan: early Iron Age (Phases 8 and 9).

rectangular. The wall in the west cubicle survived in seven courses to a height of 0.9 m, while in the east one most of the wall had slumped badly; the best preserved part was the pier forming the division between it and the south-east cubicle, being 1.0 m high in nine courses (Fig 12, bi). The northernmost cubicle was trapezoidal and lay directly facing the entrance. The south-eastern cubicle was an irregular quadrant.

Paving and floor deposits
The central floor area and the entrance passage were neatly paved. Between the passage and the house floor were two thin erect slabs forming a threshold. The paving in passage and house was at a uniform level, but this was lower than the paving level in the corridor between the two houses and still further below the level of the paving of the corridor entrance in the South House. One therefore stepped down on entering the passage into the North House. In the central floor area of the house, the paving slabs were luted, and firmly held in position, with hard yellow clay. When the paving stones of the passage were lifted, another paved floor was found directly beneath them.

The floors of the cubicles were more complex. The north alcove and the two central cubicles on the east and west were only partly floored with slabs; much of their areas were taken up by hearths of red clay and peat ash. In the north alcove were five slabs surrounding a clay area 0.8 x 0.75 m; on its eastern side was a low erect slab set in the floor so that its top was just level with the clay surface. When sectioned, the clay was found to be 0.06 m to 0.10 m thick, deepest at its centre; beneath it was a layer of soft peat ash. The red clay was bounded to the south by a strip of the yellow clay used to set the paving stones; the peat ash, however, continued under the paving slabs for 0.55 m from the yellow clay strip.

In the eastern central cubicle the red clay area, 1.1 m x 0.8 m, occupied nearly the whole cubicle, with only one set flagstone. The red clay was bounded in places by a yellow clay surround; the hearth had a dipping section, with a maximum thickness of 0.15 m, and composed of 0.01 m to 0.07 m of red clay overlying red peat ash. Under the wall on the east side of the cubicle, the hearth stopped at a patch of yellow clay, possibly intended as foundation for the lowest stones of the wall. Just inside the cubicle, against the sides of the piers, were two stone-lined slots, apparently settings for pillars.

The hearth in the western central alcove was the smallest of the three, and this was the most thoroughly paved of the cubicles, although the stones were badly shattered. The central red clay area was 0.3 m x 0.6 m, made up of an 0.4 m thickness of red clay overlying peat ash to a maximum total thickness of 0.12 m.

The south-eastern bay of the house had no obvious floor. Its bottom consisted of earth and rubble at 0.2 m below the level of the neighbouring paved floor of the central area (Fig 8). At that paving level, however, and right round the base of the wall line, a band of yellow clay was observed which probably represented a floor previously cut through. In the southern corner of this cubicle were two slabs on edge, their tops virtually level with the surface of the yellow clay; these proved to

Figure 8: North House – entrance, south-east cubicle and radial pier fronted with pillar (R. Lamb).

be relics of the earlier building. In the north-west corner was a rubble-filled stone-lined slot for a pillar.

The cubicle forming the south-western bay of the North House had not been discovered before 1974 because the slumped walls to either side of it were barely distinguishable from the rubble that filled it. The cubicle proved to be of the same shape as the south-east one, and its addition to the plan made the house symmetrical. The rubble was removed down to the level of the main paved floor, which proved to continue into the cubicle but to become more irregular within it. The gaps among the flags, and between the flags and the wall, were packed with hard yellow clay corresponding to the clay layer in the south-east cubicle. The walls were poorly preserved; to the south and west little remained above the bottom course of erect slabs.

Floor plan

The shape of the house interior therefore was a cinquefoil, with its stem represented by the entrance passage. The central area had a well paved floor but the five lobes did not. The northern three of these contained hearths; the two southern lobes had no trace of red clay or peat ash and were floored with yellow clay which in the south-west one, at any rate, was set with widely spaced slabs. The yellow clay was used throughout the interior to seal the flagstones and provide a floor where there were no flags; it may be assumed that the yellow clay was oxidised red by burning. The hearths were shallow and there is no evidence that they antedate the paving; the northernmost alcove was the only place where ash was found underlying paving, and this is explicable by the renewal of flagstones as those nearest the fires became shattered by heat.

The walls and radial piers
During the rebuilding of the North House the walls were enlarged and slightly realigned. On the west side of the house the inner face of the later wall could be seen to lie further east than that of the later Bronze Age wall (Fig 7). There was, however, congruence between the two major phases. In the north end of the entrance passage there was an edge-up threshold slab in nearly the same position as the threshold of the earlier house. The orthostatic slab forming the wall-face immediately east of the doorway was also shared with the earlier building.

Both the early Iron Age wall and the piers dividing the space within proved to have no structural foundation, their lower part being loose earth and rubble. The internal stone facing, and the radial piers, were founded at the level of the floor but, except in one place, the flagstones did not pass under the wall. This could be seen to advantage in the deeper excavation in the south-east cubicle, where the wall below the clay layer had no structure, being merely a mass of earth and stones. The exception was the north wall of the northernmost cubicle which looked to be an insertion or blocking wall. The paving stones of the cubicle's floor could clearly be seen to pass beneath it.

Each of the radial piers was finished with a large monolithic pillar – the one standing at the end of the pier between the east and south-east cubicles being 1.05 m high (Fig 8, Fig 12 bj). These pillars were held in position by basal packing stones which projected above the paving level. Upon excavation it proved that three out of four of the piers were not bonded into the main wall of the house. The fourth, the pier between the eastern and south-eastern cubicles, probably also was not bonded in, but the masonry had slumped so badly that it was impossible to be sure. The paving of the house floor did not run under any of the piers, but as the close-set paving was confined, in any event, to the central area, and the floors of the cubicles had either no or very sporadic paving, this was to be expected. The foundations of the piers did not penetrate deeper than the upper part of the rubble-and-earth layer immediately below the floor. The piers therefore are interpreted as secondary to the main wall and paved floor.

The walls can be seen to have become substantially enlarged and faced, or revetted, to the exterior (Fig 7). On the east side, there were two inner skins, concentric with the (upper) house floor, and an eastern, outer skin, which stopped at the north-east corner of the house. Where it stopped, there were two hard patches of red clay, lying immediately east of the inner two wall skins. These clay patches measured 1.2 m x 1.0 m and 0.75 m x 0.9 m.

The inner two wall skins continued around the north-east corner and then petered out in the rubble north of the northernmost cubicle. Only the inner skin of stonework, i.e. the inner face of the wall, was founded at the level of the floor paving.

The outer stonework was founded much higher up, and the wall below it had no real structure, being a mix of earth and stones (Fig 6). On the west side of the house, there was one convincing outer wall-face made of large stones laid flat, also founded at a high level; this line began on the west side of the rubble confusion north of the northernmost cubicle, and ran around to link up with the deeper-founded, coursed masonry fronting the inter-house corridor.

The exterior
The exterior of the North House had not been within the area of the SANHS excavation. Stone features were separated from the natural sand by a layer of grey sandy soil averaging 0.4 m in thickness. On the east side of the 1974 trench was a group of six heavy flagstones set around the north-east corner of the South House. These matched the massive slabs in the same relative position off its north-west corner. Lying directly upon these slabs were some other, less substantial ones; on removal, these proved to be broken halves of wide shallow trough querns placed upside-down on the paving. Through the bottom of the troughs had been punched several holes, each c. 60 mm in diameter. The purpose of these holes is not clear; the holes were not smoothed as if by rope, so the stones do not appear to have been used as tether-stones, although they may have been intended as such, and the holes seem larger than needed for that purpose. A similar example was found in the make-up of the early Iron Age wall.

On the west side of the trench were some very large paving slabs and a tumbled heap of other massive slabs (Fig 7). These were at a slightly lower level than the paved floor of the later period roundhouse and were of extraordinary size and thickness. The slabs were the continuation of those in the corner between the north-west wall of the South House and the trench side. To the west of the house they were bounded by an arc of well-coursed masonry which just projected from the west edge of the trench; this evidently belonged to some other building lying outside the excavated area (labelled z on Fig 7).

The area peripheral to the house had first of all the hard, contaminated brown soil of the 1940 surface; this was 0.10 m deep and, particularly against the stone of the west wall of the house, was full of thin (5 mm thick) lenses of sand. It gave way to softer and uncontaminated brown soil, which to the east of the house produced great quantities of shale tools and waste flakes. This was part of the area for working stone tools which is described in detail below.

On the east side of the North House, south of the section baulk, the brown soil contained few stones, except for a strip of rubble stonework adjoining the wall-face. Below here was a grey sandy soil, in which were found many more fine shale implements and stone handled clubs. North of the section baulk, curving around concentric with the stones of the wall, were bands of peat ash and coloured earth, evidently part of the heap construction of the wall. This was the only sector of the North House where these coloured bands comparable with those in the South House appeared. The bands of ash and burnt material are interpreted as rake-out from the hearth which was being dumped around the outside of the house, which when revetted became wall core. During the early Iron Age occupation of the North House it appears that ash and other rake-out was being removed and tipped at the rear of the house. Removal of the ash and soils revealed a spread of close-set rubble running north and west into the northern trench side. The stone wall could be seen to be resting on earth at a high level. To the east the grey sandy soil continued down to the natural marine sand with the lowest-level ard marks.

In the north-west corner of the trench, the removal of the upper part of the North House wall revealed a confusion of earth and rubble, with what appeared to be a short section of an internal wall-face. Also inside the wall material there was a spread of red clay. At a slightly lower level than this, a band of close-set stones ran north, and then curved north-east 1.0 m short of the northern side of the trench; this was at a level equivalent to the close-set rubble spread in the north-east corner of the trench, immediately above the level of the red clay spread and covered drain. West of this rubble band was the narrow line of stones, running due north-south which proved to be a wall, three to four courses high, with had a good face to the west (Fig 7). The provision of this wall is probably related to activity which took place immediately to the west of the excavated area. To the west was loose rubble mixed with earth and lumps of clay, with shale tools and pottery fragments.

Corridor between the North and South Houses

The corridor between the North and South Houses was paved with large flags (Fig 9). Below these was much rougher paving set in earth, overlying a drain which was visible in the western section face. The drain appeared to connect with one coming from the passage entrance from the South House, and there was the beginning of a drain going into the east section of the corridor. This, however, stopped abruptly only a few centimetres from the junction, and there was no sign of any further drain under the eastern corridor (Fig 7). There was no obvious direction of flow in any of the drains.

The west drain was made partly of slabs on edge, but mainly of large slabs laid flat, their edges forming the sides of the channel. These large slabs had their opposite, or outer, edges set tight against the walls of the houses, the curves of which they followed, so that the drain became wider, indeed funnel-shaped, to the west. Here survived one capstone laid directly upon the walls of the drain at a lower level than the paving above. That paving was laid on the earth and rubble which filled and covered the drain after it had passed out of use. West of the houses, the drain disappeared within rubble.

The large orthostats forming the north facade of the South House were founded deep in the natural sand. In the eastern section of the corridor, where no drain existed, the rubble underlying the paving also lay directly on the clean sand. The constructional form of the drain, with the flat slabs laid jammed against the walls on either side, suggests that it was made after the construction of the South House, early Iron Age heel-shaped facade and the outer wall of the North House. It became

Figure 9: View from east of early Iron Age corridor between North and Soutth Houses (R. Lamb).

apparent that the disturbance accompanying the early Iron Age phases of the South House, as well as the subsequent drain, had destroyed any stratigraphic relationship between the North and South Houses. It is probable that the east-west corridor was an innovation of the early Iron Age phase of the buildings, and it is suggested that the north-south passage linked the North and South Houses when the two were occupied concurrently (see section 4 below).

At the west of the end of the corridor was a confusion of stones, which in the corner between the trench side and the north-west facing side of the South House gave way to an area of well laid paving slabs of exceptionally massive size. They were jammed against the wall of the South House; directly below them lay the natural marine sand. At the east end of the corridor was a threshold sill-slab. There

Figure 10: View from east of South House interior showing the hearth centre picture. Sample section of secondary paving to left of hearth (R. Lamb).

were large blocks lying immediately west of this, which appeared to form steps leading upwards from the east end of the corridor onto the paved surface.

South House

Like the North House, the South House comprised two major phases of stone-built construction. The SANHS excavated the interior of the house, removing the uppermost, later phase, paved floor and the earth and rubble beneath it. A sample section of the secondary paving had been left standing to the west of the hearth (Fig 10); the rest of the interior was excavated to the lowest, primary level of paving (hence the disturbed/unrecorded area shown on Fig 7). The lowest levels of the paving were left *in situ*; consequently the stratigraphy below this floor was unexplored.

Features antedating the South House: later Neolithic and earlier Bronze Age

When the earliest wall material and blown sand were removed on the east side of the house, an enigmatic confusion of irregular stone structures was revealed which rested on the natural marine sand, which here was devoid of ard marks. These also

Plate 1: Sumburgh Airport and Sumburgh head from the north. The site lay under the runway on the right marked 60. Jarlshof is situated on the far side of the bay on the right hand side of the picture.
Copyright Kieran Murray.

Plate 2: Excavations at Sumburgh Airport by the SANHS, 1968.
Copyright Shetland Museum.

Plate 3: Ard marks predating the settlement remains at Sumburgh Airport. Photograph Raymond Lamb.

Plate 4: Drains underlying the later Bronze Age paved floor of the North House, Sumburgh Airport. Photograph Raymond Lamb.

Plate 5: Tank within North House, Sumburgh Airport. Photograph Raymond Lamb.

Plate 6: Hearth within the rear, ruined part of the North House, Sumburgh Airport. Photograph Raymond Lamb.

Plate 7: Later Bronze Age North House, Sumburgh Airport, taken from north east. Photograph Raymond Lamb.

Plate 8: Sumburgh Airport South House interior, with higher level early Iron Age paving partially removed. Copyright Shetland Museum.

Plate 9: View of Sumburgh Airport houses from south, 1970. Copyright Shetland Museum.

Plate 10: Hearth in South House, from south east. Photograph Raymond Lamb.

Plate 11: South House from north, after removal of North House. Photograph Raymond Lamb.

Plate 12: Sumburgh Airport from the east. The site lay under the runway at the top right of the picture. Jarlshof can be seen at the left hand side of the large bay.

Plate 13: Excavations at Old Scatness Broch, 1997, with site of Sumburgh Airport houses under runway in background. Copyright Kieran Murray.

Plate 14: Artefacts from Sumburgh Airport: Steatite vessel, miniature steatite axe hammer, schist armlets. Photograph Paul Belford.

Plate 15: Grooved Ware with applied decoration from Sumburgh Airport. Photograph Paul Bedford.

Plate 16: The Standing Stones of Yoxie (foreground) and the Benie Hoose, Whalsay, Shetland. Photograph Jane Downes.

Plate 17: The Benie Hoose, Whalsay, Shetland. Photograph Jane Downes.

Plate 18: Sumburgh Airport South House from the north east. 1969. Copyright Shetland Museum.

Plate 19: Clickhimin Broch, Shetland, with later Bronze Age house to exterior. Copyright Historic Scotland.

Plate 20: Sumburgh Airport view through houses from south. Copyright Shetland Museum.

appeared as partial remains of stonework during the SANHS excavation, at a low level to the east of the main paved floor. North of the section baulk, the stonework became a solid and well built lump of masonry, very competently built of close-set small stones, which incorporated a curious, open-ended slot, 0.8 m wide and 0.3 m deep. Ard marks, at first trending parallel with the stonework, then becoming criss-cross, began on the foundation level of the stonework and just to the north of it. It is possible, therefore, that this stonework represents some kind of structure or enclosure contemporary with this, the earliest ploughing on the site. But it is also possible that the enclosure is slightly later than the ploughing, the ard marks originally present having been obliterated by the disturbance. There was, however, no trace of ploughsoil under the stones, which might have been expected if the area had been ploughed before the stones were laid.

South House: later Bronze Age

The interior

The inner wall-face survived only in the western half of the stone-built house. In plan the house was oval with four cubicles on the west side formed between short radial piers (Fig 5). The passage entrance way at the north end of the house remained in use through the life of the building. At the south end of the house was a gap (between orthostats b and h, Fig 12) which also appears to have been an entrance. This part of the house underwent complex modifications which are discussed below. On the east side one cubicle survived in the south-east corner. Most of the east and north east sides had been dug out beyond the edge of the paving during the SANHS excavations in an attempt to locate traces of a wall-face or indeed of any stonework. Such remains were not located and it appears this side of the building was robbed out. On the west side the paving generally did not extend into the cubicles, all but the north-west of which had ill-defined floors of earth.

It is likely that the edge of the paving on the east side of the house did not represent the inner wall there, but merely the edge of the central floor. There may have been three cubicles north of the surviving south-east one, which, if they matched those on the west side, would not have had paved floors. It must be assumed, however, that the wall-faces behind those cubicles had been robbed out in antiquity.

Some of the paving slabs of the main floor were found to have other slabs above them. These, however, suggested not distinct floor levels, but the occasional levelling-up of the floor with new slabs, as the old ones subsided into the natural marine sand upon which they were laid.

The main feature of the floor was the large central hearth (Figs 5, 10 and 11), a rectangular area of clay surrounded by a flagstone shelf and a stone-slab kerb. Its south side was undefined. North of it was a curious keel-shaped area defined by a kerb (Fig 12, ak), and flanked on the north-east by a square-sectioned monolithic pillar (Fig 12, w) 0.91 m high above the flagstones. There was a socket for a similar pillar at the north west corner of the hearth. Other monolithic pillars occurred, most particularly between the hearth and the south end of the house (Figs 5 and

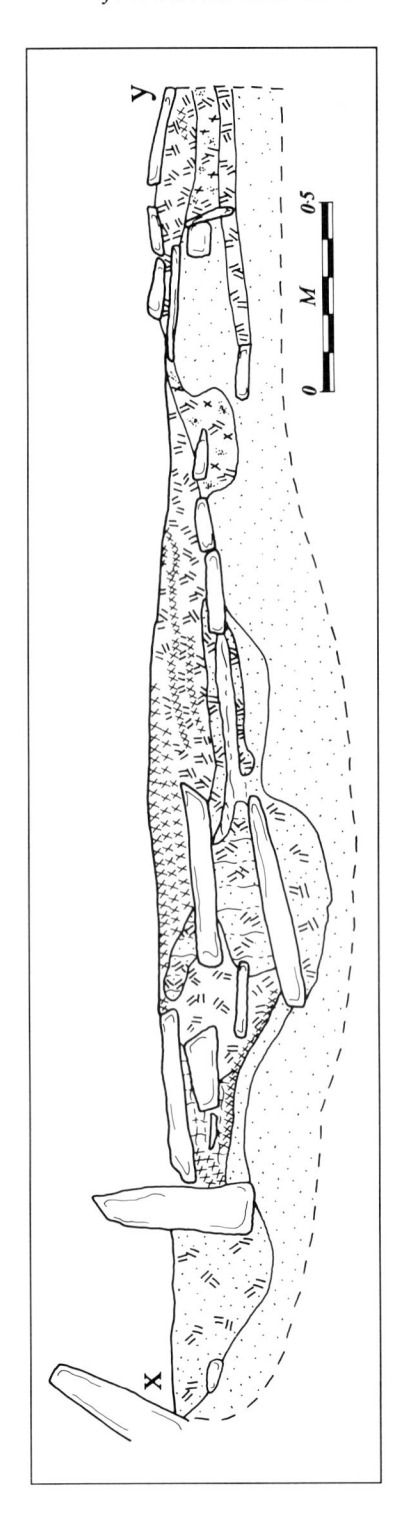

Figure 11: West-facing section through hearth of South House.

Excavations

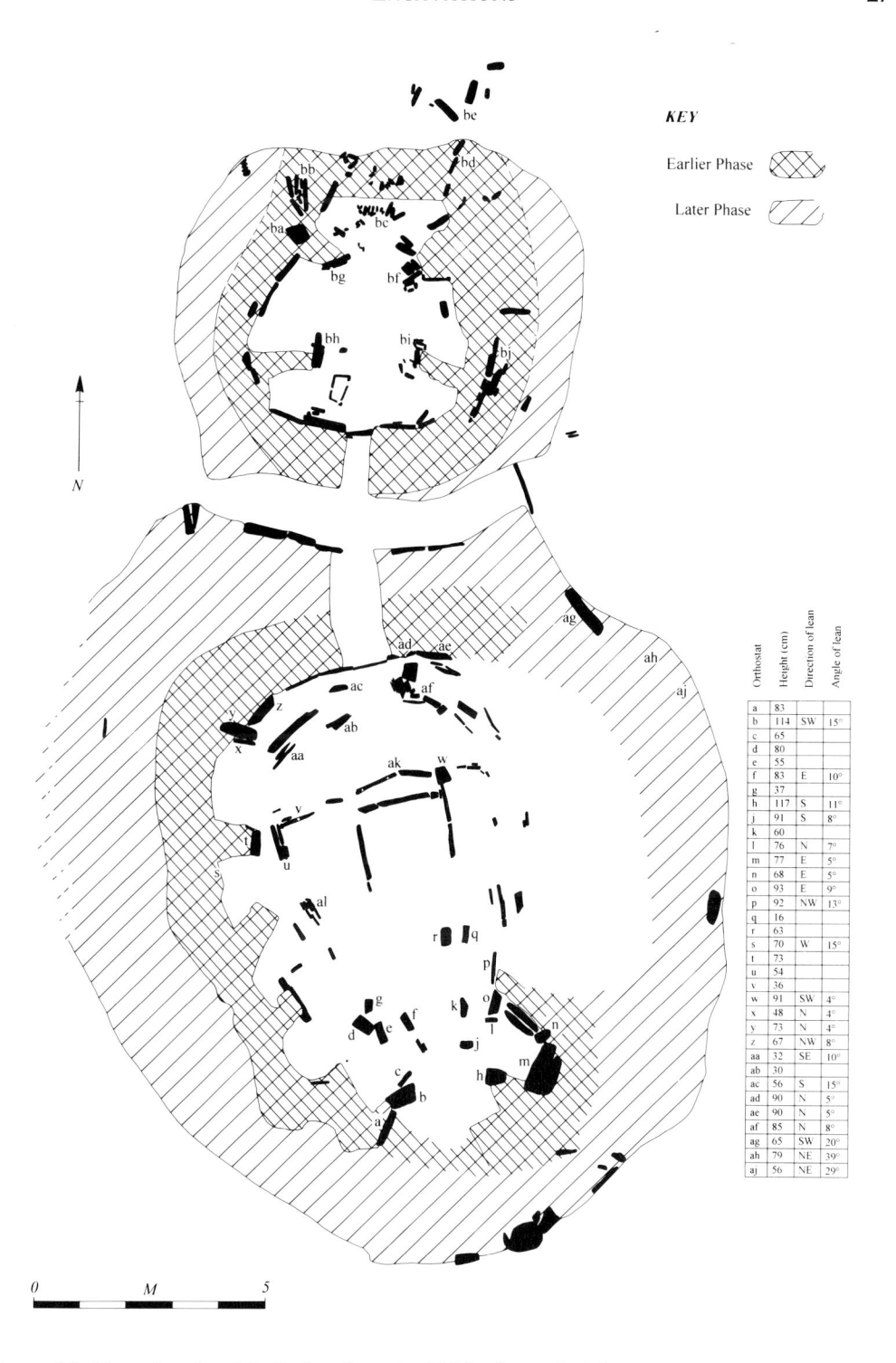

Figure 12: Plan showing labelled orthostats. Table shows height, orientation and angle of orthostats in South House.

Orthostat	Height (cm)	Direction of lean	Angle of lean
a	83		
b	114	SW	15°
c	65		
d	80		
e	55		
f	83	E	10°
g	37		
h	117	S	11°
j	91	S	8°
k	60		
l	76	N	7°
m	77	E	5°
n	68	E	5°
o	93	E	9°
p	92	NW	13°
q	16		
r	63		
s	70	W	15°
t	73		
u	54		
v	36		
w	91	SW	4°
x	48	N	4°
y	73	N	4°
z	67	NW	8°
aa	32	SE	10°
ab	30		
ac	56	S	15°
ad	90	N	5°
ae	90	N	5°
af	85	N	8°
ag	65	SW	20°
ah	79	NE	39°
aj	56	NE	29°

12). It is probable that at least some of these pillars were tether posts. There were settings of slabs on edge forming kerbs, set in a curve about 1 m within the curve of the north end of the house (Fig 12, aa and af), and in a broken, rectilinear pattern seemingly related to the hearth (Fig 12, uv and al).

The hearth itself measured 1.84 m east-west by about 1.8 m north-south within its kerb of erect slabs, its central clay area being 0.85 m x 1.2 m. The clay was yellow around the perimeter and burnt to a vivid red in the centre. The surrounding shelf of flat-laid slabs proved to have an almost identical slab-shelf immediately above it (not shown on section or plan). The yellow and red clay was only the top layer of a very complex stratigraphy; below it were thin layers of brown sandy soil, then yellow sandy clay, sandy soil, faintly reddened clay, yellow clay, rose-red clay, sticky red clay and so on to a maximum depth of 0.45m below the topmost clay (Fig 11). The keel-shaped area to the north of the hearth had the same east-west dimensions as the hearth itself, 1.84 m, and was 0.49 m wide at the centre and 0.31 m at the ends. The erect slab forming the boundary to the north west was pierced with two neat holes as if it had been intended for use as a tether stone (Fig 12, ak); a slab similarly pierced with a single hole stood in line with it, one metre to the west (Fig 12, v).

Beneath the northward entrance corridor was a stone-lined drain (Fig 7). This did not extend far into the house itself, and ran out northwards to join a drain in the west section of the corridor between the north and south houses. The entrance passage itself was 2.4 m long and 0.95 m wide at its outer end, widening to 1.1 m in the centre and narrowing again to 1.03 m at the inner end, where there was a threshold sill-slab set across the floor.

Through an examination of the contexts from the exterior (see below), it can be determined that the South House was lengthened southwards during the later Bronze Age. The south-eastern cubicle certainly, and the south-western one presumably, are additions belonging to this phase. Unfortunately, the masonry at the south end of the house was in so bad a state that it was impossible to detect a join here; but, as the wall consists of larger irregular stones haphazardly laid, it does lend itself to such patching in a way that would leave little trace. There is, however, a noticeable kink in the curve of the wall in the south-west corner (the kink occurs behind the north-west corner in the south west cubicle) and it looks as if the wall south-east from this point is a later addition

The walls
Unlike the North House with its stone walls faced to interior and exterior, the later Bronze Age walls of the South House consisted of a single thickness of coursed masonry with earth behind. There were many massive orthostats forming the basal course of the walling at the backs of the cubicles, or the ends of the piers. The entire wall structure survived for study only on the north, west and south sides. Here in places was another wall-face, facing outwards, within the thickness of the wall (Fig 5). Between this wall-face and the back of the cubicles the wall was between 0.6 and 1.7 m thick. This wall-face was founded lower down than the outer, later boulder-

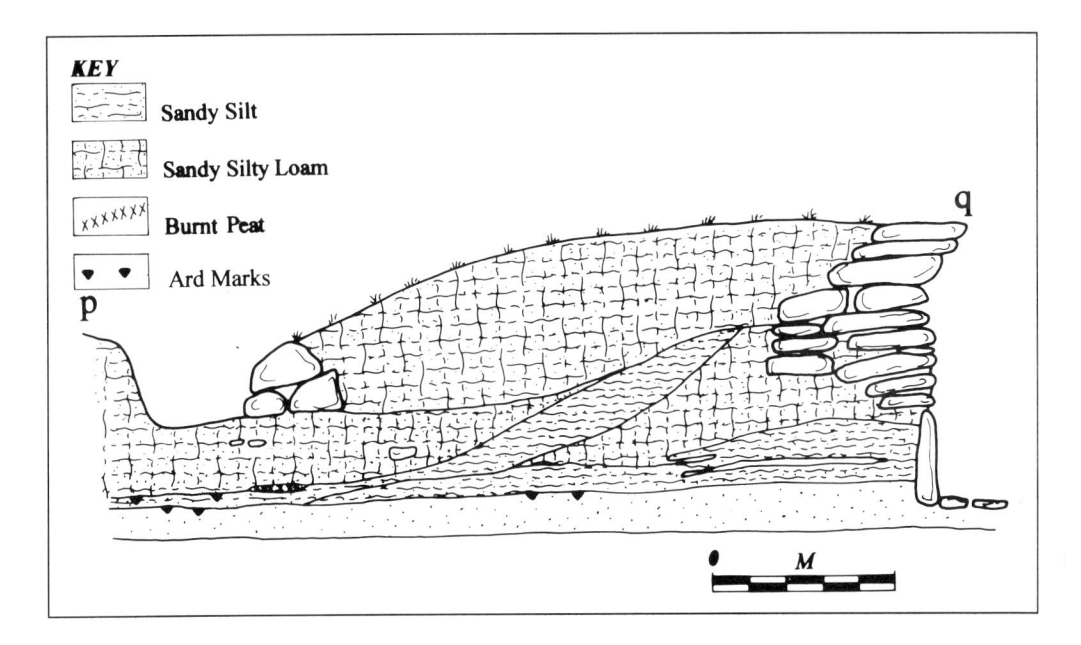

Figure 13: East-facing section through wall of South House.

wall (Fig 13); its quality was best on the north-west part of the building, becoming more rough and irregular towards the south.

At the south end of the house was a complex interrelationship between the wall material and the adjoining ploughsoil. The drawn section p-q (Fig 7 and 13) shows the stratigraphic relationship between the inner and outer lines of stone wall. The paved floor inside the house, and the orthostats forming the basal course of the inward wall-face, were founded in the natural marine sand which was the base of the stratigraphy throughout the site. Above the orthostats came courses of crude walling set in sandy silt. Heaped material, comprising red-brown soil and grey sandy soil, with lenses of burnt material and decayed turf, sloped away south from the inward wall-face. The heap material on the whole varied around the house. At the north-west corner, the material was the standard brown soil, with just one burnt layer low down in it, but over most of the west and south-west sectors there appeared vividly coloured streaks representing tips of peat ashes and burnt earth, and layers of unburnt turves. The wall heap material did not extend around the southern end of the house, and this is taken as further evidence that there was an entrance to the house from the south at this earlier phase. The quantities of ash and burnt material around the south-west and west of the house indicate that rake-out from the hearth was being brought out of this entrance and dumped against the side of the house. The walls were therefore increasing in size as the dwelling was occupied, and they were periodically revetted with stone.

The exterior deposits and accumulations (sandblow and ploughsoils discussed below) were cut by the back of the south-eastern cubicle of the house (the floor and interior wall-foundation of which is, of course, at a lower level). Thus the wall heap, which accumulated during the earliest occupation of the South House is earlier than the sandblow and the succeeding period of ploughing; but the sandblow and ploughing are earlier than the extreme south of the house, which is cut back into pre-existing levels. The south end of the South House therefore represents the enlargement of the original, shorter structure

There was no trace of any stonework representing the north-eastern wall of the house in this period to match the walling on the north-west side. This stonework, if it originally existed, had certainly disappeared in antiquity, probably being robbed out at the time the secondary wall-heap was added. However, remnants of the coloured earth layers resulting from what is being interpreted as heap construction walling could be seen. In particular, there was a vivid tawny layer (Fig 5), probably decayed turf, curving around in a quadrant from the stonework east of the entrance passage, and into the reserved section baulk which was left protruding from the east side of the trench. This tawny layer sloped steeply downwards and evidently represented the tail of a heap-construction wall.

South House: early Iron Age

The interior

The later phase of paving within the South House was laid over a deposit of earth and rubble, which appears to have been introduced to both North and South Houses at the same time that the walls were substantially enlarged. The layer comprised large irregular stones loosely packed with earth; it was approximately 0.5 m thick and contained many artefacts. The later phases of activity within the South House are less well documented than those in the North House, and the secondary paving appears on the plans of the SANHS in the southernmost part of the building only, where it is described as two or three layers of flat slabs, and in a baulk to the west side of the building. The paving sloped down in the northern end of the house towards the entrance passage where it lay above the earlier level of paving. The northern entrance passage was retained as a place of access, and the passage lengthened to accommodate the greater wall thickness (Fig 7). The southern entrance was, however, no longer in use.

The paving covered over the large central hearth, and during this period of occupation there is no evidence of a hearth within the building. Although it appears there was no longer a hearth within the house, it appears that the basic layout of the building did not change, and that the piers defining the cubicles were not modified. The monolithic pillars in the southern part of the house projected through the secondary paving, and continued to fulfil a function in these later phases of occupation, possibly as tether posts.

The walls

The walls which appear to correspond with the levelling and repaving of the floor were, in their ultimate form, at least 3 m wide and were formed by an inner facing of stone and boulders forming a massive outer face. The walls were built on top of those of the later Bronze Age South House, and on c. 0.5 m of ploughsoil which had accumulated on the tail of this earlier wall (Fig 13). The northern entrance became concave and was faced with very large orthostats. The effect of this was to convert the house from an oval to a heel-shaped plan (Fig 7).

On the east side of the house the greater part of wall was excavated by the SANHS to a level slightly lower than that of the paved floor; it is probable that this area had been much disturbed by stone-robbing in antiquity. In the west side of the house lines of stones within the wall heap were located which indicate that, as with the earlier phase wall, the ultimate form of the wall is the result of a process of material being dumped against the wall and periodically revetted with stone. Localised patches of coloured earth were seen also in the north-east part of the walls, indicating tips of different materials in the wall heap.

The exterior
As in the case of the North House, the exterior of the South House had not lain within the area of the SANHS excavation and was still covered with blown sand which had drifted over the area since the 1940 clearance. Below the sand was brown soil, its uppermost level much compacted and contaminated with coal, fragments of electrical fittings, and Royal Air Force china.

The original, first-period wall-heap merged southwards into the ploughsoil of the subsequent period, a grey sandy loam. On the surface of this level was a shallow burnt layer incorporating broken, heat-shattered slabs (Fig 13). This seemed to be a hearth, which was broken and scattered by ploughing. Plough marks were visible both within and beneath the burnt level (Fig 13). It seemed that the hearth was established on an area already under the plough, and that ploughing resumed after its brief use. The later wall rested on brown earth, but below this was a layer of clean sand.

To the north and east of the South House, criss-cross ard marks were visible. In the corner between the reserved baulk and the trench side on the east was a stone-slab box (Fig 4). This had a covering of clean sand and the ard marks cut across it. To the west of the house the clean sand could be seen to overlie the heap material of the later Bronze Age wall. The section in the east wall of the trench showed the clean sand layer becoming deeper towards the south. This sand, therefore, is interpreted as the result of a sandblow, probably due to a severe south-easterly gale, which piled sand against the exposed south-east corner of the earliest stone-built house. Ploughsoil subsequently developed on the blown sand surface. The extension of the later Bronze Age stone building southwards necessitated cutting back into the sandblow and ploughsoil.

The sandblow with its ard marks appeared also to the north of the reserved baulk, when the overlying orthostats had been removed. Here the sand had drifted over some buried masonry of an earlier structure, and some of the stones projected. But the ard marks showed that the implement had been manoeuvred around these obstructions.

In the north-east corner, the outer wall-face of the heel-shaped house, curving away southwards from the corner of the entrance facade, was built of orthostats rather than boulders. Immediately north-east of the line of orthostats was a concentration of large flat slabs, which followed the line of the orthostat wall, and had a north-east-facing limit about a metre from it (elevated paved work area, Fig 7), the northern edge of which was not clear. This may have been a broad plinth to buttress the orthostats (which it effectively did), or a pathway; but to the north, the slabs merged into a confusion of stones east of the end of the corridor between the two houses. In the acute angle between this stone feature, the trench side, and the baulk reserved for a section, was a spread of red clay. The clay lay directly on top of a spread of yellow clay which ran underneath the slab feature.

In the brown earth north-east of the orthostat wall and its accompanying slab pathway was a great profusion of shale tools and the waste chips from their manufacture. The brown earth with shale tools and chips occurred again under the yellow clay, but in places there was a further layer of red, then another of yellow clay, before the brown earth again was found. The clay spreads appear to have been laid as floors, most likely outdoor ones; they varied in thickness between 0.3–0.6 m. They probably served as working surfaces in this area devoted to the making of shale tools.

It is significant that the ploughing seen on the sandblow came right up to the wall-slope of the later Bronze Age house. Unlike the later ploughing seen in the ploughsoil south of the house, this did not run in one direction parallel to the house wall. The general trend of the sand-surface ard marks is north-south, but they are crossed by some oblique ones, mostly trending north-east to south-west and apparently skimming the slope of the wall; there are even a few marks running east-west straight into the wall material. This may have implications concerning the technique of ploughing employed.

POST-ABANDONMENT ACTIVITY

The latest prehistoric activity within the excavated area was represented to the south-east of the South House. Here, at a high level within the brown soil, but not quite high enough to be clear of the boulder-wall of the heel-shaped house, were two slab-formed drains, one running from the east, the other from the south (Figs 7 and 14). They penetrated the boulder-wall and met at a point just on the edge of the cutting left by the previous excavation. The drains were covered by paving slabs, and this paving was extended east to cover the boulder wall also. This level was very close to the 1940 ground surface and to the medieval ploughing, and the paving was disturbed; it may once have covered a wider area. A wall-face, facing east, diverged from the north-south drain and disappeared into the side of the trench. But if there was a building at this level, no floor deposits survived; both above and below the drains and stonework was the ordinary brown soil. It is presumed that the South House was out of use by this time, and was being used as a sump, the drains serving some new occupation area away to the south and east, with which the high-level paving and wall-face may well be associated.

Figure 14: Later drain running north-south (R. Lamb).

Upon abandonment both houses and corridors were filled in with a mixture of rubble – presumably collapsed walling – and black soil which in places contained layers of ash. The black soil contained many artefacts. The SANHS encountered a much more compact mixture of black sand, clay and loam soil lying over the rubble and black soil, which appeared to have overlain the walls and exterior of the buildings. This was interpreted as cultivated soil which had become compressed under the weight of overlying deposits. After the settlement was abandoned the site was levelled for agriculture, earth and stones being tipped into the remaining hollows. The site became a field and was ploughed on an east-west alignment, with a plough which scored and displaced the buried orthostats. Some of these orthostats had fallen and were leaning towards the east; their top edges bore east-west striations made by an iron-shod plough. The ploughing presumably knocked the upstanding orthostats outwards from their original positions. This ploughing continued until the disastrous sand-blow of the late 17th century put an end to farming in the district.

Summary Account of the Sequence of Activities by J. Downes

During the early Bronze Age one or more timber structures occupied the site. This activity overlay Neolithic settlement and/or agricultural activity. A hiatus between this activity and the stone houses has been identified through artefact studies and is indicated stratigraphically by the existence of a ploughsoil between the earlier and later Bronze Age phases.

The later Bronze Age stone-built North House is thought to have been constructed before the South House, and it had drains under the paving and a tank as the central feature of a circular paved area. The paved part of the building appears to have been an outer area of the inner part of the house to the north-east. The north-east part of the North House was probably a small inner area which could have had a recess to either side, and one at the rear. Although it is not possible to tell its form, the structure appears to have had a hearth on the west side.

The South House appears to have acted as a forecourt to the North House, before its southern end was enclosed, at which time the inner chamber of the North House may have been blocked off, and the paving and tank clayed over. The substantial stone-built hearth was central to the later Bronze Age phases of the South House, and would have dominated the interior of the house. The space within the South House was divided and each space used for different activities.

The interior of the buildings was repaved and the walls rebuilt at the end of the Bronze Age. At the time the hearth of the South House was paved over, the South House was not accessible through the southern entrance, as the wall now encircled this end of the house. Hearths were situated in the bays of the North House which were formed by the insertion of piers.

The east and west passages between the North and South House were constructed at this time, and, whereas access to the North House had probably always been gained through the South House, during the later occupation subsequent to the rebuilding, access to either house was gained via the central linking passages. The outside areas were, by this time, substantially raised above the level of the house interiors (Figs 4 and 6) through a combination of midden accumulation, sandblow and movement of soil through ploughing, and a work area was established to the east (Fig 5) for the making of stone tools.

Ultimately these aspects of architecture and material culture reflect, and influence, the nature and structure of the community which inhabited these houses. This is discussed more fully below.

3. SITE SEQUENCE AND CHRONOLOGY

J. Downes

A provisional site phasing was developed during the post-excavation programme. This was based in part on that developed and used by Raymond Lamb, but it was modified to take into account the amalgamated stratigraphic record. The phasing was put together on the basis of the perceived structural sequence, and the specialists worked with the phasing as a framework. At the same time the phasing was tested against the results of the artefact analysis. The aim of this work was to produce sequence and chronology for the site, and during the process it was possible to reduce the phasing to the simplified broad scheme used in the foregoing text. The working site phasing is illustrated in Table 1 alongside the simplified phasing.

Artefact analysis with regard to the chronology of the site was aimed at attempting to discern the duration of the occupation of the houses as a whole, whether occupation was continuous with modifications and rebuildings occurring without break in the occupation, or whether structural changes indicated hiatus in occupation. It was for this reason that the phases were subdivided into the *event* of building, and the *occupation* within the building, for it was hoped that differences in the assemblages might indicate the longevity of each period of occupation. This analysis permitted an understanding of the chronological relationship between the structural elements of the two buildings. The form of the architecture permits an interpretation of the use of space and the location of activities; changes to or modifications of the architectural form may indicate a change in the way people occupied the space.

The Pottery as a Chronological Indicator

The pottery is particularly crucial in respect to the lack of stratigraphic relationship between the North and South Houses. However the analysis was undertaken with an awareness that redeposition of material and post-depositional processes would make the establishment of a pottery sequence problematic. For instance, the majority of the pottery derived from the heap walls, exterior of the buildings, and the upper layers of the site and, in the case of the North House, 72 % of the pottery came from the wall fill, compared with 28 % from the interior of the house itself. Only a small

Table 1: Provisional Phasing and Simplified Phasing.

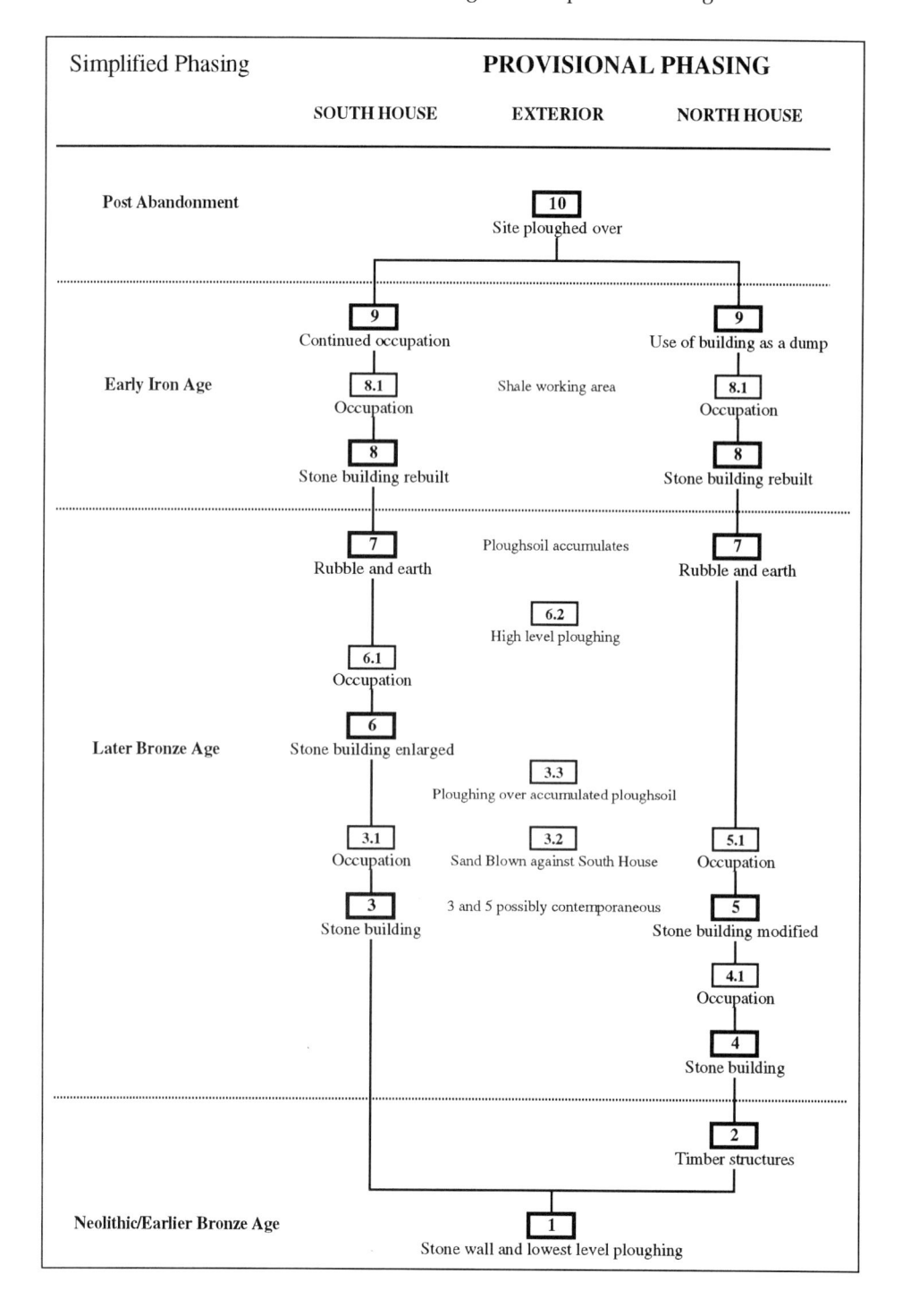

Simplified Phasing	PROVISIONAL PHASING		
	SOUTH HOUSE	EXTERIOR	NORTH HOUSE

Post Abandonment
- **10** Site ploughed over

Early Iron Age
- South House: **9** Continued occupation — **8.1** Occupation — **8** Stone building rebuilt
- Exterior: Shale working area
- North House: **9** Use of building as a dump — **8.1** Occupation — **8** Stone building rebuilt

Later Bronze Age
- South House: **7** Rubble and earth — **6.1** Occupation — **6** Stone building enlarged — **3.1** Occupation — **3** Stone building
- Exterior: Ploughsoil accumulates — **6.2** High level ploughing — **3.3** Ploughing over accumulated ploughsoil — **3.2** Sand Blown against South House — 3 and 5 possibly contemporaneous
- North House: **7** Rubble and earth — **5.1** Occupation — **5** Stone building modified — **4.1** Occupation — **4** Stone building — **2** Timber structures

Neolithic/Earlier Bronze Age
- **1** Stone wall and lowest level ploughing

proprotion of pottery could be considered to have been left be *in situ*, or to constitute even primary refuse.

Aims of the analysis

The aims of the pottery analysis were close to those outlined in recent guidelines by the Prehistoric Ceramics Research Group (PCRG 1995). It was felt that the pottery would be central to an understanding of formation processes, and thus to an understanding of the site as a whole. The use of pottery as a chronological indicator was understood to be important not only in terms of inter-site comparison, but as an aid to understanding the sequence of activities at Sumburgh Airport. Analysis of the pottery as an indicator of settlement organisation was also a major consideration and is detailed below, as is the account of the function and use of the pottery.

Methods of analysis by J. Downes and C. Yarrington

Through post-excavation processes the pottery was analysed on two different occasions and from two different perspectives. The original pottery report by Sylvia Stevenson was continued in 1981 by Clare Yarrington. This report was based on the pottery catalogue, which details fabric type, vessel form, the number of sherds and their weight, vessel dimensions, surface treatment and decoration, surface adherences, and manufacturing technique for each sherd/pottery group. The authors divided the pottery into broad fabric groups, and a description of vessel forms, methods of construction, surface finish and decoration was written.

The assemblage included a large number of badly abraded sherds and many encrusted with carbon. Thus surface finish and decoration were difficult to assess. The handmade nature of the pottery means that many of the rims are uneven and estimations of diameter in the catalogue are approximate, this is also the case for the base sherds. The original study had to be carried out by examining the material from the SANHS and 1974 excavations separately, since the parts of the assemblage were located in Shetland and Edinburgh, respectively.

Having combined the contextual information from both excavations of the site during the most recent post-excavation analysis, contexts were targeted for further analysis of the pottery. As the material now all resides in Shetland, the assemblages from both the excavations could be looked at together. The contexts targeted were those deriving from the interior of the structures, and those that could be identified with each rebuilding, modification or phase of occupation. The pottery was analysed in terms of its context, type, condition and relationship to other pottery and artefacts. The internal and structural contexts were prioritised above those from external contexts as it was not possible to include all contexts in this stage of post-excavation analysis, due to the size of the assemblage. A vessel form series was devised, which was then placed in sequence against the stratigraphic information. The pottery was then compared to other assemblages from Shetland.

Fabric groups by C. Yarrington

The pottery was divided into seven groups based on fabric. Examination was by binocular microscope only, hence the broad grouping. There is considerable variation within the larger groups e.g. F3 and F4. Of the total assemblage by weight 4.9 % (5013.4 g) has not been assigned a fabric group as this material fell between two or more groups.

Table 2: Summary of the fabric groups by weight/percentage

Total weight of pottery			101386.3g	(c. 100 kg)
F1	vesicular pottery		4.4%	(4483.9g)
F2	coarse pottery		3.4%	(3422.3g)
F3	steatite gritted pottery		38.9%	(39422.5g)
F4	mixed rock gritted fabric		47.7%	(48365.8g)
F5	grass tempered pottery		0.08%	(79.4g)
F6	crumbly – similar to soil concretions		0.4%	(371.2g)
F7	dense and micaceous – all but one sherd cord impressed	0.2%	(227.8g)

F1 (vesicular pottery)
The fabric is generally thick (10–14 mm) hard, well fired and fairly heavily gritted. The organic or similar inclusions have mostly burnt away in firing or dissolved during deposition leaving characteristic large (< 10 mm) and angular vesicles. Some sherds were very heavily gritted and the now vesicular fabric crumbles readily. It is likely that much of this pottery was not retrieved. Where the grits have survived they are dull white or yellow, soft and angular in shape. One possible identification is bone. A few, similarly shaped grits are of a hard rock. The numerous, fine mixed rock grits which are also present were probably part of the original clay matrix.

F2 (coarse pottery)
This group of sherds is similar to F1 except in that the large angular inclusions are fragments of various hard rocks and a few grits of steatite are also present. Many of the grits protrude through the surface of this very coarse ware.

F3 (steatite-gritted pottery)
The sherds of this group are largely or wholly gritted with steatite. The finely to coarsely crushed steatite is found in varying proportions from sparse to heavy, but most sherds are well to heavily gritted. A few sherds are so heavily gritted that they were mistaken on excavation for parts of steatite vessels. Both fragments of steatite vessels and steatite-gritted sherds are of a similar softness. The few small grits of mixed rock were probably part of the original clay matrix. The surfaces vary from no obvious treatment to highly burnished. Most are smooth, the steatite often giving a greasy feel to the sherds. Steatite is readily available in Shetland and

is soft and easily ground down; its high temperature resistance would have assisted in the firing process and the number of fine-walled and well burnished examples indicate the ease of working the clay and finishing off of the pots. A number of sub-groups could be identified on the basis of grit size and frequency, together with particular surface treatment.

F4 (mixed rock-gritted fabric)
The filler is of ill-sorted fragments of various rocks with steatite occurring only in small quantities or absent. However, due to the varying proportions of steatite there is significant overlap between fabric groups F3 and F4. The majority of sherds are well to heavily gritted with quartz as the prime constituent. Sand may have been a source of filler. This micaceous fabric ranges in hardness from soft to hard, with most being hard. The colour of the fabric shows incomplete oxidisation, the core is usually grey and the surfaces are patchy brown, orange and yellow. No great care appears to have been taken finishing the surfaces, which are usually either sandy or smooth, possibly finished with a wet hand. Five sub-groups could be distinguished where only one type of grit (e.g. shale, schist, mica) or a limited range of rock grits were used; some of these may represent a single vessel.

F5 (grass-tempered pottery)
A very small group of sherds of probably grass-tempered or chaff-tempered pottery.

F6 (crumbly)
A group of sherds notable for the difficulty in distinguishing them from soil concretions. The fabric is soft and crumbly requiring consolidation in most cases. There are a few possibly incidental small rock fragments. The dark grey surfaces are smooth but uneven and cracked. One sherd is decorated with an applied moulding and cord impressions.

F7 (dense and micaceous)
The hard black-brown fabric is slightly micaceous with some medium to fine dark grey rock grits. There is no apparent surface finish, but the dense texture of the fabric gives a smooth finish, although all the pieces are abraded. All but one of the sherds are decorated with cord impressions.

Vessel forms by J. Downes

Using the illustrated pottery, a vessel form classification was undertaken. The classification of vessels was based on the scheme created for the classification of pottery from Danebury (Cunliffe 1984), a scheme which has since been widely used for the analysis of later prehistoric pottery. This scheme has the advantage of being infinitely expandable, thus allowing for the insertion and addition of other pottery from elsewhere in Shetland and beyond. Reference to parallels discernible within other pottery assemblages from Shetland is made within the pottery type descriptions.

Each vessel is classified at as many as four levels, depending on the degree of survival of the vessel and how many recognisable traits it comprises. The levels of classification are class, type, form and variety. Two classes of vessel were identified in the Sumburgh Airport assemblage: jars and bowls. The distinction between a jar and a bowl has been made on the criterion that the height of a jar will normally be in excess of the maximum diameter, whereas the height of a bowl will usually be less than the maximum diameter (Cunliffe 1984, 232). Where only part of the profile is reconstructible the distinction cannot be clearly drawn, and the small size of many rim fragments compounded this difficulty. There may be overlap between the two classes. It should be noted that the vessel form classification does not relate to the chronology of vessel forms; Jar Type 1 does not necessarily precede Jar Type 2.

Within the two classes of vessel identified, five types of jars and three types of bowls were distinguished. The form is the subdivision of the number ascribed to the type, and the variety the final subdivision (rarely used). Variety can be used to describe such differences as vessel size, but, due to constraints of time, vessel size is not a factor consistently used in the interpretation of the assemblage. (This information is contained within the archive.) Where size of vessel is referred to these are the criteria devised by Clare Yarrington:

small	= up to 120–150 mm rim diameter, c. 70 mm base diameter
medium	= c. 150–280 mm rim, c. 100 mm base
large	= over 280 mm rim, over 100 mm base.

Jars

Jar Type 1 – Carinated (Fig 15)
Carinated jars occur in both fabrics F3 and F4, but are predominantly F3 with a large amount of steatite temper, and they exhibit a variety of sizes from small to large vessels. Surface finish varies between the very rough to the most highly burnished and fine-walled of all the Sumburgh Airport assemblage. Jar Forms 1.2 and 1.3 derive solely from the South House.

These jars have clear parallels in several sites which have been placed within the early Iron Age. Pottery from Jarlshof is the largest assemblage of closely comparable material, with carinated jars deriving from the Late Bronze Age Village II, Phases I and II, dwellings IVc, V, and VI (Curle 1934; Hamilton 1956, 37–38) which were early Iron Age round houses.

The Early Iron Age Farmstead pottery from Clickhimin contains a range of comparable carinated vessels (Hamilton 1968, 42, Fig 19, 1–5), and the assemblage from the early Iron Age house at Mavis Grind consisted almost solely of carinated vessels with steatite temper (Cracknell and Smith 1983).

Although Jar 1 (Fig 15, 2.96) has no surviving rim, its form can be seen to be distinct from that of the other carinated vessels as it has a high carination or shoulder than to the angular, lower carination of all other forms. Through its similarity in form to sherds from later Bronze Age contexts (Phases 3.1 and 6) this vessel type is thought to be earlier than other carinated vessels. The form and

Site Sequence and Chronology

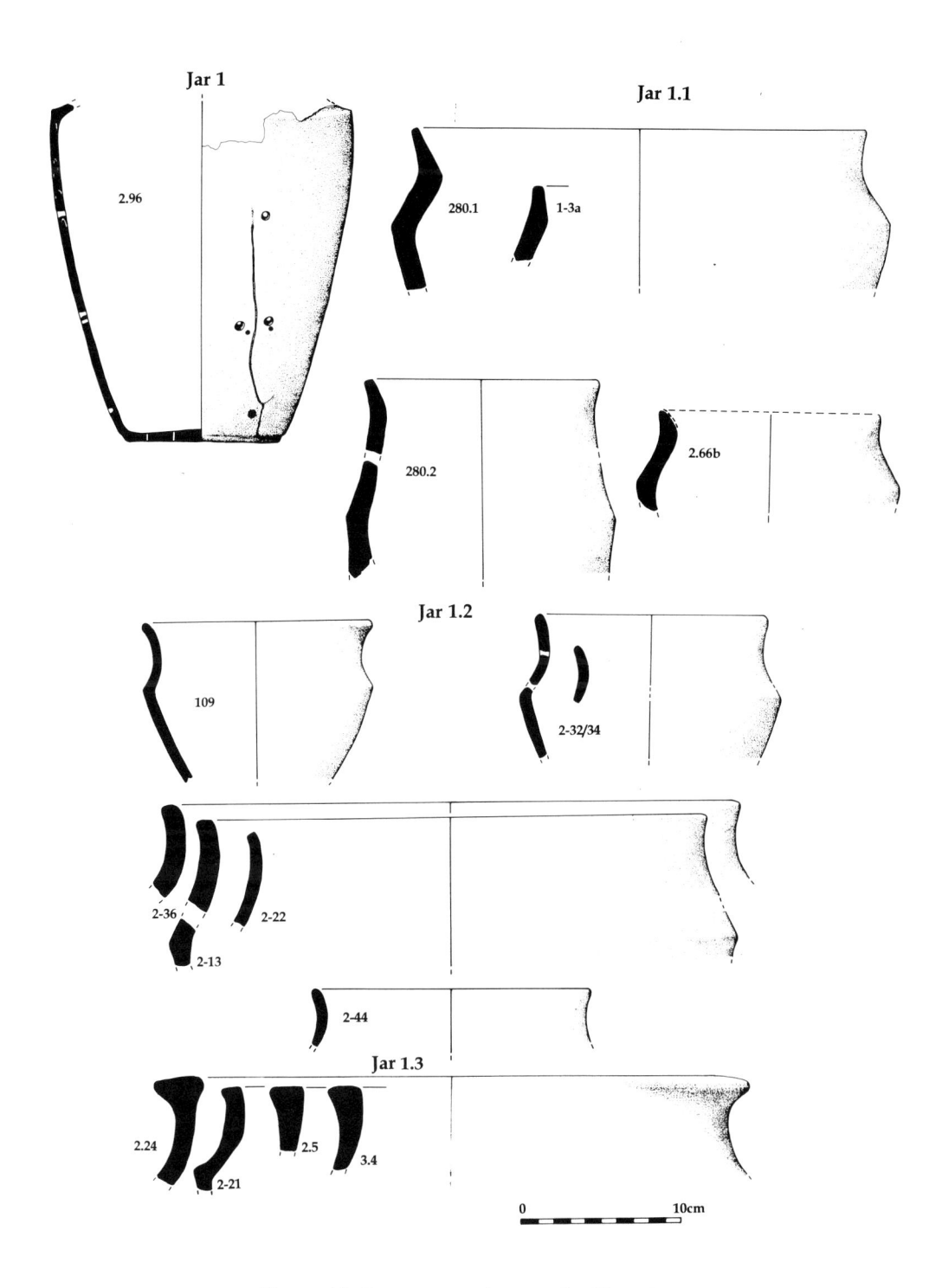

Figure 15: Pottery vessel types: Jar Type 1.

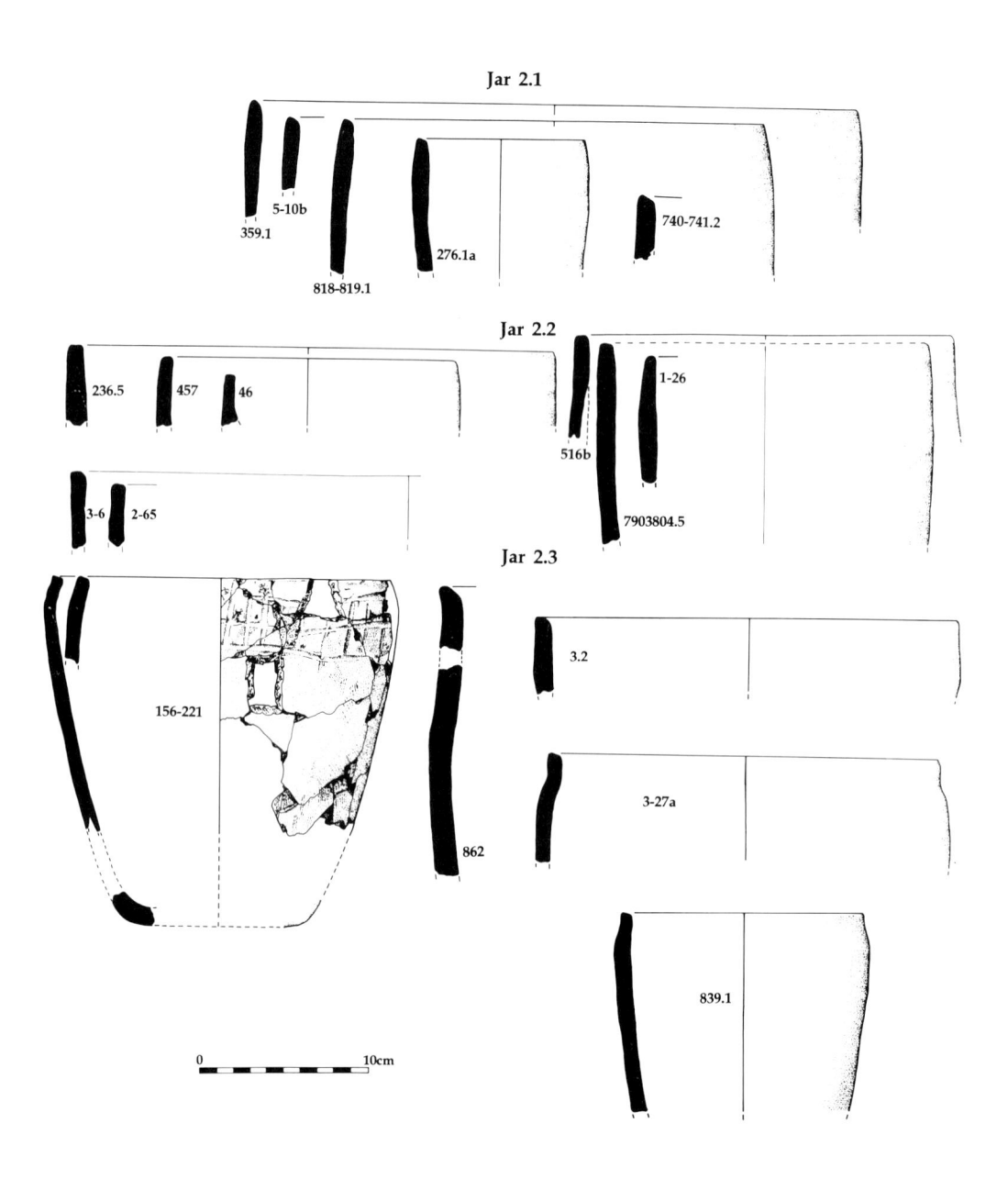

Figure 16: Pottery vessel types: Jar Type 2.

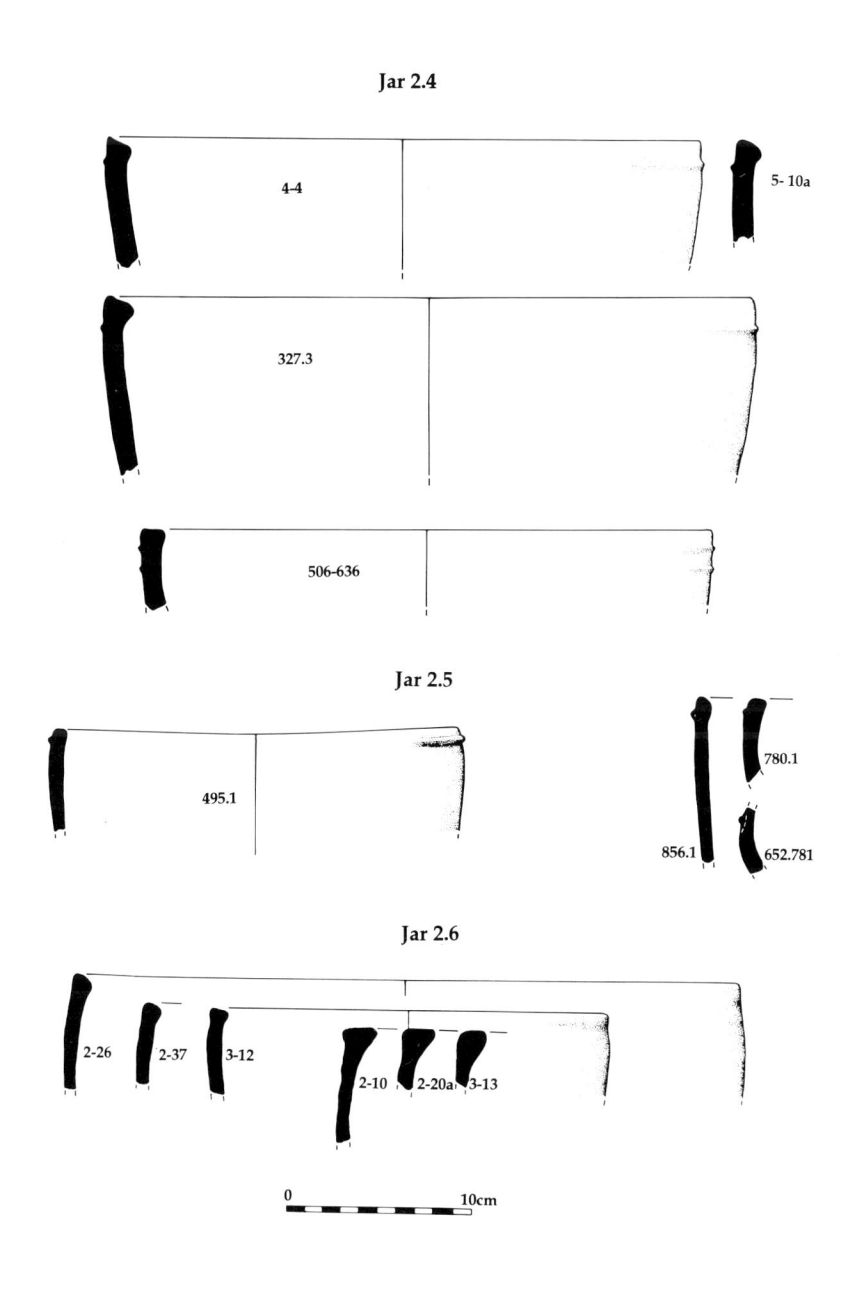

Figure 17: Pottery vessel types: Jar Type 2.

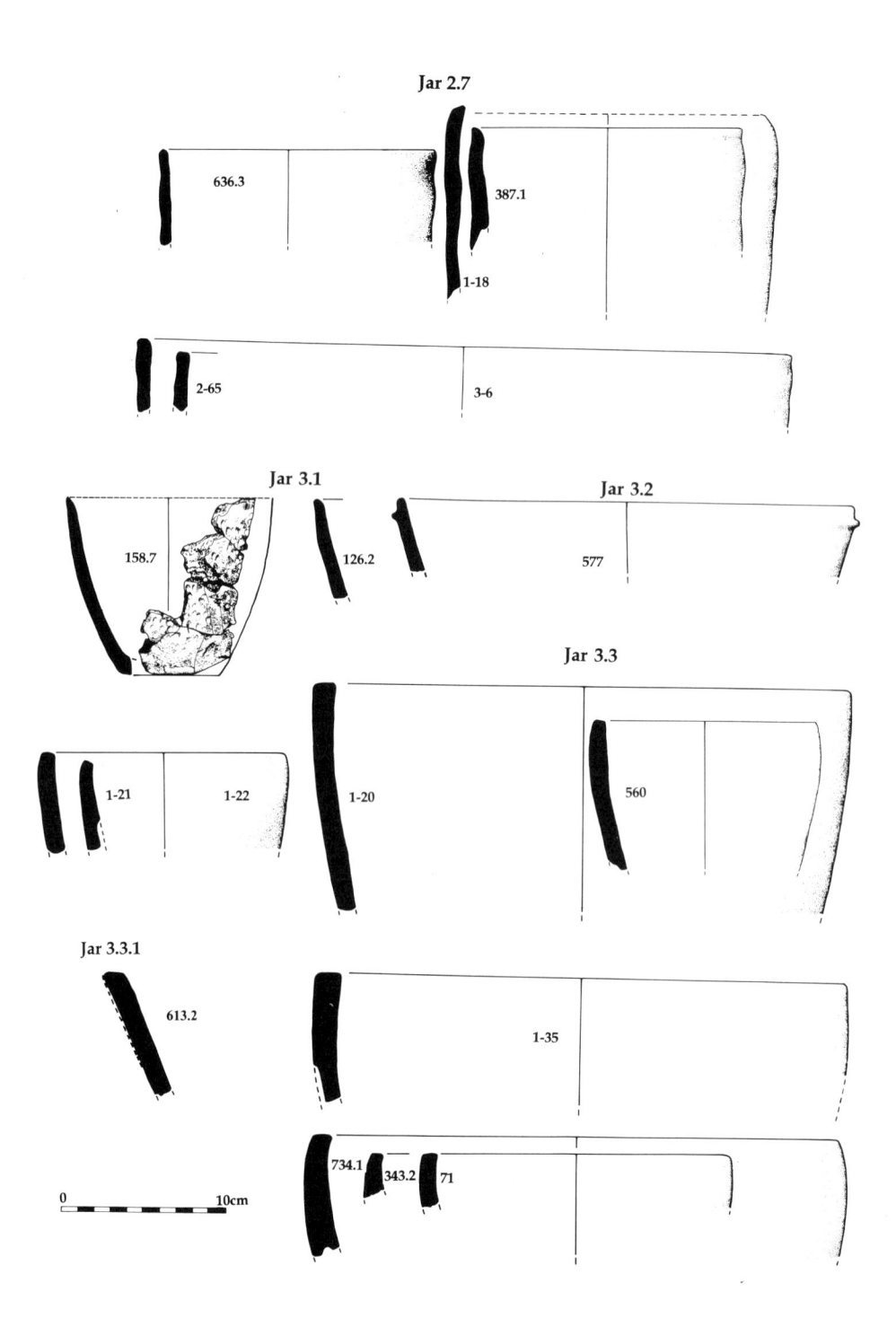

Figure 18: Pottery vessel types: Jar Types 2 and 3.

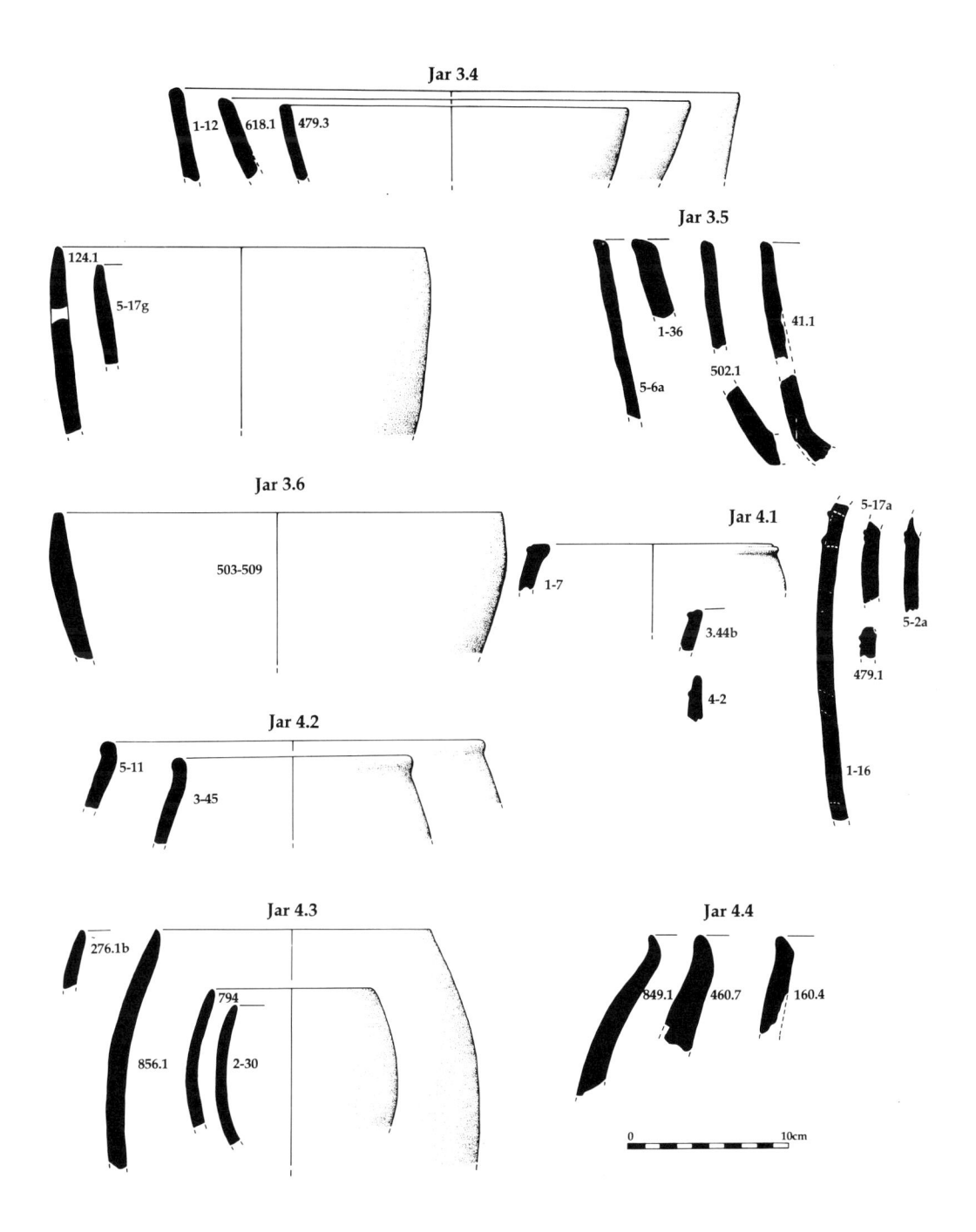

Figure 19: Pottery vessel types: Jar Types 3 and 4.

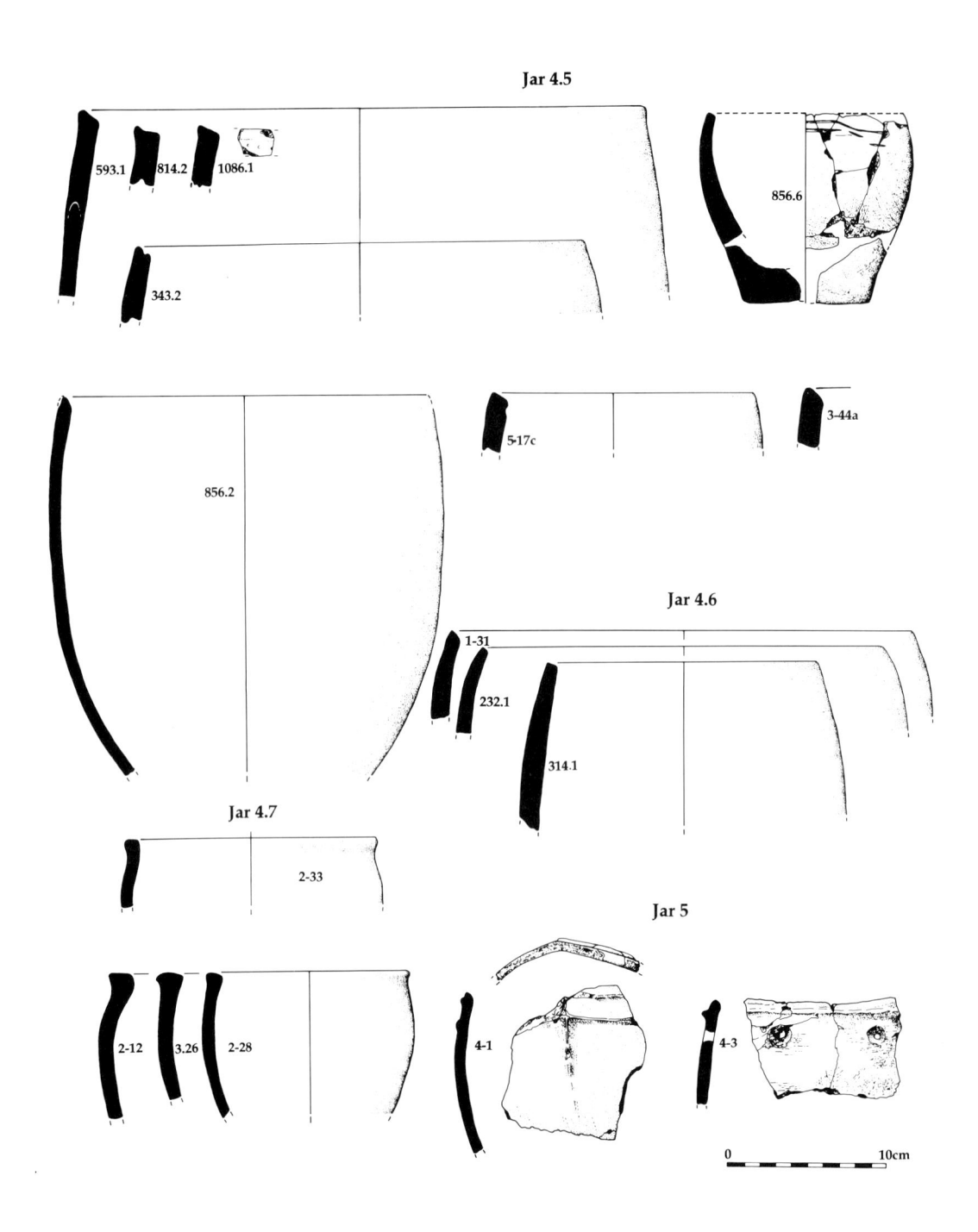

Figure 20: Pottery vessel types: Jar Types 4 and 5.

SITE SEQUENCE AND CHRONOLOGY 47

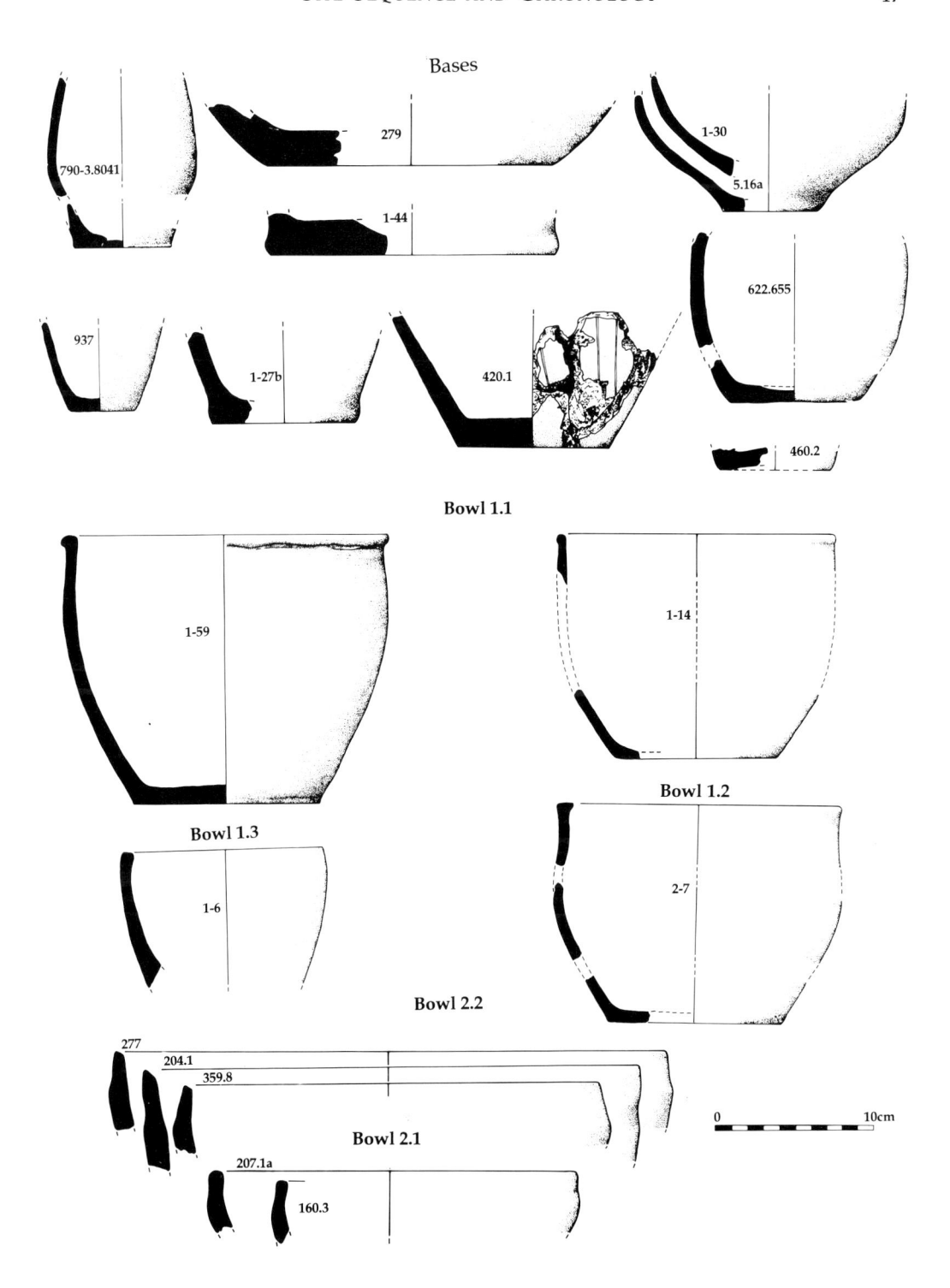

Figure 21: Pottery vessel types: Bases and Bowl Types 1 and 2.

highly burnished, metallic quality of the finish give the impression that this jar type is a skeuomorph of later Bronze Age bronze buckets.

    Jar Form 1.1   (Fig 15; 280.1, 280.2, 2.66b, 1–3a)
        Distinctive shoulder carination and outward turned rim; internal rim angle.
    Jar Form 1.2   (Fig 15; 109, 2–32/34, 2–44, 2–13, 2–22, 2–36)
        Distinctive shoulder carination and simple outward turned rim
    Jar Form 1.3   (Fig 15; 2.24, 2.5, 3.4, 2–21)
        Distinctive shoulder carination with expanded rim

Jar Type 2 – Straight-sided (Figs 16, 17 and 18)
These vessels are numerous and exhibit a limited variety of rim forms – simple and modified – of which the modified is either thickened or bevelled. Fabric types and vessel sizes vary. These vessels appear to be both the earliest type to derive from the stone-built structures and the most widespread.

    Parallels to Jar Type 2 can be found in the Late Bronze Age Village I at Jarlshof (Curle 1934; Hamilton 1956,), where this type is associated with the 'courtyard houses', and with the Late Bronze Age clay moulds. However, Jar Form 2.6, with a thickened rim, has closest affinities with pottery from the Jarlshof Late Bronze Age Village II Phases I and II. At Sumburgh Airport this group is all of Fabric Group 3, and all derives from the South House. Vessel Type 2 is also similar to the pottery from Clickhimin designated Late Bronze Age (Hamilton 1968) and to simple forms from the Benie Hoose (Henshall 1963).

    Jar Form 2.1   (Fig 16; 359.1,5–10b, 818–819.1, 276.1a, 740–741.2)
        Flat-rimmed with internal bevel
    Jar Form 2.2   (Fig 16 and 25; 236.5, 457, 46, 516b, 2–65, 3–6, 7903804.5, 1–26, 793/888)
        Flat rim
    Jar Form 2.3   (Fig 16: 156–221, 3.2, 3–27a 839.1)
        Straight-sided with shoulder below rim
    Jar Form 2.4   (Fig 17; 4–4, 327.3, 506–636, 5.10a)
        Straight-sided with internally expanded bevelled or flat rim; one or more plain external slight ridges below the rim
    Jar Form 2.5   (Fig 17; 495.1, 856.1, 780.1, 652.781)
        Straight-sided with one or more applied cordons
    Jar Form 2.6   (Fig 17; 2–26, 2–37, 3–12, 2–10, 2–20a, 3–13)
        Straight-sided with thickened rim
    Jar Form 2.7   (Fig 18; 1–18, 636.3, 387.1, 2–65, 3–6)
        Rounded rim

Jar Type 3 – Open (Figs 18 and 19)
This type derives from later phases of the site, and Jar Form 3.3 in particular has a very specific grouping in that it is all from the North of the site, is all of fabric group F4, and is very distinctive in appearance. This type is similar to pottery from Jarlshof Late Bronze Age Village I material (Curle 1934; Hamilton 1956).

    Jar Form 3.1 (Fig 18; 158.7, 126.2)
        Open with thinned rim
    Jar Form 3.2 (Fig 18; 577)
        Open with simple rim; applied cordon

Jar Form 3.3 (Fig 18; 734.1, 343.2, 71, 560, 1–22, 1–20, 1–35, 1–21)
  Open with curved sides and flat rim
Jar variety 3.3.1 (Fig 18; 613.2)
  Open with straight, splayed sides and flat rim
Jar Form 3.4 (Fig 19; 479.3, 618.1, 1–12, 5.17g, 124.1)
  Open with rounded rim
Jar Form 3.5 (Fig 19; 5.6a, 1–36, 502.1, 41.1)
  Open with slightly everted and flattened rim
Jar Form 3.6 (Fig 19; 503–509)
  Open with slight carination below rim

Jar Type 4 – Ovoid (Figs 19 and 20)
Forms of this type vary from simple rims, to thickened rims, to small applied cordons. Closed vessel forms were found in the Jarlshof Late Bronze Age Village I, and parallels to forms 4.2 and 4.7 derived from the Jarlshof Late Bronze Age Village II Phase I. Pottery similar to vessel form 4.2 was also found at Mavis Grind (Cracknell and Smith 1983).

Jar Form 4.1 (Fig 19; 1–7, 3.44b, 1–16, 4–2, 5–17a, 479.1, 5–2a)
  Ovoid with simple rim; one or more applied cordon
Jar Form 4.2 (Fig 19; 5–11, 3–45)
  Ovoid with rolled rim
Jar Form 4.3 (Fig 19; 2–30, 794, 276.1b, 856.1)
  Ovoid with rounded rim
Jar Form 4.4 (Fig 19; 849.1, 460.7, 160.4)
  Ovoid with everted rim
Jar Form 4.5 (Fig 20; 856.2, 856.6, 593.1, 814.2, 1086.1, 5.17c, 3–44a, 343.2)
  Ovoid with slight internal bevel
Jar Form 4.6 (Fig 20; 1–31, 232.1, 314.1)
  Ovoid with flattened rim
Jar Form 4.7 (Fig 20; 2–12, 3–26, 2–28, 2–33?)
  Ovoid with thickened everted rim

Jar Type 5 – Square vessel (Fig 20, 4–1, 4–3)
Four sherds (one rim, one base and two body sherds) survive to indicate the presence of cornered or squared vessels. Unfortunately the sherds are small, and no idea of overall vessel shape or size can be deduced. The application of a decorative narrow cordon along the corner of the rim sherd 4–1 emphasises that this pot shape was obviously intended.

Fragments of square shaped pottery vessels were found at Jarlshof from the wall material of Dwelling III, which is of Late Bronze Village I phase. Square steatite vessels were recovered from both Jarlshof and Sumburgh Airport (see below). The square pottery base from Jarlshof was associated with rim sherds with small cordons below the rim (Curle 1934, 284). The sherd from Sumburgh displays small cordons and was associated with a mended rim sherd with a cordon below the rim. These sherds are essentially of Jar Form 4.1, and in fabric F3, the steatite content allowing the production of a highly burnished surface.

Bowls

Bowl Type 1 – Deep bowls (Fig 21)
These bowls derive from the interior of the houses, mainly the North House early Iron Age phases, and appear to relate to the last phase of occupation within the South House (see below).

The profile of Bowl Form 1.2 is markedly similar to that illustrated as part of the Jarlshof Late Bronze Age Village II Phase II (Hamilton 1956, 38, Fig 19, 6). An example of Bowl Form 1.1 can also be seen in the material from Jarlshof, described as from between dwellings IV and V (National Museum of Scotland), which is Hamilton's Late Bronze Village II. Bowls which appear similar also occur at Clickhimin, from the Early Iron Farmstead (Hamilton 1968, 42).

> Bowl Form 1.1 (Figs 21 and 22; 1–59, 1–14)
>   Deep, smooth profiled bowl with external expanded rim
> Bowl Form 1.2 (Fig 21; 2–7)
>   Deep bowl with distinct belly angle and internally bevelled rim
> Bowl Form 1.3 (Fig 21; 1–6)
>   Deep bowl with flattened rim

Figure 22: Bowl: Form 1.1, vessel 1–59 (Copyright Shetland Museum).

Site Sequence and Chronology

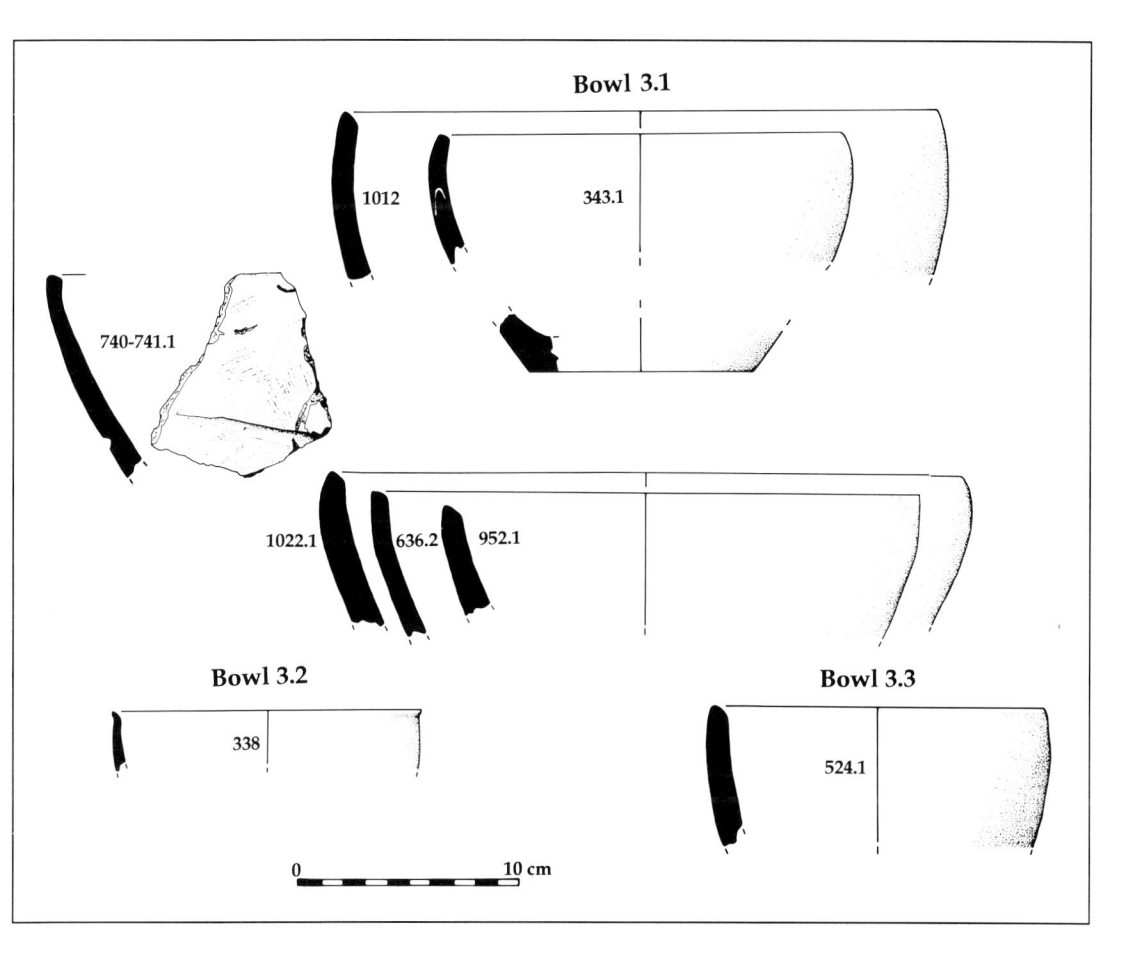

Figure 23: Pottery vessel types: Bowl Type 3.

Bowl Type 2 – Open bowl
Open bowls appear more dispersed through the site both in terms of phase and location. Parallels are not easy to define, as where only part of a vessel survives, the angle at which the rim is drawn is crucial in determining how the vessel is interpreted. However, open bowls, particularly those of Form 2.3, were found at Clickhimin from the Early Iron Age Farmstead (Hamilton 1968, 42), and representatives of Form 2.1 were found at Jarlshof Late Bronze Age Village I (Hamilton 1956, 30).

> Bowl Form 2.1 (Fig 21; 160.3, 207.1a)
> Open-mouthed with thinned rim forming a shoulder; simple rounded rim form
> Bowl Form 2.2 (Fig 21; 359.8, 204.1, 277)
> As 2.1 but rim with flattened internal bevel

Bowl Type 3 – Ovoid bowls (Fig 23)
Ovoid or closed bowls derived from the later phases of occupation at Sumburgh Airport. A small cooking pot from Jarlshof Late Bronze Age Village I (Hamilton 1956, 30) is similar to this vessel type, particularly to Form 3.1, as are the bowls from Clickhimin Early Iron Age Farmstead (Hamilton 1968, 42).

> Bowl Form 3.1 (Fig 23; 636.2, 952.1, 1012, 343.1, 1022.1, 740–741.1)
>   Closed-mouthed with internally bevelled flattened rim
> Bowl Form 3.2 (Fig 23; 338)
>   Closed-mouthed with small everted lipped rim
> Bowl Form 3.3 (Fig 23; 524.1)
>   Ovoid with internally bevelled flattened rim

Bases by C. Yarrington

(Fig 21)
The majority of base-body profiles are flat with flared walls (e.g. 279, 460.2). The angle of flaring varies. Most walls flare slightly, as in the small vessel 937, or near 45 %, as in the decorated base 420.1. The latter has a very sharp profile. Others flare widely. Base 1–44 may have had a vertical wall or a developed foot. A few bases have a slight foot from which the wall flares out (e.g. 1–27b). Sufficient body sherds are associated with bases 622–655 and 790–3.804/1 to suggest round bodied vessels. Base 5–16a, and the body sherd 1–30 come from vessels with footed bases and wide-flared and sinuous or globular bodies. The reconstructed vessel 2–96 has only the rim missing and is of a flat-based bucket-shaped pot with flared walls with a high-set ledge carination.

Decorative techniques by J. Downes and C. Yarrington

The decorative techniques described here are those concerned with such methods as applying and impressing designs upon a vessel. These techniques are useful as signatures in the development of a chronological sequence. It should be remembered that the use of colour, slip and burnishing are also important considerations in the design of a vessel. For instance, it has been proposed that steatite was included in the vessel matrix so that the pot could be burnished to an attractively glossy finish (Fojut 1993). Surface finish is discussed more fully below.

Impressed decoration

Four distinctive methods of impressing patterns into the clay surface were used: cord; pitting; jabs; 'finger' marks.

Cord (Figs 24 and 27; 78.1a, 79–81, 185, 194.3, 195.1, 254, 387.4, 417.1, 437.5, 454.1, 1041, 1062.2, 1080; 2–66d and e)
There are thirteen examples of cord-impressed decoration, all of fabric group F7. The impressions are consistent in being elongated in shape and, on several sherds, are arranged in close set bands of lines, often paired. These bands are placed either

horizontally or diagonally, sometimes forming a V shape which may have originally been part of a chevron pattern. These V shapes can be infilled by more horizontal cord impressed lines. The carinated flanged rim 2–66d has faint traces of a herringbone pattern across the carination and the interior is completely covered with sets of opposing diagonal and horizontal lines. Sherd 454.1 is decorated only on the interior, and 254 and 437.5 are decorated on both sides.

The five rims are all everted with 2–66d and e, 254 and possibly 78.1 being distinctively flanged. Sherd 454.1 is distinctive in the unusual flattening off of the brim. Five of the sherds demonstrate rounded (convex) walls, with 185 S-shaped, and on each the decoration is visible only above the maximum point of curvature. Wall thickness varies from thin to thick, but most sherds are about 9 mm thick. Only two rim diameters could be estimated, those of 2–66d and 454.1; they are from a medium-sized and a small/medium-sized vessel, respectively.

Cord decoration occurs on pottery from a number of other sites in Shetland, all of which have earlier Bronze Age components. At South Nesting, from a cairn with a cremation came a sherd of cord-impressed pottery, with cord impressions running horizontally around the vessel (J. Bond and S. Dockrill, pers. comm.). From Tougs, Burra Isle, a sherd of pottery associated with the burnt mound and structure (Phase 1 activity) is decorated with cord impressions and is described as part of the neck of a large coarse Beaker (Hedges J. 1986). In a discussion of the ceramic assemblage of Tougs, Hedges notes that at Ness of Gruting, and at Stanydale House and Temple, 'Beaker influence, if not presence' is evident (ibid., 30). The earliest occurrence of cord-impressed ware at Sumburgh Airport was from the early Bronze Age activity below the stone buildings. Although only small portions of the vessels survive, it is possible that the S-shaped profile is indicative of Beaker vessels. The carinated flanged rim, 2–66d, is similar in form to a rim from Jarlshof Midden II (Hamilton 1956, 16), which contained artefacts of early Bronze Age types.

Pitting (Fig 25; 793–888)
Five examples representing at least two vessels are similarly decorated with all-over random pitting of the exterior wall made by a round-ended tool (a bone?). The decoration starts just below the rim. Patchy burnishing has partly obliterated the pitting in places. The rim, 793–888, is from Jar Form 2.2, fabric F3, Phase 10.

Jabs (Fig 27; 78.1b)
There are three very different examples of this form of decoration: sherd 5–17b (not illustrated) has very rough and random stab-like marks across the surface; the applied cordon of 78.1 (associated with cord-impressed decoration) is decorated along its length with single round pits or jabs; and there are faint jab marks on the upper surface of rim 1086.1 (not illustrated). Each sherd is of a different fabric and from a different phase.

'Finger' marks (Figs 18 and 25; 128.1, 158.7, 160.14, 246.1, 418–818–819, 999.1, 160.6, 874.1)
There are fourteen examples with a similar but distinctive form of decoration where the marks were very likely made using part of a finger, although a specialist tool

could have been used. Most are thick, slab-like body sherds with roughly vertically arranged oval and round finger-end impressions which cover the exterior surface. The impressions were made when the clay was still soft. Sherds 160.14 and 246.1 have horizontally placed finger-end impressions and 160.14 is decorated on both surfaces. The small fine vessel 158.7 has the whole of the outside decorated with small oval impressions arranged roughly vertical. These sherds derive on the whole from Phase 10 and are all in fabric group F3.

Sherd 999.1 is decorated with faint, irregular, elongated and vertical impressions. The surface has been highly burnished, so a ripple effect is made by the contrast of the shiny surface with the dull hollows. Sherd 160.6, a very thick body sherd from a fairly small vessel, is covered on the exterior by random finger-nail impressions, most of which are arranged almost horizontally. Although 874.1 exhibits a strictly excised technique, it is included here, as the small double-oval pits may have been made by the pinching of the clay with two finger nails. Such decoration would also serve to give a better grip when handling the vessels.

The 'finger mark' decoration is found on a sherd of pottery from the putative late Bronze Age phase of activity at Kebister; parallels between this pottery and that from the Benie Hoose, Whalsay, and late Bronze Age phases at Tofts Ness, Orkney are drawn in the Kebister report (Dalland and MacSween, forthcoming). A sherd of similarly decorated pottery was found in the Neolithic House 2 at Scord of Brouster (Whittle 1986), although the fabric appears to have been different from the examples cited above.

Incised and grooved decoration
Incision and grooving are distinguished by the breadth of the scoring tool used. Gashed lines of varying width are treated here as incisions. It is possible, particularly of gashes, that some of these marks were caused by accident rather than by process of deliberate decoration. This is the largest category of decoration, with 34 examples, and has been subdivided according to motif: single and multiple incised lines; single and multiple grooved lines; grooved panels; grooved lattices; grooves with cordons. All are of fabric groups F3 or F4, except the group of sherds decorated with cordons which are of F1. Twelve examples are from the South House and derive from later phases. Of the 24 examples from the North House, 21 are from late phases. Both incised and grooved lines could have assisted in the handling of a pot as well as a being a decorative device. Likewise horizontal grooved lines could have been used for hanging or carrying using a thin rope or strap. However such decoration on the interior would indicate a decorative purpose only.

Single and multiple incised lines (Figs 16, 20, 21, 22 and 26; 1–14, 156–221, 256, 327.2, 365.1, 406.9 420.1, 740–741.1, 856.3, 856.6, 887)
A simple form of decoration. Of interest are the rough horizontal lines incised on the exterior of the rim of bowl 856.6 and on the interior of the rim 543.1. The body sherd 365.1 is also decorated on the interior. Sherd 420.1 offers an example of lines possibly made up of dashes, but the decoration is very abraded and may have

Site Sequence and Chronology

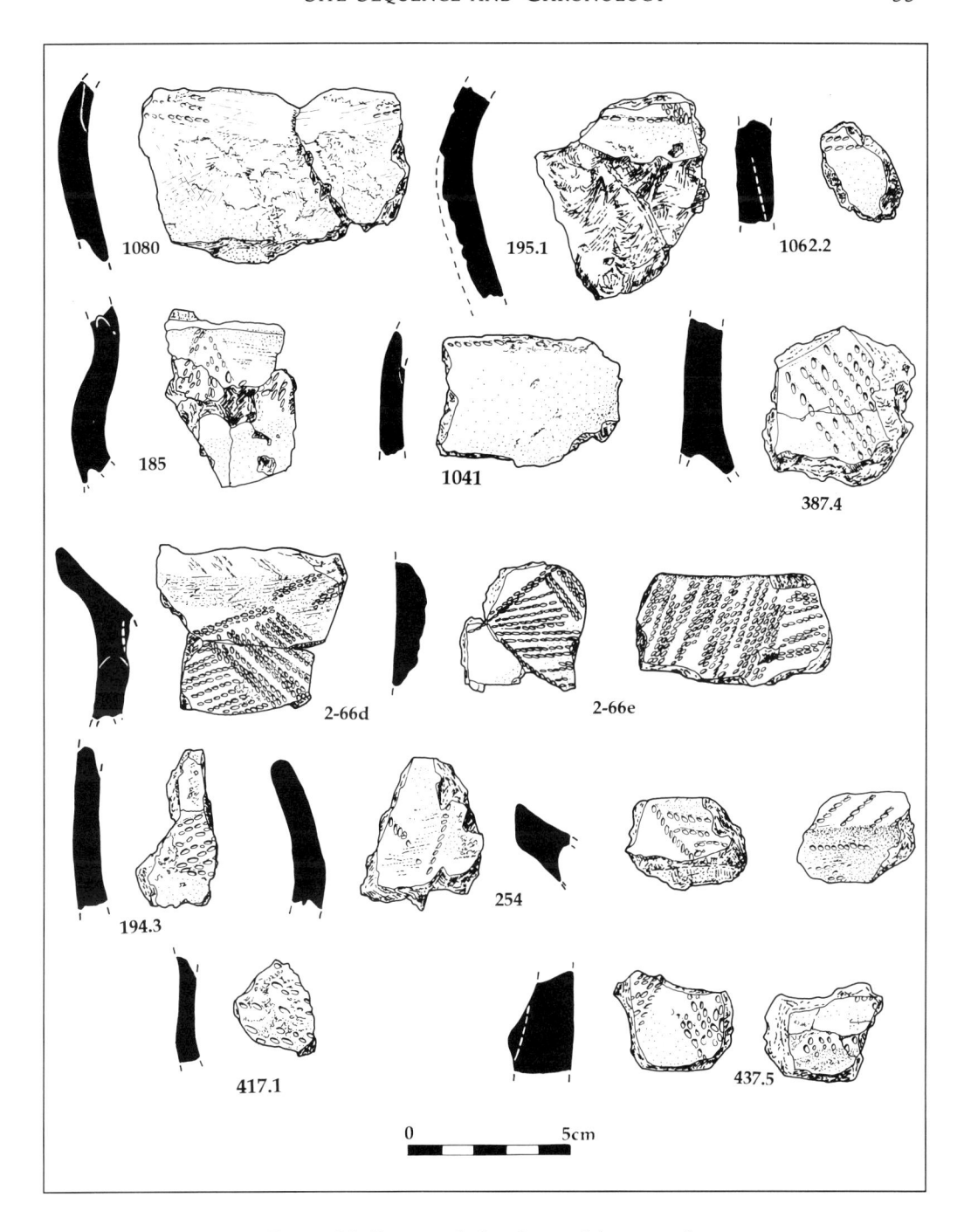

Figure 24: Decorated sherds: cord-impressed.

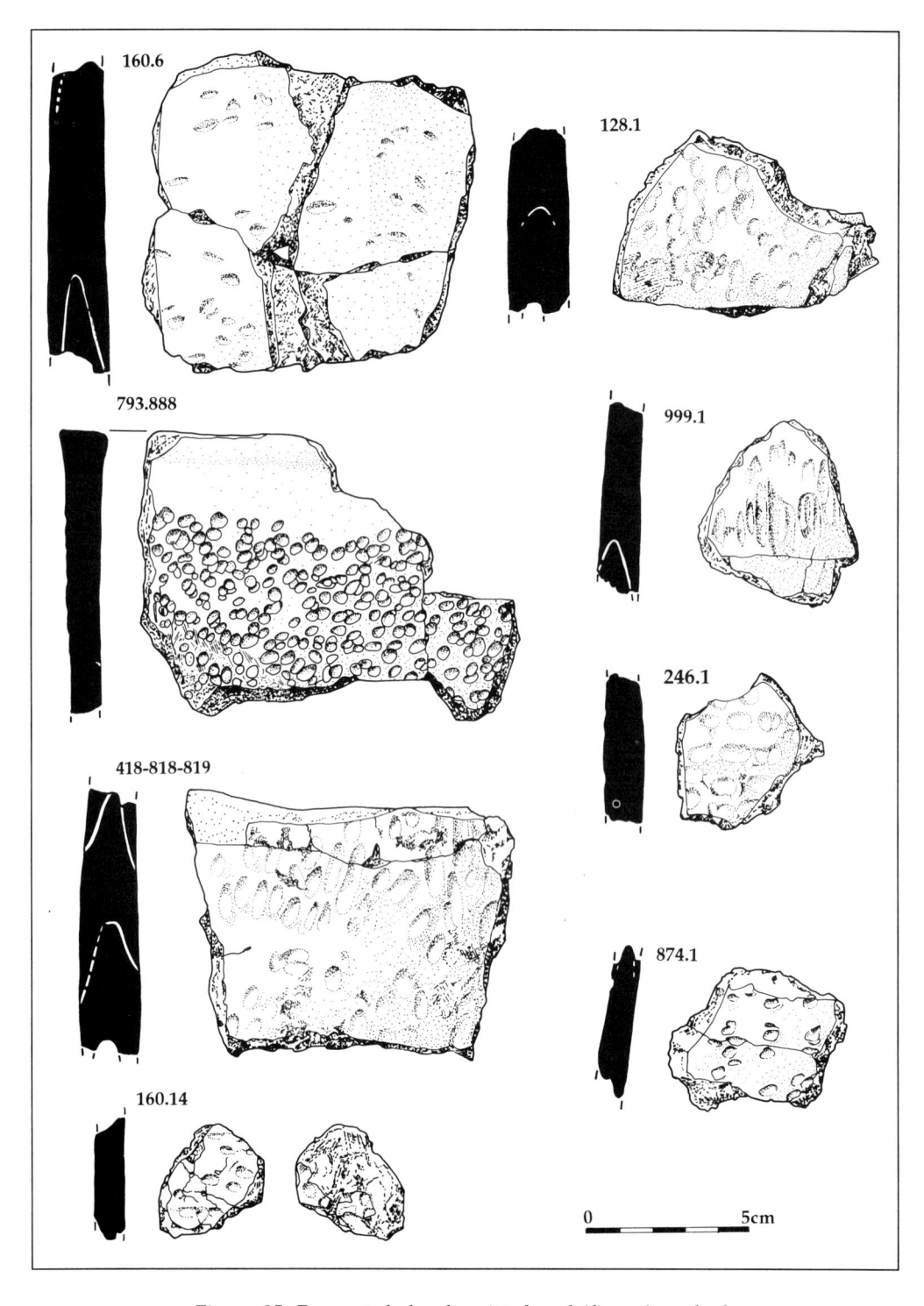

Figure 25: Decorated sherds: pitted and 'finger'-marked.

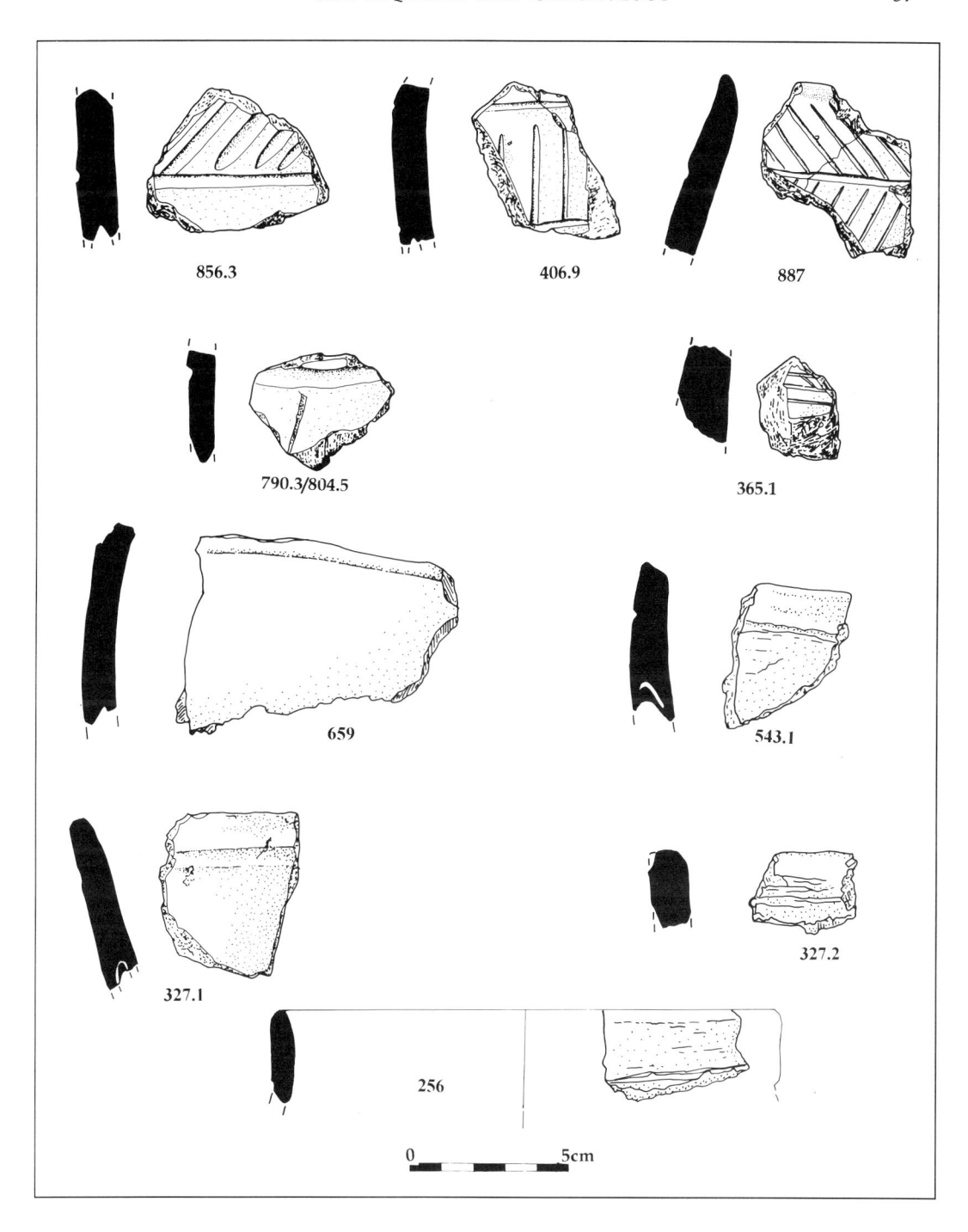

Figure 26: Decorated sherds: incised, grooved and 'finger'-marked.

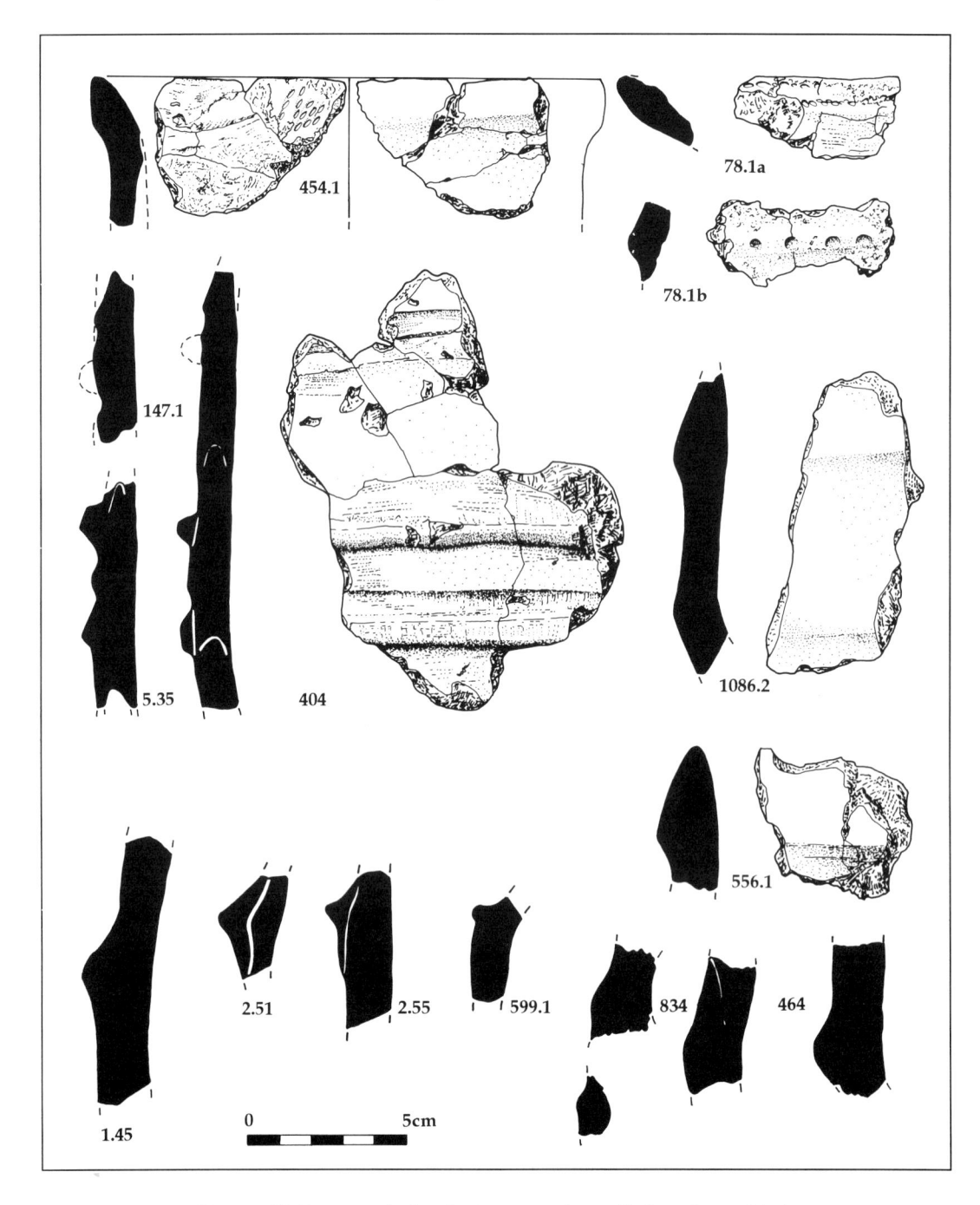

Figure 27: Decorated sherds: impressed, applied and moulded.

originally consisted of continuous lines. Sherd 740–741.1 has part of a large gash below the rim.

Single and multiple grooved lines (Figs 19, 26 and 27; 147.1, 327.1, 404, 479.1, 543.1, 556.1, 790–3 804.5, 659)
The occurrence of grooved lines is similar to that of incised lines. The body sherd 659 has a groove with a domed section and is from Phase 8.1.

Grooved panel (Fig 26; 406.9, 856.3, 887)
The small rim sherd 887 shows part of a horizontal incised herring bone with central line design placed immediately below the rim. Of the two body sherds only 406.9 is clearly decorated with a panel of two horizontal grooved lines infilled with vertical grooved lines; 856.3 has only one horizontal line visible abutted by a series of diagonal lines. All are from the final Phases 9 and 10, and are of fabric group F3.

Grooved lattice (Fig 16; 156–221)
There are two examples of this form of decoration, both from the same vessel or very similar vessels (Jar Form 2.3). A large part of 156–221 survives and shows a band of a fairly roughly drawn lattice pattern below the rim. It is quite difficult to see as the black surface has been highly burnished and the grooves are shallow. The medium-sized pot has flared walls and a flat rim inturned to form a slight shoulder. It is of fabric group F3, Phase 10.

Grooves with cordons
(See below under applied decoration: cordons and grooves, also doubled narrow cordons.)

Grooved rims
Two examples, not illustrated: 1061 of Jar Type 3; and 342.1 of Jar Type 4. There is a possibility that the groove on 1061 is accidental modern damage.

Incised and grooved decoration occurs as a decorative form in pottery assemblages from other sites in Shetland, but there are no markedly close parallels, and the designs cannot be said to provide chronological indications. There are pottery sherds from the earliest levels of occupation at Jarlshof, amongst which was a small sherd of pottery decorated with herring-bone incisions, but with no bounding line as in the sherds from Sumburgh Airport. This decoration runs vertically, not horizontally (National Museums of Scotland). From Ness of Gruting there are many examples of herring-bone incisions, some of which are bounded by parallel lines (Henshall 1958). The herring-bone decoration runs both vertically and horizontally on the pottery from Ness of Gruting, and some is formed by the use of a comb. There are also many examples of grooved lattice decoration from the Ness of Gruting assemblage. However, the form of the pottery from Ness of Gruting is different from that of the assemblage at Sumburgh, being highly decorated and dominated by large cordoned jars (see below). The iron smeltery at Wiltrow, a site thought to have been occupied from the late Neolithic/early Bronze Age to the Iron Age, yielded pottery with a plain, inturned rim, which was decorated with herring-bone incisions running vertically and diagonal incisions within lozenges (Curle 1936).

Applied decoration
There are three main forms of applied decoration: narrow cordons; cordons (and grooves); mouldings.

Narrow cordons (Figs 17, 18, 19 and 20; 1–7, 1–16, 3–44b, 4–1, 4–2, 4–3, 4–4, 5–2a, 5–10a, 5–17a; 327.3, 479.1, 495.1, 506–636, 577, 780.1)
This is the dominant form (24 examples) of applied decoration. Narrow cordons occur on jars of types 2.4, 2.5, 3.2, 4.1 and 5 and are discussed in relation to vessel form above. Such cordons would have served well for easy handling or securing of the pot. These vessels are of fabrics F3 and F4.

Cordons (and grooves) (Fig 27; 2–55, 2.51, 147.1, 404)
Sherds 147.1, 404 and 535 may be from the same large vessel of fabric F1. The decoration is a series of horizontal cordons and grooves. Sherd 404 has been identified as a sherd of late Neolithic Grooved Ware, parallels for which are found in Orkney and other parts of Britain. This sherd derived from Phase 8 and is an example of the redeposition of material.

Mouldings (Figs 24 and 27, 1–45; 78.1b, 437.5, 464, 556.1? 599.1, 834, 1086.2;
This includes those sherds with a wide thickening or moulding which may or may not have been applied. The mouldings all run horizontally across the vessel. The rim 556.1 may have a moulding just below the rim or was part of a very thick-walled vessel with a horizontal groove in the same position. The now detached moulding of 78.1 was additionally decorated with circular pits or jabs; 437.5 is also decorated with cord impressions.

Neither of the two main fabric groups is represented: 1–45, 78.1, 464, 599.1 are of F1; 556.1, 834, 1086.2 are of group F2 and 437.5 is of group F6. Pottery with similar mouldings and vessel wall size was also discovered at Ness of Gruting (Henshall 1958), Stanydale and the Benie Hoose (Henshall 1963), and Yoxie (National Museums of Scotland).

THE CERAMIC SEQUENCE BY J. DOWNES

The establishment of a ceramic sequence at Sumburgh Airport is made difficult because of the complexity of the formation processes (involving considerable amounts of redeposition), the lack of datable material from the stone-built phases, and the lack of a prehistoric ceramic sequence for Shetland. Nonetheless, through the examination of pottery from internal contexts and building episodes it has been possible to identify the earliest occurrence of key diagnostic sherds, as well as of particular pottery types, and thereby to construct a generalised sequence. However, overlap in types cannot be interpreted as continuity in the sequence, for it is clear through the examination of the stratigraphy and the occurrence of pottery types that pottery which is indisputably early, for example, can persist in use in late phases and in association with later pottery types. It has also been possible to trace broad changes in the fabric of the pottery through time.

Bronze Age phases

In total there were fifteen finds of pottery from Phase 2, the timber structures, all of which derived from the features cut into the sand lying beneath the North House. The fabrics were mixed: four finds of F1, four of F2, three of F3, two of F4, and two of F7. There was very little steatite content in the sherds of F3. The only vessel of a recognisable form from Phase 2 is represented by a small sherd 1086.1, F2 (Fig 20), of Jar Form 4.5, the ovoid jar which also occurred in Phases 7, 9 and 10.

Sherd 1080 (Fig 24), the earliest occurrence of cord impressed pottery of fabric F7, also came from Phase 2. This key sherd is attributable to the early Bronze Age; that the other sherds of this form (see above) derive from Phases 9 and 10 in association with later types of pottery is indicative of the movement of material through both cultural and natural formation processes.

Pottery from Phase 4 (later Bronze Age North House) derived from the sand below the paving, from within and on top of the drain, and from within the wall make-up. Although small amounts of material derived from these contexts (c. 10 small finds of pottery), there was an apparent difference between the pottery from Phase 3, the South House, and Phase 4, the North House. Three sherds from within the North House Phase 4 were classified as fabric group F3 but have little steatite content, and on the whole there was very little steatite filler in the pottery, in contrast with the pottery of Phase 3, the South House. A large rim sherd (392.1, not illustrated) derived from this phase. It is of Jar Form 2.4 and fabric group F4, and it is decorated with a narrow ridge below the rim, which is internally bevelled (cf. Fig 17, 4–4 (Phase 9), 5.10 (Phase 10); Fig 17, 327.3 (Phase 8)). This is the earliest occurrence of this distinctive pottery, the distribution of which was restricted to the area in or around the North House. Pottery comparable with this type was found at Jarlshof and is described as being from the Late Bronze Age Village I (Curle 1934, 296; Hamilton 1956, 30).

Only one or two finds of pottery can be attributed to Phase 4.1, later Bronze Age occupation of the North House, none of which is assignable to a vessel form type. Sherd 1016 (not illustrated) is from a coarse large vessel, of fabric F3/4. The base of a small vessel 937 is illustrated (Fig 21). One find of pottery was made from each of Phases 5 and 5.1, North House, neither of which is diagnostic or assignable to a vessel type.

The finds of pottery from Phase 3, the later Bronze Age construction of the South House, are few (five), and represent only fabric groups F1, F2 and F5. The earliest occurrences of the straight-sided, flat-rimmed, Jar Forms 2.1 and 2.2 are from within this phase. Jar Form 2.1 is represented by sherd 1095 (not illustrated), as are all other examples from Phase 10. Jar Form 2.2 is represented by 3–6 (Fig 10), a sherd from a large vessel of a type also found in Phases 8, 9 and 10.

The finds of pottery that can be identified as being associated with Phase 3.1, the occupation of the South House stone building, number only c. 11 finds, but are notable in that for the first time steatite temper (fabric group F3) is present in significant quantity. The whole of the assemblage is composed of fabrics F3 and F4. Of the vessels of F3, 532 (not illustrated) is a thick sherd with little steatite temper, whereas 3–23 and 3–18 (not illustrated) are both sherds of fine ware with highly burnished surfaces, 3–18 displaying a sharp-angled shoulder. This pottery is the same as Jar Type 1, 2–96 (illustrated in Fig 15, Phase 9; see below).

Of the vessels of F4 group in Phase 3.1, 3–22, 3–31, and 3–36 (not illustrated) appear to be all sherds of one large storage jar with coarse sand temper. Sherd 3.2 (Fig 16) is a rim of Jar Form 2.3, a straight-sided jar with a shoulder, also found in Phase 6 and Phase 10.

Fragments from no more than ten vessels were recovered from contexts thought to be associated with Phase 6, the construction of the South House extension during the later Bronze Age. These were all of fabric F3, with heavy steatite content and varied in form from fine highly burnished pottery of Jar Type 1, to coarser vessels with straight sides and simple, flat rims. An example from this phase of Jar Form 2.3, 3–27a, is illustrated (Fig 16); this sherd was part of a medium-sized vessel.

There were c. 5 finds of pottery from Phase 6.1, the occupation identified with the extension of the South House, either of fabric group F3 or F4. Sherd 3–21 is a rim sherd (not illustrated) similar to 3–26 (Fig 20, Phase 9), and represents the earliest occurrence of Jar Form 4.7.

In analysis it appeared that the pottery from Phases 3.1, 6 and 6.1 was similar and comparable, and different from that of Phase 3. Another observation to be made at this point is the differences in form and fabric between the pottery from the later Bronze Age phases of the North and South House. There is a much lower incidence of the use of steatite as temper in the North House, and the vessel types from both houses differ.

There were c. 20 finds of pottery from amongst the rubble from the interior of the houses in Phase 7, of which only one came from the North House. The find from the North House comprised one sherd of soft sandy pottery, of undiagnostic form and with no obvious parallels to the fabric.

From the South House there were several finds which were assignable to vessel types and are illustrated. Sherd 2–66b (Fig 15) is the earliest occurrence of Jar Form 1.1, of which there two examples from Phase 10. Sherd 3–44b is part of a vessel type Jar Form 4.1 (Fig 19), the earliest occurrence of this type of which there are two other examples from Phase 9. Jar Form 4.5 is represented in this phase by 3–44a (Fig 20). Sherds 5–11 and 3–45 (Fig 19) are of the Jar Form 4.2; this vessel type only occurs in Phase 7.

It is possible that there was a brief hiatus in activity in one or both of the houses, as the pottery types do not correlate with those of the preceding phases, but do continue into succeeding phases. However it must be noted that there is coincidence in pottery types and forms between phases preceding 7 and Phases 8–8.1. Based on the pottery evidence, there does not appear to be a significant time lapse between the later Bronze Age phases and the rebuilding of the houses.

Early Iron Age phases

There was a larger amount of pottery from this (Phase 8) than from any of the preceding phases (c. 40 finds). The assemblage derived in the main from the wall make-up and could include material that had gathered around the wall through dumping of midden material (see below). There were more finds of pottery from the South House than the North (24 versus 6 respectively), the former being the thicker walls of a larger structure.

From the North House derived the earliest bowls: Bowl Form 3.1 (Fig 23; 1012); and Bowl Form 3.2 (Fig 23; 338). The earliest occurrence of Jar Forms 2.4 (Fig 17; 327.3) and 4.6 (Fig 20; 320) derived from Phase 8 North House, as did two incised and grooved sherds 327.1 and 327.2.

The earliest occurrences of Jar Form 3.2 (Fig 18; 577– sole example of this type), Jar Form 2.5 (Fig 17; 495), and Bowl Form 2.2 (Fig 21; 277) came from the passages in Phase 8. From the South House Phase 8 the earliest occurrences of Jar Form 2.6 (Fig 17; 3–12, 3–13), Jar Form 2.2 (Fig 16; 457), and Jar Form 1.3 (Fig 15; 3–4) were found, as well as the Grooved Ware (Fig 27; 404).

Thus from this phase no concurrence of vessel types can be identified between the North House, Passages and South House. Material attributed to this phase could have resulted from different processes and therefore need not be exactly contemporary – some of the deposits within walls may have been brought from elsewhere and used as building material, whereas other deposits could have resulted from the dumping of refuse against the walls. However, certain vessel types can be seen to occur only in either the North or the South House, for example Jar Form 2.4 (all F4), which only occurs in the North House and north-west exterior and Jar Form 2.6 (all F3) whose distribution is restricted to the South House.

There was a total of c. 45 finds of pottery from Phase 8.1, the early Iron Age occupation the houses, of which the majority came from the South House. No vessel types from the North House are illustrated, but there are two decorated sherds: 417.1 (Fig 24), decorated with cord impression, and 659 (Fig 26), decorated with grooves.

The South House contained the earliest occurrences of Jar Form 1.2 (Fig 15; 2.32/ 34, 2–36), and Bowl Form 1.2 (Fig 21; 2–7, sole example). Jar Forms 1.3, 2.6, and 4.6 were also found in the South House.

Types of vessels from the South House are the most internally consistent groups from the site. There is concurrence between Phases 8 and 8.1 in Jar Forms 1.3, 2.6 and 4.6. Through Phases 8 and 8.1 the difference in fabric types between the houses continues to be apparent, with F4 more common in the North House, F3 in the South House.

It is a possibility that Phase 9 also contained elements of Phases 8.1 and 10, as in some instances it was difficult to separate the contexts. Fabrics F1, F2, F3, F4 and F5 were represented in this phase. Finds of F3 dominated; there were 126 finds of F3 from this phase, and 76 finds of F4. Many pottery vessels of Phase 9 are illustrated (a reflection of how many large parts of vessels survived), but they will not be detailed here.

There is a continuation of many types seen in previous phases, but some new types appear. Earliest occurrences include Jar Form 3.3 (Fig 18; 1–20,1–21, 343.2), which is characterised by a hard, well fired, smooth matrix, and is similar in appearance to a modern flowerpot. Of the seven examples of this type of pottery, six are from Phase 9, and one from Phase 10. All examples are of fabric F4, and all derive from the North House or North House exterior contexts. Other earliest occurrences are of Bowl Forms 1.1 (Fig 21; 1–14, 1–59) and 1.3 (Fig 21; 1–6), both types from the North House. The sherd size and condition of the sherds from the North and South Houses are indicators that the South House continued to be used during Phase 9, while the North House was filled with refuse (see below).

Post-abandonment phase and ploughing

A vast amount of pottery derives from Phase 10 which, although much of the illustrated material comes from this phase, will not be described in detail. Fabric types represented are F1 (16 finds), F2 (7 finds), F3 (185 finds), F4 (156 finds), F5 (2 finds) and F6 (5 finds) – finds numbers approximate. The majority of finds of fabric F4 came from contexts outside and to the north-west of the North House (118 finds) as did the majority of those of F3 (87 finds).

The vessel types represented are Bowl Forms 2.1, 2.2, 3.1, Jar Forms 1.1, 1.2, 2.2, 2.3, 2.4, 2.7, 3.3, 3.5, 3.6, 4.3, 4.4, 4.5, 4.6, of which Bowl Form 2.1 and Jar Form 3.6 are earliest occurrences of their kind. Some Jar Forms only derive from Phases 9 and 10 – 2.7, 3.5, and 4.3. These represent later, or the latest, types of pottery vessels on the site.

Summary of the ceramic sequence

Through the identification of key pottery types and their earliest occurrence within the stratigraphic sequence, it is possible to refer to a ceramic sequence at Sumburgh Airport. The early Bronze Age timber structures are associated with fine cord impressed ware from small to medium-sized vessels, and a single small sherd of an ovoid jar (Jar Form 4.5). There is then a considerable hiatus in activity on the site, broken by the appearance of later Bronze Age pottery within the wall material of both the North and South Houses. This pottery consists of straight-sided jars (Jar Type 2) with variations in rim form and decoration suggesting that the North House was slightly earlier than the South. Straight sided jars continue to be used during the earliest phases of occupation of the South House, and pottery with a sharp-angled shoulder (Jar Type 1) and the ovoid form (Jar Type 4) also occur.

In the rubble layer antedating the repaving and rebuilding of both houses further forms of ovoid jars occur, and open jars (Jar Type 3) are also found. Early Iron Age carinated jars occur from the rebuilding of the houses onwards. No bowls appear until the early Iron Age phases of occupation. Straight-sided, ovoid and open jars continued to be used during the early Iron Age.

In terms of changes in temper within pottery through time, it can be seen that the coarsest pottery fabrics and organic temper are indicative of the earlier pottery (fabrics F1, F2, F5, F6), some of which is very similar to late Neolithic/early Bronze Age pottery from other Shetland sites such as Stanydale, Yoxie, and Jarlshof early middens (National Museums of Scotland). The fabric group F7 describes only the early Bronze Age cord decorated pottery. Fabric F4 is a very broad description that occurs throughout the sequence at Sumburgh Airport. The steatite temper, fabric F3, also encompasses a wide range of fabrics but does not occur until the later Bronze Age. There is an increase through time both in the amount of steatite used as temper, and in quantity of sherds found containing steatite as temper.

Through the analysis of fabric and vessel types, and specific forms of decoration, it has been shown that pottery was found which dates to the late Neolithic, earlier Bronze Age, later Bronze Age and early Iron Age. That earlier types of pottery occur throughout the stratigraphic sequence is indicative of the complexity of redeposition and formation processes.

STEATITE AND OTHER FINE STONE OBJECTS AS CHRONOLOGICAL INDICATORS by P. SHARMAN

Table 3: Summary of the steatite assemblage.

Type	No. of finds	%
vessels	34	62
plates	1	2
battle-axes	1	2
pendants	1	2
armlets	4	7
smoothers	2	4
fragments	12	22
Total	55	101

Vessels

Steatite vessels derived from a range of phases. Less than 25 % of the vessel fragments were in any way indicative of the vessel shape. Two of the fragments were from round vessels – 948 from a collared vessel with upright walls and a rim almost flat in section (Fig 28, Phase 1/2), and 479 (not illustrated, Phase 10) from a wide-mouthed vessel with walls curving in section and a rough but basically flat rim. Find Pre-1974 U/S 1 (not illustrated) is a wall fragment from the corner angle of a four-sided vessel, whilst A494 (Fig 28, Phase 9) is over half of a wide-mouthed, four-sided vessel with the walls curving to a more vertical angle near the rim, which is slightly convex in section. B151 (not illustrated, Phase 7) is a fragment of a vessel with almost vertical walls and an uneven, roughly flat rim. Rim fragments 426 (Fig 28, Phase 10) and 239 (Fig 28 Phase 9) were slightly less certain in shape, but appeared to be from either four-sided or oval vessels rather than round ones, with steep almost vertical walls and flat or slightly convex rim sections. Including those described above, all the rim sections (12 in all) were undecorated and very simple with flat or slightly convex chunky sections (B230 and A92; Phase 10), the sandstone vessel, had slight bevels on the exterior), or with tapering irregular or convex rim sections (e.g. 752, Fig 28; Pre-1974 U/S 4–5). The rim forms and tooling on the sherds indicated that a minimum number of 10 vessels was represented in the assemblage.

Table 4: Occurrence of steatite vessels.

Vessel shape	Amount	% of vessels	% of total assemblage
round	2	6	4
four-sided	3	9	5
oval/four-sided	3	9	5
indeterminate	26	76	47
Total	34	100	61

Fragment 948 (Fig 28), the collared vessel fragment from the early Bronze Age phase, has almost exact parallels in a rim fragment found at the Benie Hoose on Whalsay (Henshall 1963a, 43, Fig 7.33) and one found at Kebister (Sharman, forthcoming). The fragment derives from a context assigned to Phases 1/2/2.1, which associates the find – assuming it is securely located – with an early Bronze Age radiocarbon date.

The four-sided vessel B151 from Phase 7 is paralleled in a domestic context by the four vessels recovered in a cache in a late Bronze Age structure at Jarlshof (Curle 1934, 92–3; Hamilton 1956, 20) and by a rim fragment from a subrectangular vessel also found in a late Bronze Age deposit at Tofts Ness on Sanday, Orkney (Smith, forthcoming). Four-sided vessels have been found in a funerary contexts, such as the urn from a cist at Little Asta, Tingwall and 3 vessels from a cist in a cairn at Muckle Heog on Unst (Corrie 1932, 73; Henshall 1963b, 150 and 256). The other rim and vessel sherds (apart from A494), with such simple rims and uncertain forms, are too small and undiagnostic to try to draw any definitive parallels, although one might perhaps compare those with finer, tapering irregular or convex rim sections like 752 (Fig 28) and Pre-1974 U/S 4–5 with the 2 rim sherds found in the late Bronze Age/early Iron Age structures on the Calf of Eday, Orkney (Stevenson 1939, Figs 4.18, 4.19 and 5.11).

Although A494 (Fig 28) is a square vessel, of which there are indisputable Bronze Age examples, this vessel is more akin to the Late Norse (12th to late 15th centuries AD) four-sided vessel, peculiar in form to Shetland, with many parallels, such as the pieces from Jarlshof (Hamilton 1956, 165–6 and passim) and the Catpund soapstone quarry (Sharman, in prep.). The vessel is perhaps an indication of the extent to which the later phases 9 and 10 have been mixed and later material has intruded.

Sandstone vessels are rare, although a four-sided sandstone vessel was recovered from late Bronze Age contexts at Jarlshof (Hamilton 1956, 26). Most other sandstone vessels are more like cups, usually lamps, and usually from Iron Age contexts such as those from Jarlshof and Clickhimin (Hamilton 1956, 54; Hamilton 1968, 79 and 113).

Plate

Find B221 (not illustrated) was identified as a plate rather than a vessel fragment because of the way in which it had been worked. The two flat faces had been worked using a blunt pointed instrument in short percussive strokes, in a way which indicated that the piece was flat, with no upright walls to hinder the process, producing grooves in random directions on one side and a diamond lattice effect on the other. This style of tooling has only so far been seen on Norse products such as those manufactured at the Catpund soapstone quarry (Sharman, in prep.) and found at settlement sites such as Jarlshof, Kebister and Sandwick on Unst (see, respectively, Bigelow 1985, 107; Buttler 1984, 23; Sharman, forthcoming). However, as the piece appears to have been found in an early Iron Age context, it is unusual. Bakeplates have not been recognised from prehistoric contexts before; indeed they are usually seen as a Late Norse item, dating to the 12th century AD or later (Buttler 1989, 195).

Battle-axe

Find numbered 723 (Fig 29) is a type of asymmetrical battle-axe, with a curved blade larger than the roughly semicircular butt and belongs to Roe's Crichie group of battle-axes (Roe 1966, 212, Fig 7b). It is, in fact, closest in form, though not decoration, to the battle-axe from Broomend of Crichie itself (Dr A. Sheridan, pers. comm.). This was found within a stone circle, near a group of cremation deposits (Clarke et al. 1985, 89, 272, fig 4.10; Dalrymple 1884) one of which was associated with what appears to be a Food Vessel Urn (Dr A. Sheridan, pers. comm.). Such urns are not well-dated, but the Crichie type of axe is regarded as contemporary with the middle Bronze Age Snowshill group in Southern England (Roe 1966, 212). Miniature battle-axes of different form (Roe 1966, 242–3) have also been found at the late Neolithic/early Bronze Age settlement at the Ness of Gruting (Henshall 1958, 392, Fig 19, B and C) and with a child's inhumation in a cist at Doune, Perthshire (Hamilton 1959).

Thus the parallels to the battle-axe are, in general, from the early to middle Bronze Age, whereas the other artefacts from Phase 8.1 point to the occupation of the houses being later Bronze Age. It is possible that the battle-axe was passed down as an heirloom, or found during the later occupation and kept.

Pendant

Find B223 (Fig 29), a slender subrectangular pendant, is a carefully crafted but very simple object and as such has no close typological parallels. A possible diamond-

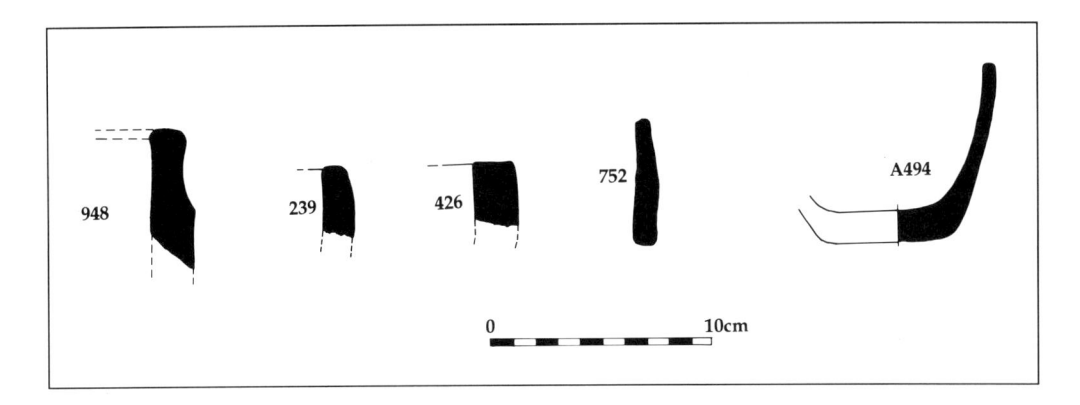

Figure 28: Steatite profiles

shaped pendant with curved edges was found at Yoxie on Whalsay (Henshall 1963a, 45, Fig 8.2) and vaguely similar objects were recovered from Clickhimin for example, where a heart-shaped or leaf-shaped sandstone pendant was recovered from early Iron Age contexts and where several rectangular and circular garnetiferous schist plaques were also found in Iron Age contexts (Hamilton 1968, 40, 85, 115). The pendant must therefore be dated by its context (364, Phase 8.1), rather than the reverse.

Armlets
Two of the armlets (B226, Phase 7, and B227, Phase 9; Fig 29) were only small in diameter – 45–50 mm – the other (B228, Phase 9) being 80 mm, but neither the size nor, indeed, the section of such objects are diagnostic in terms of date. Parallel artefacts are found at the late Bronze Age/early Iron Age site of Mavis Grind (Cracknell and Smith 1983, 27, Fig 9), from the Iron Age round house at Jarlshof (Hamilton 1956, 37, Fig 17) and deposits associated with the broch at Underhoull (Small 1967, 234, Fig 9). The fact that they were made of local schist rather than jet or cannel coal suggests that they are pre-Norse in date (Batey 1988).

Possible smoothers
The polished facets on finds Pre-1974 U/S 7 and 8, and the clean, shiny and slightly scratched break face on the collared urn fragment 948 (Fig 28) find parallels at late Bronze Age Jarlshof where two such items were recovered, albeit of unidentified stone (Curle 1934, 98–100; Hamilton 1956, Fig 12.9). Such items are undiagnostic and have been interpreted as polishers. Smoothers and burnishers of pumice, pebbles and other types of stone have been found, for example, at Yoxie (Henshall 1963a, 45).

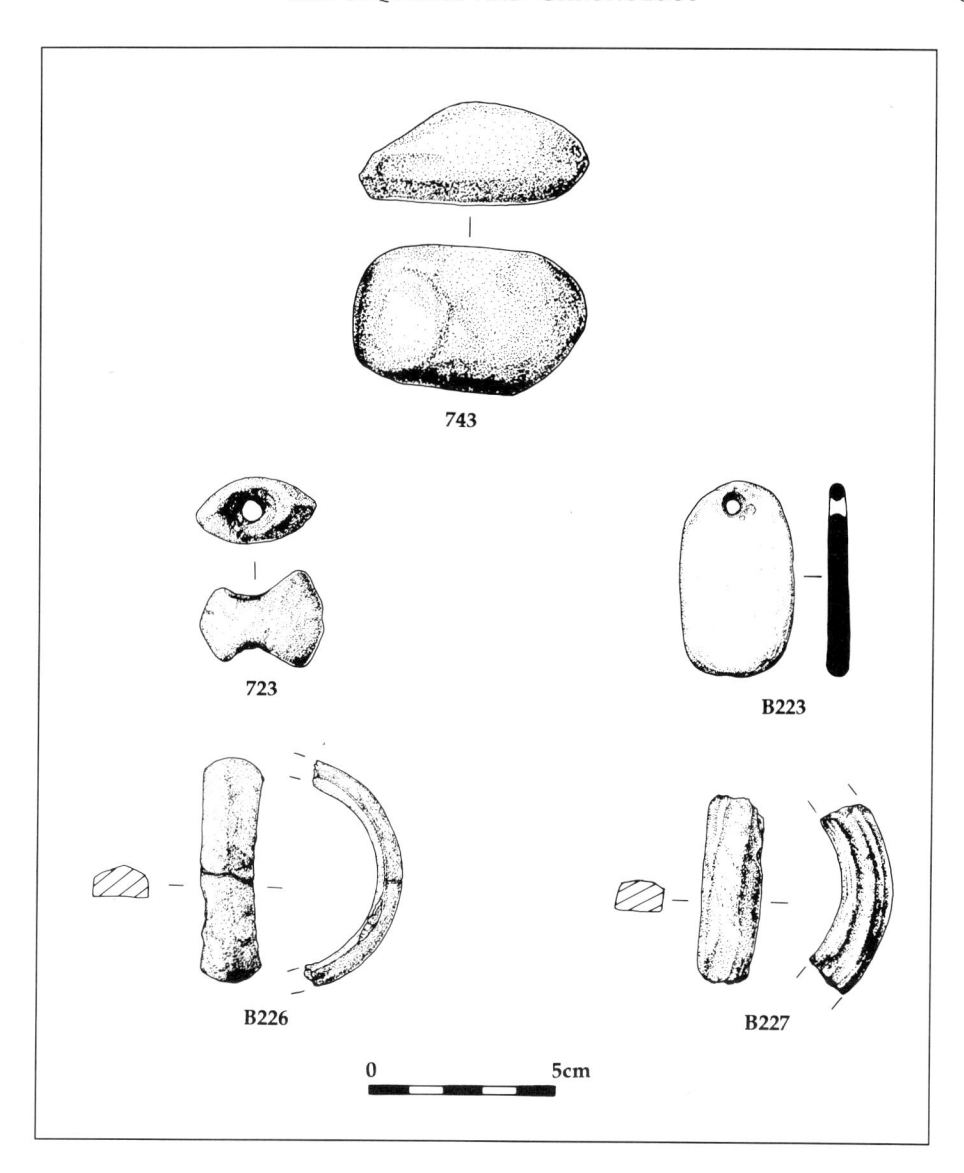

Figure 29: Steatite and fine-stone artefacts.

Coarse Stone Tools as Chronological Indicators by A. Clarke

The assemblage of coarse stone tools comprises over 1000 artefacts and a similar number of shale fragments, both unworked and worked. The artefact types are described fully in the following section this report, as are aspects of the assemblage concerning raw materials and use. The context of the artefacts is considered here, both as an indicator of the chronology of the site and with respect to changes in the use of different parts of the site through time.

Methods of analysis

As in the case of the pottery, the coarse stone tools were analysed at two different times and by two different specialists. Raymond Lamb carried out preliminary analysis and classification of the stone tools from his 1974 excavations, except the ard points, for which Sian Rees produced a report. Ann Clarke subsequently studied the whole assemblage except for c. 80 artefacts, most of which were from the SANHS excavations. There existed an earlier catalogue of this material, and the artefacts are included in Ann Clarke's report with the proviso (shown by bracketing) that it was not known how they would compare to her assignation of artefact types. Shale tools from these 80–odd artefacts have not been included in this concordance as it was not possible from the descriptions to assign a type. The main discussion of the artefact types and the phasing is confined to the artefacts which Ann Clarke has examined, although a summary of the additional artefacts is given, and where necessary these are referred to in the discussion.

Summary of contexts and phasing

Only one stone artefact, an ard point, is present in a Phase 1 context. There are few artefacts from the houses themselves before Phase 7 (Table 5); from the North House, Phases 2 and 4, there are only ard points and shale flaked stone bars, as well as a club and a stone disc. The finds from the walls of Phases 4 and 5 are similar in composition as are the artefacts from external contexts in Phase 2 (Table 1). The use of the clubs continues throughout all phases of the site, but they are particularly associated with the North House, either in internal contexts or else in the wall heaps. There were even fewer artefacts from the South House in Phases 3 and 6 comprising ard points, a shale flaked stone bar and a sandstone flaked stone bar. Phase 7, the deposits between the primary and secondary floors, shows little change from earlier use in the North House and passages as here only flaked stone bars and an ard point are present. In contrast, Phase 7 of the South House comprises a larger number of artefacts, which forms a varied assemblage including, amongst other things, waisted stone slabs and countersunk pebbles. They also mark the first use of heart-shaped pieces and other types of shaped slate, and the main use of the sandstone flaked stone bars. The assemblage composition of Phases 8 and 8.1 in each of the houses is similar to their previous Phase 7 composition, and in this respect the assemblages from the passages are more varied than those of the North House. Cleavers and Skaill knives make their first appearance, in the South House, and here there is a further number of heart-shaped pieces. Artefacts from the external contexts of Phase 8 and 8.1 are similar to those from the North House with ard points, flaked stone bars, cleavers and clubs.

Phase 9 indicates a change in assemblage composition in the North House, as there is a greater variety of artefact types, and there are more points of comparison

Table 5: Phase and distribution of coarse stone artefact types. (See Fig 30 for location areas)

Phase	Area	Ards	Flaked shale bars	Flaked sandstone bars	Cobble tools	Skaill knives	Stone discs	Cleavers	Clubs	Shaped slate	Heart-shaped pieces	Misc.	Perforated
2	NH	-	2	-	-	-	1	-	-	-	-	-	-
	Ext	1	4	-	-	-	-	-	2	1	-	-	-
2.1	Ext	-	2	-	-	-	-	-	-	-	-	-	-
3	SH wall	3	1	1	-	-	-	-	-	-	-	-	-
4	NH	4	8	-	-	-	-	-	1	-	-	-	-
	NH wall	4	5	-	1	-	-	-	2	-	-	-	-
4.1	NH	-	1	-	-	-	-	-	-	-	-	-	-
5	NH wall	3	6	-	-	-	-	-	1	-	-	-	-
6	SH	1	-	-	-	-	-	-	-	-	-	-	-
	NH	1	11	1	-	-	-	-	-	-	-	-	-
7	SH	6	7	5	4	1	2	-	1	2	3	2	-
	PASS	-	7	-	-	-	-	-	-	-	-	-	-
	NH	8	15	3	1	-	-	-	3	-	-	-	-
	NH wall	7	7	-	-	-	-	-	-	-	-	-	-
8	SH wall	1	7	1	-	1	-	1	-	1	-	-	-
	PASS	-	14	2	2	1	1	-	-	1	-	-	-
	Ext CW	-	-	-	-	1	-	1	-	-	-	-	-
	NH	-	2	-	-	-	-	-	-	-	-	-	-
8.1	SH	2	17	1	2	6	4	-	-	-	5	-	1
	PASS	1	1	-	-	-	-	-	1	-	-	-	-
	Ext CE	7	47	1	1	-	-	4	2	-	2	1	1
	Ext NE	8	80	2	-	-	-	2	4	-	-	-	-
	NH	9	29	5	35	4	3	-	1	1	1	1	2
	NH wall	28	122	4	5	-	2	4	5	4	1	-	2
	SH	22	17	6	16	7	1	-	3	-	-	1	1
9	PASS	5	13	6	6	2	-	1	-	-	-	-	-
	Ext NE	-	6	-	3	2	-	-	-	-	-	-	-
	Ext CW	-	1	-	1	-	-	-	1	-	-	-	-
	Ext S	5	30	5	2	-	2	1	-	-	-	1	-
	Ext E	-	3	-	-	-	-	-	1	-	2	1	1
10	Ext N	36	73	3	3	-	1	2	2	1	1	4	-
	Ext W	2	8	1	-	-	-	-	1	-	-	1	-
	Ext S	2	1	-	-	-	-	-	-	-	-	-	-

with the assemblage from the South House. The main differences between the houses in this phase is the larger proportion of ard points appearing in the South House and the larger proportion of shale flaked stone bars from the North House. Phase 9 is also marked by the greater number of cobble tools from all internal and external contexts and this observation is supported by the numbers of the cobble tools which were not seen during this analysis. The following comments on the cobble tools are based solely on those which were available for study. As there are so few cobble tools from earlier phases, these have not been mentioned previously: a quern rubber and a notched cobble come from a passage Phase 8 and the rest are quite plain forms with no evidence for faceting. The few pounders/grinders that are present are from both internal and external contexts of Phase 9. Because of the rather indefinable nature of much of the cobble tool assemblage it is difficult to note any differences or similarities between the houses. In Phase 9 both the houses have sub-spherical cobbles of granite which may be unused. Whilst the same phase of the North House has a number of the heavily flaked cobbles, these are absent in the South House. The flat oval, side-faceted cobbles and the domed cobbles with flat bases occur in external contexts of Phases 9 and 10, and, with the exception of one from a passage, are not present internally. In the external contexts of Phase 9 and 10 there are some differences between the deposits by the walls and those further out, most notably in the greater quantity of tools of most types from the wall heaps. In the wall heaps too are heart-shaped pieces and shaped shale, although Skaill knives are lacking.

From the evidence given above there appear to be three main 'episodes' within the stone assemblage: before Phase 7; Phases 7 and 8; and Phase 9. These three episodes follow the broad chronology of the use of the site and show an increasing variety in the types of tool in use, particularly because each artefact type appears in all subsequent phases after its point of introduction. Although clear differences in assemblage composition are apparent between the different phases of the houses before Phase 9, it is uncertain to what degree these reflect chronological differences. This is particularly true of the assemblages before Phase 7 which are so small, particularly from the South House, that little comparison can be made between them. The association of the handled clubs with the North House and northern and central external contexts may be a functional rather than a chronological difference with the South House. It is likely that the assemblage from Phase 7 was formed directly through use inside the structures rather than as imported rubble to make up the secondary floor; this observation is based on the close similarity in composition between Phases 7 and 8 in each house. If Phase 7 is concurrent in both the houses and passages, then the differences in assemblage composition are most likely functional, reflecting the different uses of the houses. Phase 9 in all contexts is confused by a certain degree of mixing with the products of a probably earlier manufacturing area and also by wall collapse. However, the similarities in assemblage composition between the houses suggests that the functional division which was noted before Phase 9 is not so clear and that there was a degree of merging of activities in the last phase.

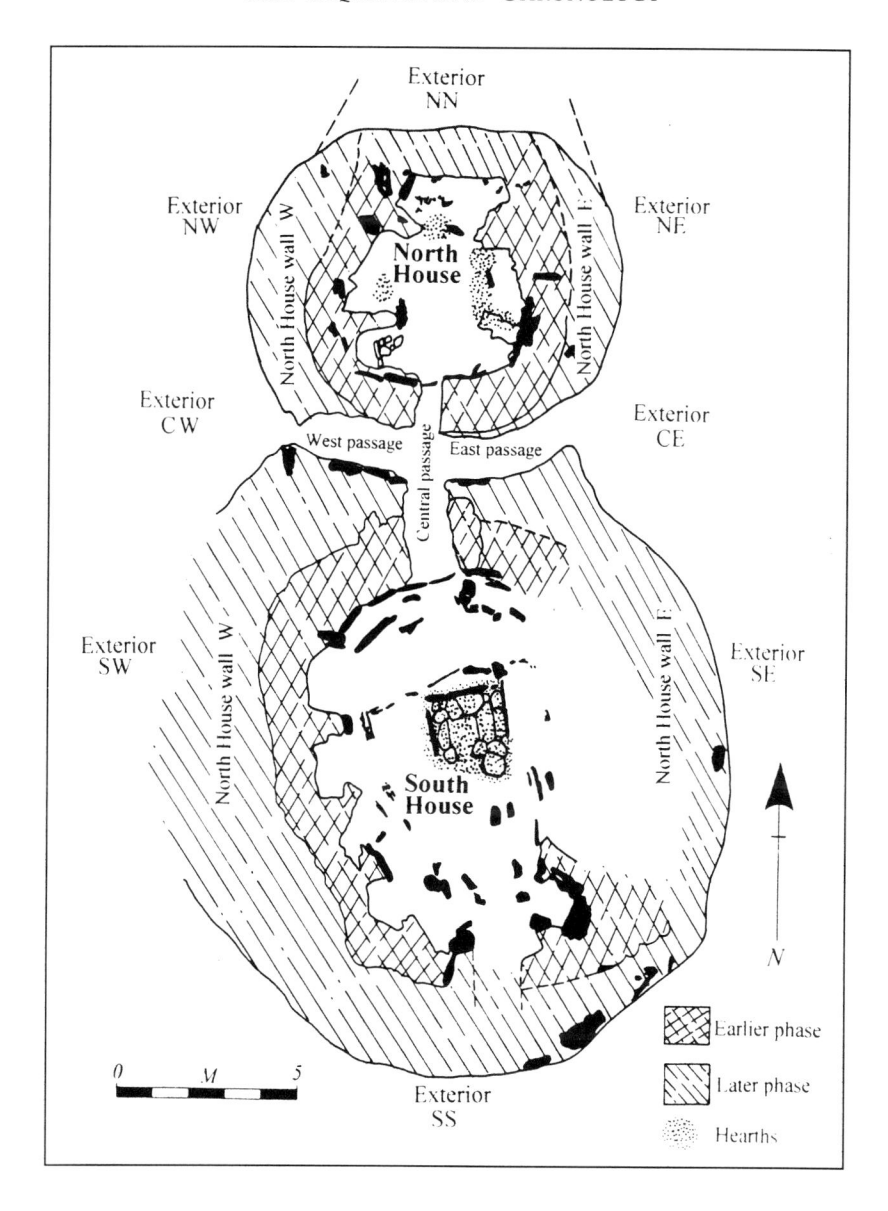

Figure 30: Plan showing areas of site referred to in text.

Inter-site comparison

With the exception of a few artefact forms, the assemblage from Sumburgh Airport is one that is typical of the Bronze Age/early Iron Age of Shetland: it is composed mainly of flaked blanks (flaked-stone bars and ard points), with handled clubs, cleavers and shaped shale (including the heart-shaped pieces) also present. At all sites, with the exception of Clickhimin (Hamilton 1968), both flaked-stone bars and ard points are present, whilst cobble tools and stone discs are also common. The broadest pattern is that which associates handled clubs with the shaped slate pieces. At Sumburgh Airport, Jarlshof (Hamilton 1956) and Kebister (Lowe and Owen forthcoming) the handled clubs are associated with lobate objects, heart-shaped pieces, cleavers and knives whilst at Benie Hoose (Calder 1963) the former two types are present. At Clickhimin heart-shaped pieces were numerous. Stone balls occur at the sites of Scord of Brouster (Rees 1986), Stanydale Temple and Ness of Gruting (Henshall 1958), and only at Scord of Brouster are these associated with handled clubs. A comparison of the stone assemblages with the different ceramic assemblages therefore suggests that the stone balls are of an early Bronze Age date whilst handled clubs and/or shaped shale appear later in the Bronze Age.

This is clearly a very broad chronology for the use of the stone tools and any attempts to refine it are confused by the functional differences which are apparent within site phases themselves. At Kebister there are two different excavated areas within the same phase which exhibit different assemblages: one with handled clubs and shaped shale, and the other without. At Sumburgh Airport the contrast between the assemblages of each house before Phase 9 is most probably functional rather than chronological. This suggests, for example, that if only the North House had been excavated, then the use of many of the tools which are in fact present earlier in the South House would have been dated later on the basis of the North House deposits. Since it is likely that the assemblages which were retrieved from earlier excavations were subject to similar differentiation in spatial and functional deposition around the site then, without knowing what was not excavated, it is impossible to develop a more detailed chronology on this basis.

The greater use of cobble tools, noted in Phase 9 at Sumburgh, is normally an indicator of Iron Age date. At other sites such as Kebister (Lowe and Owen forthcoming), Mavis Grind (Cracknell and Smith 1983) and Scalloway (Clarke 1998) in Shetland and at several Orcadian sites the use of cobble tools is observed to increase dramatically during Iron Age phases where they are often the most dominant tool type (Clarke 1995). Where 'earlier' artefact types, such as flaked blanks and shaped shale pieces, are present in these Iron Age deposits these are normally at sites with earlier Bronze Age contexts such as Kebister, Tofts Ness and Bu and are therefore most likely to be residual (ibid.). Of the cobble tools from Sumburgh Airport the pounders/grinders could be of either a Bronze Age or Iron Age date. Two distinct cobbles (105, 321) are reminiscent of Knap of Howar grinders found in some Grooved Ware contexts in Orkney, although the latter are smaller and circular in plan. The larger, flaked cobbles are perhaps more common to the Iron Age. A few flat cobble tools with faceted sides are similar to a large assemblage of this type from Scalloway, but without the associated gloss residue. A cylindrical stone with flattened ends from Phase 9 of the North House is similar to single pieces from Tofts Ness, Punds Water, Calf of Eday and Upper Scalloway thus giving it a probably early Iron Age date (ibid. 1995). A few other artefacts may be attributed to the Iron Age, and these are the perforated pieces. There is very little evidence for perforated stone objects before the Iron Age, and it is certainly not until this later period that they become common. At Sumburgh Airport most of the perforated pieces are unidentifiable, but there is a small shale ring and a probable weight. All but one of these pieces come from Phase 9 or 10 deposits, and the perforated oblong stone comes from Phase 8.1 of the South House. It is likely then that the Phase 9 and 10 deposits are in part formed by activity during the Iron Age. Neither a clear dating of this phase nor its relationship to the previous activity can be determined from this change in use of the stone tools.

SUMMARY OF THE ARTEFACTS AS CHRONOLOGICAL INDICATORS
BY J. DOWNES

The dating of later prehistoric settlement at Jarlshof is crucial to our understanding of the chronology of Sumburgh and so will be outlined here. The likelihood of the Late Bronze Age Village I occupation being long-lived is stressed by Hamilton (1956). Rather than being built contemporaneously, the four courtyard houses are interpreted as being built sequentially, each time replaced by an adjacent house in a more southerly location. This building sequence does not preclude contemporaneous or overlapping occupation of the buildings. The most readily datable artefacts which have placed this settlement within the late Bronze Age are the moulds for making bronze artefacts and the bronze artefacts themselves. The bronze working probably took place over a fairly long period of time, within two successively built structures, Dwellings III and IVa; the central and southernmost of the recessed 'courtyard houses' (Fig 40). Typologically, the bronze artefacts and moulds have been attributed to Ewart Park industrial phase. The bronze working was not undertaken until the sixth phase of the eight major structural phases defined in the Late Bronze Age Village I (Hamilton 1956, 4). It is possible therefore that the origins of the Late Bronze Age Village I lie centuries before the first metalworking on the site. Our knowledge of how many centuries of occupation this represents depends, of course, on unknown factors such as the length of intervals between the changes in spatial organisation, and, as pottery is regarded as a sensitive indicator of chronological sequence, the regularity with which pottery vessels were broken and replaced and the amount of time to which any particular pottery style was adhered. In a discussion of the artefacts from Scord of Brouster, Whittle suggests that pottery vessels may have had a long lifespan, and he cites ethnographic examples of storage vessels lasting up to 12.5 years (Whittle 1986, 136).

The pottery, coarse stone artefacts and steatite objects all provide a broad date range from early Bronze Age to early Iron Age, for the occupation at Sumburgh Airport, with some late Neolithic material which appears in residual contexts. The chipped stone assemblage accords with this date range, being typical of the later Neolithic and Bronze Age quartz assemblages of the Northern Isles. The ceramics from the site are the most sensitive indicator by which a period can be assigned to phases, and provide the clearest indication of a hiatus between the early Bronze Age timber structures and the later Bronze Age stone houses. This said, the traits of middle Bronze Age pottery in Shetland are undefined. The analysis of both the pottery and the coarse stone artefacts shows a close correlation of artefact types from before and after the rebuilding of the stone houses, which indicates that there is no definable break in the occupation around this event. The evidence from both these categories of artefact also accords with the identification of the material from Phase 9 as refuse from the final occupation of the South House.

The discovery of artefacts which are significantly earlier than the contexts from which they derived is common throughout the history of the site, and is indicative of the extent to which material was moved through processes such as ploughing (both during the occupation of the site and subsequent to abandonment), and the deliberate movement of midden material either to dispose elsewhere or to use as building material. A clear example of this redeposition is the late Neolithic Grooved Ware which was found in the wall fill of the early Iron Age stone buildings. This sherd could have moved by ploughing, but since it is large and unabraded, it is perhaps better interpreted as being brought in with material derived from extant midden that was used as wall fill. It has also been possible to identify, in two instances, artefacts which occur in contexts later than their date of manufacture, perhaps because they had been kept as heirlooms. The first instance is the early-middle Bronze Age miniature steatite battle-axe (Fig 22, 723), found on the paved floor of the early Iron Age South House. As has been suggested, this artefact may have been inherited, or found and kept as a treasured possession. The second example is the pot (Fig 15, 2–96) which was found smashed *in situ* on the paved floor of the early Iron Age South House. This type of vessel dates to the later Bronze Age phases of this building (see above). The repair holes on either side of the crack in this vessel show careful efforts to curate a vessel of antiquity which could have been made generations before its final use.

4. THE MANUFACTURE, USE AND DEPOSITION OF ARTEFACTS

J. Downes

A wide range of artefacts was recovered from Sumburgh Airport, made from a variety of materials, including pottery, steatite, coarse stone, chipped stone (quartz and flint), and pumice. These were the more durable items that were preserved; bone did not survive, neither did other organic material apart from some charred plant remains. From the surviving artefacts it is possible to gain an idea of where materials were being obtained, how, and in some instances where the artefacts were being made, what function they fulfilled and where they were being used. The context of the artefacts is considered in an attempt to distinguish between redeposited and *in situ* material. These attributes and issues will be discussed with each of the artefact types in turn under the headings (i) sources of material, (ii) method and location of manufacture, (iii) range and use, (iv) context.

Throughout this report the North and South Houses have been referred to as such for ease of identifying the structures and ascribing finds locations. However, through this section the artefact analysis will focus on an account of the use of space within the buildings. It will be seen that the two 'houses' functioned as one dwelling space, within which the focus for activities shifted through time.

THE POTTERY

Sources of materials used; method and location of manufacture by C. Yarrington

As there was no thin-section analysis of the pottery it is not possible to say where the clays derived from. For the sources of the steatite used as temper see below.

All the fabric groups – except F5 and F6, whose few sherds are in poor condition – show evidence of only one construction method: ring or coils built up on a solid base of clay. Frequently the sherds have broken along the line where the rings were joined, sometimes so cleanly that they look like rims. Where there is clear evidence this is shown in the section of the illustrated examples. A number of post-firing repair holes are represented, indicating the value of the pots to the users.

Surface finish
Many of the sherds show that the potters took some care over the finish of the vessels with the grits carefully covered with a slurry of clay or smoothed over. However, there is considerable variation: some vessels are very roughly formed, as are most of those of F1 and F2 (thought to be earlier Bronze Age); and some sherds of F3, though thin, are very roughly made. At the other extreme some sherds were very well finished and burnished to a high lustre. More than a hundred individual sherds or small groups of sherds are burnished black, usually on the exterior, and occasionally on the interior (e.g. 1–8b; 406.1, not illustrated). The greater proportion of these are of fabric F3. The steatite filler is conducive to smoothing to a high lustre and faceting from the burnishing tool is sometimes visible. The black surface may have been made by a slip but the presence of a slip is difficult to establish without thin-sectioning. An even all-over blackening of the exterior surface could also have been deliberately produced by smoking.

There is one black burnished rim of fabric F1, 117.1 (not illustrated), and nineteen examples of F4 sherds. Some 28 examples of F3 and F4 sherds are burnished either pink or brown. The final colour of the majority of the pots represented very much depended upon the fabric used and the completeness of the firing. For example where a large amount of steatite is present in the clay (e.g. F3) the overall colour is grey, and a well fired quartz based fabric (e.g. F4) is orange in colour, with grey cores where oxidation was not complete. Therefore, examples of burnished pink and grey and burnished black sherds are indicative of a deliberate choice of colour by the potter.

Lumps of clay were noted in both the SANHS and the 1974 excavations. However, it is not possible to say whether these are indicative of pottery making being carried out on site, as clay was being brought in to the houses for other purposes such as for use as flooring. Furthermore, there is no evidence of wasters. Very close similarities between the pottery from Jarlshof (see above) and that from Sumburgh Airport suggests that in some instances both communities were obtaining their pottery from the same source.

Range and use of pottery vessels by J. Downes

The types of pottery vessels are described in detail in the preceding section. Broadly speaking the range of jars and bowls represent varying sizes and degrees of fineness and coarseness, which must have been employed for a variety of activities: cooking, serving food and drink, or storage. A crude indicator of the use to which vessels were put is the size of a vessel (e.g. large vessels for storage of water or grain) and sooting on the exterior of the base which could demonstrate that a vessel had been used for cooking. Information concerning the size of the vessels and the presence of sooting is contained within the archived catalogue, but it is not possible to present this information in detail here. However, from the examination of the pottery from the stratified layers within the houses, it could be seen that, in general, pottery base sherds with external sooting of a gritty F4 fabric were present in and around the

South House in the later Bronze Age phases (Phases 3–6.1), when the large hearth was in use within this house, whereas there was little or no soot-encrusted pottery from the North House during these phases of occupation (Phases 4–5). After the rebuilding of the houses (Phase 7) – when the hearths were present in the North House, and the South House no longer contained a hearth – much soot encrusted pottery of gritty F4 fabric was present in the North House (Phase 8.1) and derived particularly from the east cubicle. There was a dearth of such pottery from the South House, but an abundance of large jars with a very high steatite content (fabric F3). In general these large vessels, and indeed F3 vessels as a whole, were not soot encrusted, and it is suggested that these vessels were predominantly used for storage, and that steatite vessels were not often used for cooking. The use of steatite as temper does not make a vessel function less well as a cooking pot, and steatite-tempered vessels have frequently been found to have been used as such. The notable variation in use of vessels according to the main fabric groups from Sumburgh Airport, F3 and F4, may relate to how material was classified by the settlement's inhabitants, to distinctions drawn between the appearance and feel of vessels of different fabrics.

The implication of this observation is that during the early Iron Age phases of occupation the South House was used as a storage area and for such activities as crafts (discussed below), whereas previously it had been a place where food was prepared and perhaps where people slept. The role of the North House in its earlier phases is not clear, but it does appear that food preparation was being carried out in this house in the early Iron Age phases.

Context of the pottery vessels

Although a detailed analysis of sherd size and condition of pottery from all contexts was not undertaken it was possible to ascertain that the pottery from within the houses varied between very abraded sherds (recovered from contexts such as those within the drains and amongst paving stones), and large parts of whole vessels in fresh condition. The former may be regarded as what Schiffer (1987) has termed 'primary residual material', which probably remained after cleaning of the house floors, and the latter could be classed as primary refuse, that is material discarded in the area where it was used.

Table 6 shows the overall distribution of pottery sherds in terms of type and weight. The grouping of the phases in the table does not concur exactly with the broader grouping of the site phasing (Table 1) because the counts were undertaken in the earlier stage of post-excavation analysis before the phasing had been established. Details of the type and weight of sherds per phase are contained in the archived catalogue. The data contained within Table 6 are not broken down into internal and external contexts; the information presented is a generalised view of distribution of material not only from within the houses and the walls, but from the ploughed layers surrounding the houses (external contexts).

An interpretation of the mean sherd weight (Table 6) at this level of detail is not easy, as there are many different factors affecting sherd size within the external and

Table 6: Summary distribution of pottery sherds.

Position	Sherd	Phase 1 to 3	Phase 3.1 to 6	Phase 7 to 10	u/s	Totals
North House	Rims	5	10	171	18	204
	Bases	1	12	83	12	108
	Body	16	102	1555	191	1864
	Frags.	17	85	573	21	696
	Totals	39	209	2382	242	2872
	Weight (g)	444.5	2956.8	55314	8035.6	66751
	Mean Weight (g)	11.39744	14.14737	23.22166	33.20496	23.24199
South House	Rims	2	30	103	9	144
	Bases		9	49	5	63
	Body	8	114	646	56	824
	Frags.	4	21	152	7	184
	Totals	14	174	950	77	1215
	Weight (g)	80.1	3241.8	24267.4	1006.5	28595.8
	Mean Weight (g)	5.721429	18.63103	25.54463	13.07143	23.53564
Passage	Rims			42	6	48
	Bases			17	1	20
	Body			426	15	468
	Frags.			184		184
	Totals			669	22	720
	Weight (g)			11984.5	1061.8	13801.5
	Mean Weight (g)			17.91405	48.26364	19.16875

internal contexts. However, the gradual increase through time in mean sherd weight can perhaps be attributed to two factors: first, that the later material would have been subject to less abrasive effects such as trampling and plough damage; and second, greater sherd size in the later phases is indicative of primary refuse and *de facto* refuse (usable artefacts abandoned *in situ*) (ibid). Check counts of the percentage distribution of the diagnostic sherds in each of the main structures (mean percentages: rims = 11.3%, bases = 4.2%, body = 84.1%) showed no significant differences in their occurrence, indicating that breakage and disposal of particular parts of pottery vessels was random across the site.

There are several observations to be made concerning the deposition of pottery when phase and context are considered together. The larger amount of pottery from the North House than the South in Phases 1 to 3 (Table 6) can be accounted for by the evidence of Neolithic/early Bronze Age activity recovered from underneath the North House, while deposits beneath the floor of the South House remained unexcavated. During the later Bronze Age (Phases 3.1–6 in Table 6) the amounts of pottery from the two houses are closely comparable, and this is a reflection of the synchronous use of both buildings. The count includes both primary residual refuse from within the floors and drains, and secondary refuse (material moved from its place of use and put elsewhere) from the makeup of the walls.

In Phases 7 to 10 (Table 6), both the amount of sherds and the weight of pottery from the North House far exceeds that from the South House. The grouping of these phases masks the fact that in Phase 7, the rubble layer within the houses, there was significantly less pottery from the North House. It is suggested that the pottery from Phase 7 is a combination of primary residual material and of primary refuse – material which was left *in situ* and covered by the paved flooring in Phase 8. The argument for the presence of primary refuse, or even usable artefacts abandoned *in situ* (*de facto* refuse) is strengthened by the amount of pottery from this phase which comprised large parts of few vessels.

Of the pottery from early Iron Age Phases 8 and 8.1, the greater number of finds from the walls and interior were from the South House. Conversely, there was a significantly greater amount of pottery from within the North House than the South (83 finds and 35 finds, respectively) in Phase 9. The pottery from the North House was characterised by large parts of large vessels, whereas that from the South House was more worn and comprised smaller sherds. It is likely that the pottery from the North House is secondary refuse, whereas that from the South House is of a more of a residual nature. This evidence, combined with that of the close parallels of many of the vessel types (see above), suggests that during Phase 9 the South House continued to be occupied, while the North House was used as refuse dump for material from the South House.

Although a greater area around the exterior of the North House was excavated than the South House, there is very little pottery from the external contexts of Phase 9 from around the North House, whereas there were c. 25 finds of pottery from the external contexts of the South House, particularly to either side of the southern entrance. This is taken as a further indication that there were activities being carried out within the South House during Phase 9, from which refuse was being removed, unlike the North House which is not thought to have been occupied at this time.

By far the greatest amount of pottery from any phase comes from Phase 10, predominantly from the exterior of the North House, and it is these finds which lead to the impression that so much more pottery appears to derive from the North House than the South House in Table 6. This impression is almost certainly the result of more of the area around the North House having been excavated. There is a wide mix of vessel types and fabric from Phase 10, which is consistent with the movement of material firstly through disposal of refuse, and secondly through ploughing.

The majority of the pottery from Phase 10 (c. 207 finds) was found to the west of the North House, and may be indicative of the presence of a midden, either associated with the occupation of the North and South Houses, or belonging to a neighbouring house. Middens were observed in close proximity (c. 4m distance) from the Dwelling IVa Late Bronze Age Village I at Jarlshof (Hamilton 1956). At Sumburgh Airport a significant quantity of pottery (c. 75 finds) was also recovered from outside the end of the east passage, and smaller quantities from outside the end of the west passage.

On a more general note, the pottery from the walls is of varying sherd size and condition, and varying dates. This is a reflection of the way in which the walls seem sometimes to have been formed by the bringing in of earlier midden material, and thus its secondary reuse, and at other times to have been enlarged through the process of dumping refuse from within the houses onto the walls (see below).

Steatite and Other Fine Stone Objects by P. Sharman

Sources of steatite and other fine stone

There are minor outcrops of steatite in the north and west of Scotland, north-west Ireland, Anglesey and Cornwall (Ritchie 1984, 64–73), but the most important sources of soapstone in the British Isles are all in Shetland, where it occurs in several places associated with blocks of serpentine and metamorphosed basic igneous rocks, mostly on Unst, Fetlar and in North Roe and Dunrossness on Mainland (Mykura 1976, 119–20; Moffat and Buttler 1986, 103, Fig 1). Steatite and soapstone are the common names for soft, ultrabasic talcose rocks with varying mineralogical composition, but always having a greasy or soapy feel. Shetland steatite, which was formed by the hydrothermal metamorphism of serpentinite, is a mixture of talc with varying lesser amounts of chlorite, amphibole, carbonates and opaque minerals.

Although ancient soapstone quarries in Shetland have been recorded since the 19th century (Gordon and Mitchell 1877), it was Hamilton and MacGregor in connection with the soapstone finds at Jarlshof who made the first real attempt to connect artefacts with possible sources and discuss the possible dynamics of the movement of pieces from source to settlement site (Hamilton 1956, 206–210). The geochemical analysis of North American and Scandinavian sources appears to have been fruitful (see Allen et al. 1975; Resi 1979; Rogers et al. 1983; Turnbaugh et al. 1984), but not so for Shetland (Moffat and Buttler 1986) until recent work at the Scottish Universities Research and Reactor Centre. A suite of methods has been developed which may be able to distinguish steatite from different geological provinces within the British Isles (there are two such steatiferous provinces in Shetland), but not to the level of individual quarries. Material from Scandinavian sources was not included in the study (Bray 1994).

The study of specimens from the various sources, combined with tooling techniques used has made it possible to correlate artefacts, usually vessels and bakeplates, with certain quarries but this tends to be for Norse rather than prehistoric artefacts (Buttler 1984, 277–8; Moffat and Buttler 1986, 114; Sharman 1990). However, this approach, unsatisfactory as it may seem, currently provides the best results for the study of much of the material found in Shetland.

There have been no physical signs of pre-Norse working identified at quarries in Shetland, presumably because all traces have been obliterated by later quarrying. There are too few prehistoric soapstone objects and the working on them tends not to be distinct enough to be able to draw any conclusions about the sources of most of these artefacts. This also applies to many of the finds from Sumburgh Airport. The nearest potential sources of soapstone to Sumburgh are extremely small outcrops, none of which shows any traces of exploitation – one to the west of Garths Ness on the south side of Fitful Head, two in the vicinity of Scousburgh and another to the north-west of Clumlie – all within a 9 km radius of the site (Buttler 1984, 189; Moffat and Buttler 1986, 102–3). At The Berg near Hoswick 12.5 km to the north of Sumburgh, is an area of worked steatite partly in the intertidal zone at the very tip of the point, with numerous extant vessel bosses (ibid., 186). This is an outcrop of very minor importance, especially compared to the quarry beside the Catpund Burn near Cunningsburgh, 16.5 km to the north of Sumburgh. In terms of both area and potential production, the steatite resource here outweighs all the others in Shetland combined and was heavily exploited during the Norse period (Moffat and Buttler 1986, 102–3). Although it is not possible to say whether the majority of the soapstone found at Sumburgh Airport came from Catpund it was possible to identify 5 finds which definitely were (A494 (Fig 28), 421, B221, pre-1974 U/S-1 and Pre-1974 U/S-2). Two finds are highly likely to have come from Catpund (B151 and pre-1974 U/S-7). Four are unlikely to have come from there (948 (Fig 28), 479/1, 479/2 and 485). Eighty percent was of indeterminate origin. Having eliminated Catpund as a source of the majority of these objects it is most likely that the stone came from outcrops in North Roe, Fetlar or Unst, especially Fethaland, Houbie on Fetlar or Clibberswick on Unst, which are the largest outcrops, the others being so small they may not have had anything more than an immediately local significance (Moffat and Buttler 1986, 102–3). This implies that the material would have had to travel (in whatever form and by whatever process) some distance – at least 90 km – before reaching the settlement at Sumburgh Airport.

Apart from the outcrops of riebeckite-felsite on the slopes of the Beorgs of Uyea in North Roe, with associated working floors and abandoned pre-forms (Fojut 1993, 82), no traces of prehistoric quarrying have been noted for non-steatitic rock. The vessel rim fragment A92 is made of sandstone which occurs extensively in Shetland and actually forms the underlying geology of the Sumburgh area (Mykura 1976, 62–4). The pendant, B223 (Fig 29), is made from mica-schist whilst the armlets – B226 (Fig 29), B21, B227 (Fig 29) and B228 – are of actinolite talc-schist (these were all kindly identified by Dr Alex Livingston of the Geology Department, Royal Museums of Scotland). These metamorphic rocks occur naturally in Shetland (Dr A. Livingston, pers. comm.), although there is little schist in Dunrossness (Mykura 1976, 24–31). There is more on Yell, Unst and Fetlar (ibid., 32–39), but schist is especially abundant west of the Walls Boundary Fault in west and north Mainland (ibid., 16–23). It should be noted, however, that although the base geology of the

Sumburgh area indicates an origin for these objects elsewhere in Shetland, one cannot ignore the possibility of glacially deposited stone being the source material (ibid., 109).

Method and location of manufacture

The control of the outcrops, the organisation (if any) and the location of manufacture and the dynamics of the dissemination of the artefacts produced are all unknown quantities for the prehistoric period. Excavations have shown that soapstone vessels and plates were made at the quarry site in the Norse period – usually on a domestic rather than a professional basis – most probably because a solid block of steatite is laborious to transport and due to the fact that the likelihood of an unwanted fracture along a cleavage plane in the rock was quite high (Buttler, in prep.; Sharman, in prep.). It seems likely therefore that the same could have been true in prehistoric times. It would have been more convenient, however, to make smaller objects at home, whether of steatite or other kinds of material; steatite debris bearing tool marks was recovered from Bronze Age contexts at Kebister, for example (Sharman, forthcoming). However, there is scant evidence for this from the Sumburgh Airport finds; there were only a few fragments of steatite, none of which was distinctly identifiable as manufacturing debris. Whilst the armlets, pendant and battle-axe could have been whittled and polished anywhere, perhaps at home beside the fire (finds Pre-1974 U/S 7 and 8 may have been used for fine-finishing or polishing), these objects may have been desirable or unusual enough to have been obtained by gift, trade or payment.

Tools with wide blades were used to whittle objects into shape, such as the armlet fragment B21, and the technique of whittling may also have been used on the exterior of vessels, although these could also have been chipped using a more pointed tool; unfortunately it is difficult to be certain because the exterior surfaces of vessels are often obscured by accretions. Sharp, pointed tools were certainly available to the Bronze Age artisan, used both in a percussive manner and hand-held for gouging and incising, allowing objects like the pendant and the battle-axe to be pierced, or to create vessels in a way similar to the Norse method (Buttler 1989, 200–202; Sharman, in prep.), evidenced by the parallel vertical and diagonal 1–1.5 mm-wide, V-shaped grooves and pecks on the walls of 948 and B151. Stone such as quartz or felsite would have been able to provide the requisite kind of tools mentioned above. Several of the objects had been smoothed or polished as a finishing technique. It is not possible to distinguish with any degree of certainty the difference between deliberate smoothing and scouring or just plain use wear on the inside of a vessel, but the armlets and the outside of 948 all bore fine striations from deliberate smoothing, presumably by a fine abrasive such as pumice or sand – or even soapstone, such as finds Pre-1974 U/S 7 and 8. Soapstone would presumably have been more useful for polishing or burnishing than for smoothing, similar to the finishes on the axe or armlets B226 and B228.

These techniques are in evidence through the Bronze Age and early Iron Age at Sumburgh Airport, and the finds retrieved from later contexts assigned to Phases 9 and 10 show little difference from the methods of manufacture described above, though some tools (those with points and blades, for example) change with technology, from stone to iron. Certain finds do, however, show a distinctly Norse style of tooling prevalent at the Catpund soapstone quarry, especially the four-sided vessel A494, also 426, Pre-1974 U/S 1 and 2, the last 3 also probably from four-sided vessels. The method involved blunt-pointed iron chisels used in short percussive strokes in parallel sets. The exterior of the vessel was created whilst the block of stone was still attached to the quarry face, from what became the base, downwards to what became the rim once the block was separated from the bedrock. The vessel pre-form was then hollowed out, using the same technique but from the rim down to the inside base, until the walls were of a satisfactory thickness. It was rare to attempt to smooth out the tool marks on the resulting vessel, which was usually four-sided (Sharman, in prep.). The tool marks on prehistoric four-sided vessels tend to be slightly more unsteady and perhaps sharper and the walls tend to be more upright. The fact that four-sided vessels are a shape peculiar to Shetland both in the Bronze Age and the late Norse period may be a function of trying to cope with the highly laminated, coarse-grained soapstone prevalent at Catpund.

The range and use of steatite and other fine stone artefacts

The high talc content means that the stone is easily carved (it can be scratched with a fingernail) and that it is heat-resistant (Buttler 1984, 2; note also comments on use of steatite as filler above). The properties of steatite have been recognised and exploited since the Neolithic period by the inhabitants of Shetland, although it was mainly used during the Norse period for the manufacture of funerary urns, cooking vessels, bakeplates, lamps, metalworking moulds, weights, whorls, toys, and even into the twentieth century for firebricks and the industrial extraction of talc. However, despite the variety of items produced in the prehistoric period, these were not huge in number, and steatite was predominantly used crushed as a temper in pottery (ibid., 6–9).

The assemblage of finds from Sumburgh Airport is not large, but it is noteworthy for containing vessel fragments from an early Bronze Age domestic context rather than a funerary one, and especially because of the recovery of a miniature battle-axe of a type which has parallels on mainland Britain, setting the inhabitants of Sumburgh in their wider cultural milieu within the British Isles.

Vessels

Over half of the vessel fragments had burnt accretions or sooting on the exterior, whilst five more had burnt accretions on the interior, indicating that many of the vessels had been used for cooking rather than storage. Unfortunately it was not certain whether the fragments with no such accretions had been thoroughly scrubbed after excavation or not, so conclusions about their storage function may well be invalid. Finds 17, 479 and 497 may have actually broken while in use because some of their break faces are accreted. Attempts were made to prolong the life of some of the items – B151 had been crudely retouched, whilst 61 and 752 (Fig 28) had been pierced, possibly to strap the vessels after they had cracked. Such curative technology appears also to have been practised at the Benie Hoose (Henshall 1963a, 43) and was common in the Norse period (see Hamilton 1956, 113; Hunter 1986, 189–90). It seems likely that the smooth, worn nature of most of the vessel interiors was caused by scouring them; the interior of the collared urn 948 bears horizontal scratches, for example. The vessels may have been cleaned out using something like sand or pumice and water.

It is an enigma how prehistoric domestic vessels of soapstone were regarded. They are scarce, but this may indicate that they were not in demand because pottery was preferred, or that they had a specific function in the home rather than because they were of high status, although they appear to have been in demand and of some importance in Bronze Age funerary practices both in Shetland and Orkney. Further research is required.

Plate
All the tool grooves on the plate fragment were filled with burnt accretions, indicating that it had been well used over an open fire. From the late Norse period on, plates were used for the baking of such food as flatbread (Buttler 1989, 195). The grooves may have served to spread the heat more evenly, or perhaps to help prevent the mixture sticking to the stone. There seems to be no technological reason why the stone equivalent of a modern griddle could not have been used over a Bronze Age fire, as opposed to a Norse one, and this example may be the first evidence of such a griddle.

Battle-axe
The battle-axe (723) may have been worn as an amulet, being a symbol of power, or as a simple personal ornament. It may have also have been a toy or a combination of both interpretations, with reference especially to the context of the axe found at Doune (Hamilton 1959).

Pendant
The function of this pendant is uncertain, especially because there is no real sign of suspension wear. It may be some form of personal adornment.

Armlets
Two of the armlets appear to have been made for exceedingly small limbs (B226/B21 and B227), perhaps, like the battle-axe, hinting at artefacts for children. The actinolite in the stone is a form of amphibole which gives the armlets their green and black colour, whilst the talc content meant that the objects were comparatively easy to carve and polish (Dr A. Livingston, pers. comm.). The stone may therefore have been chosen specifically because of these properties, although it may be that this type of stone was thought to have or impart a specific spiritual quality. The objects may have been made as gifts or as desirable items for trade or exchange.

Possible smoothers
The faceting and striations on these objects indicate that they must have been used, presumably to smooth, burnish or polish artefacts made of material such as bone (pins), fine stone (armlets), pottery or steatite vessels.

Fragments
The actual function of the fragments found on the site is uncertain. They may have been for grinding up into temper for pottery, or they may have been the debris of breakage or working, though no tool marks were found on any of the fragments.

Context of the steatite and other fine stone artefacts

The collared vessel, 948, was recovered from an early Bronze Age context to the north-east of the North House. B151, the four-sided vessel with late Bronze Age parallels, was recovered in Phase 7 rubble infill within the South House. B21, the armlet fragment which joined B226 was from the same phase in a context in the area of the south hearth. The other pieces of armlet, including B226, were from a black soil deposit assigned to Phase 9. The pendant B223 was from the same context as the miniature battle-axe, that is the secondary paved floor within the South House, Phase 8.1. However, the lifespan of the battle-axe could have been a long one.

The majority of the assemblage (64 % of the finds) was found in contexts assigned to Phase 9 or 10, which may explain the small size and poor state of preservation of many of the vessel fragments. 42 % of the assemblage, all vessel fragments, came from contexts outwith the houses. Later disturbance may also account for the fact that many of the fragments were quite worn but sometimes had quite fresh-looking breaks.

COARSE STONE ASSEMBLAGE

Sources of coarse stone by R. Lamb

The greater number of artefacts is made of the fine-grained grey siltstone of the Middle Old Red Sandstone Series and probably derives from an outcrop near Grutness Voe, some 2 km from the site. For convenience this material is referred to as 'shale' throughout the report. It is likely that this material was quarried, as there is little evidence in the form of cobble cortex to suggest that rolled beach deposits were used, and, as the shale is laminated and splits easily across the bedding planes, this would enable it to be quarried directly with relatively little effort.

The shale is used for a number of different artefact types, most notably the flaked stone bars, and the more finely bedded material, which gives a flatter cross-section, tends to have been selected particularly for pieces such as stone discs, heart-shaped pieces and other shaped shale objects. A number of the flaked stone bars are made of the more coarsely grained sandstone and here beach cobbles are preferred.

Sandstone beach cobbles are also the most likely source for pieces such as the handled clubs. A few tools are of mica schist which does not occur in the Old Red Sandstone Series but could have come from Fitful Head or anywhere further north along the west coast of Dunrossness, and it is probable that this material was transported to the area during the Ice Age. The querns are made on the Devonian flagstone, which is also the main building stone; this is available at coastal outcrops at West Voe of Sumburgh and east and south of Grutness Voe.

Range and use of coarse stone artefacts and the method and location of manufacture by A. Clarke, with S. Rees on the ard points

For the coarse-stone assemblage the description of the artefact by type and use attributed to the artefact are written together with the method of manufacture. This is because the method of manufacture and the signatures of function, such as wear, are integral to the description and interpretation of many of the artefacts.

Flaked stone bars (Shale Total = 647; Sandstone Total =52)

The flaked stone bars are of two particular types: those made on slabs or large flakes of shale; and those made on slabs or cobbles of sandstone. All of the shale tools, and those made on slabs of sandstone have been shaped by flaking around the edge of a rather flat, tabular blank. In contrast, those made on cobbles of sandstone have either been flaked around the edge of a flat cobble leaving cortex on both faces (B174, Fig 32) or else have been made on a cobble which has been split down its length leaving remnant cortex on one face only (C56, Fig 32, and 281, Fig 33). Both types share the common characteristics of being long and narrow and are usually a tapering rectangle (851, Fig 32), parallel-sided (984, Fig 32) or converging (42.8, Fig 32), in plan. Several of those made on shale are in fact rather more oval in plan than others. The shale flaked stone bars have a wider size range than those made on sandstone (100 mm to 350 mm in length), but both types cluster between 150 mm and 250 mm.

There is clear evidence for hafting on 7 % of the shale tools and this takes two forms: either a single notch which has been flaked on one or both sides of the tool (B80, Fig 33 and 42.23, Fig 32); or as an area of rounding, smoothing and occasionally gloss on one or both sides of the tool (855.3 and 570.1, Fig 32). Both forms suggest that the flaked stone bar was attached somehow to a haft, most probably by binding with a cord or leather. Some of these notched bars may be tethering pegs, as they resemble waisted sandstones from Skaill, Deerness, which were set into paved floors.

Wear traces, which were formed through the use of these flaked stone bars, are evident on 40 % of the tools from Sumburgh Airport. This is a high proportion in comparison to other site assemblages and reflects the physical nature of the shaley stone which is fine-grained and relatively soft and therefore more likely to be altered by physical use than the harder sandstones and schists which were used at other sites. There are no illustrations to accompany this discussion of wear traces.

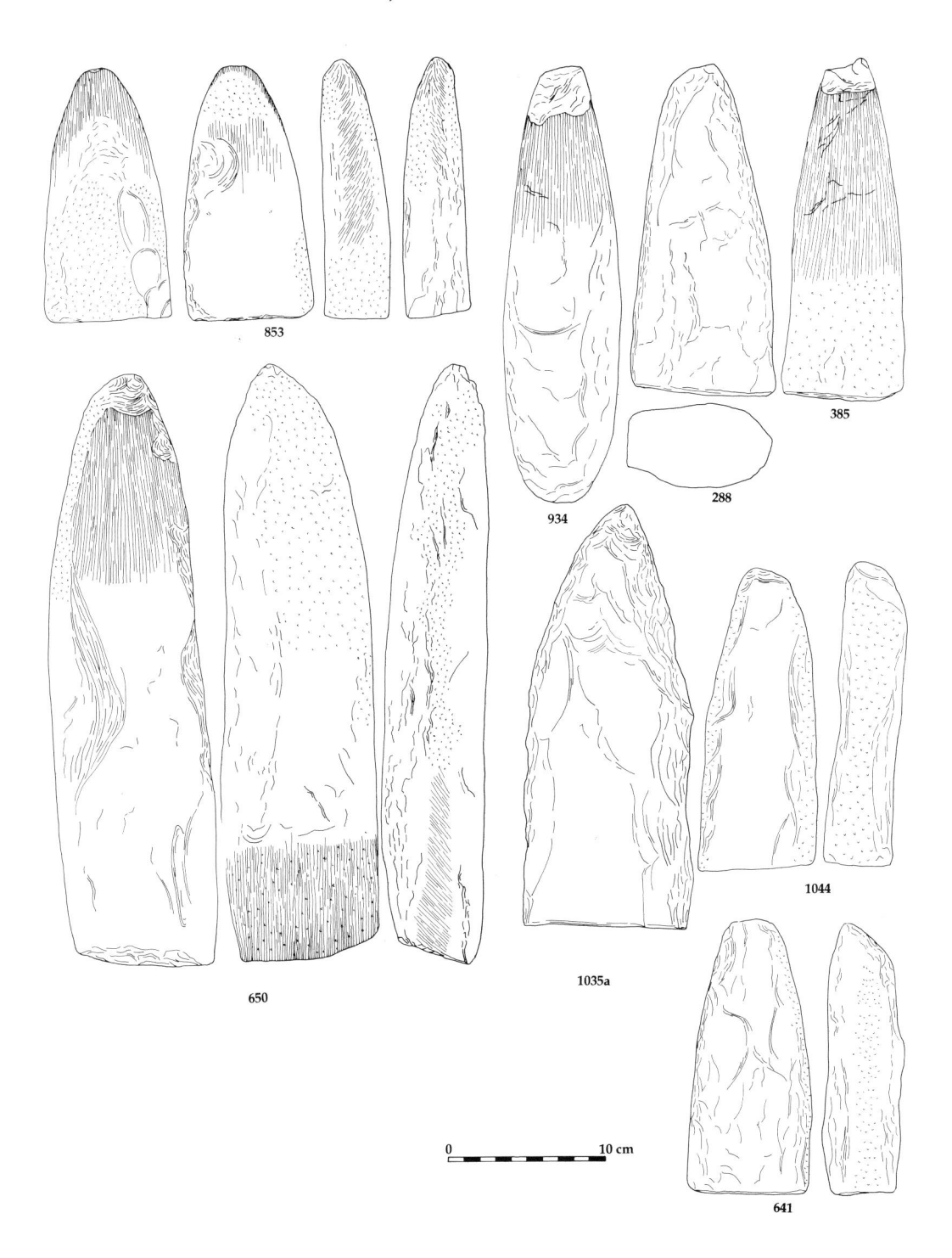

The Manufacture, Use and Deposition of Artefacts

Figure 31: Coarse stone artefacts: ard points.

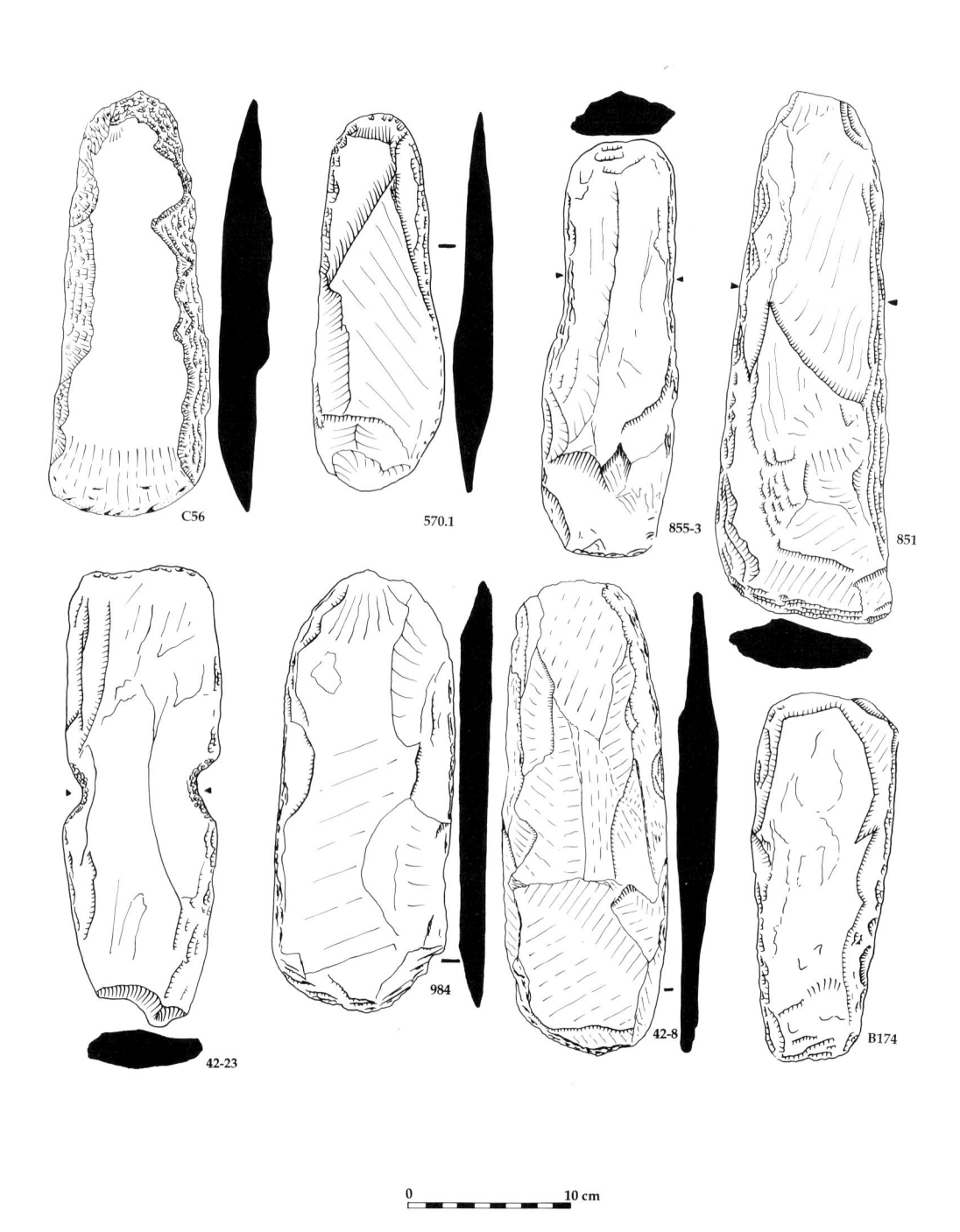

Figure 32: Coarse stone artefacts: flaked stone bars.

The wear traces take the form of smoothing and striations on the end on one or both faces of the tool, or of a 'polish' or 'gloss' placed likewise. This is usually accompanied by edge rounding on the smoothed end or down the sides, or both. On the complete tools the wear patterns occur on one end only, most often the broadest end. The ends of the bars are varied in outline, including a variety of forms from squared, curved and pointed and many are asymmetrical in plan, exhibiting a diagonally placed end, as if the tool was intended to have been used from the side rather than head on. That these tools were used like this is supported by the edge rounding which tends to be more extensive down one side than the other.

Considering the variety of sizes and shapes within the assemblage, it is doubtful that all of the flaked stone bars were used in the same way but it is almost impossible to divide this assemblage objectively into particular shape categories as they are not distinctive enough from each other. There is, however, some evidence for the differential use of particular forms, as those tools which exhibit wear traces have a different size and shape range to those that are unworn. The worn flaked stone bars tend to be longer than the unworn tools and are more uniform in the proportion of width to length. In contrast the unworn tools have a more scattered distribution and tend to be wider in relation to their length. Although fewer in number, the tools with hafting traces have a similar size/shape distribution to the worn tools. This suggests, at least, that the more elongated tools were selected for particular types of use, most probably as a hafted mattock or hoe, whilst those that are unworn may represent tools intended for different purposes which would not leave distinctive wear traces, as well as unfinished or unused rectangular tools. Over 60 % of the complete flaked stone bars exhibit wear traces whilst only a third of the broken tools are worn. However, since the evidence suggests that only one end of the tool was normally used, then it is assumed that the broken pieces must represent either end of the original tool and therefore that the proportion of broken tools which have been worn actually doubles to over 60 % of the potential assemblage, a similar proportion to the complete tools. The flaked stone bar assemblage may therefore be assumed to be dominated by tools which were used in a similar fashion with mattocking and hoeing being possible or even probable functions. The functions of the remainder cannot be determined so readily.

Ard Points (Total =187)
Stone ard points, sandstone bars which form the working part of the wooden bow ard, appear to have been the main tillage implement used in prehistoric Orkney and Shetland. They have already been discussed in previous papers (Fenton 1962–3; Rees 1978) and will not be described in detail here.

Experience has shown it to be difficult in some cases to distinguish between very crude roughouts of ard points at a very early stage of manufacture and those of other stone implements, and thus two tables have been drawn up for each group, one which includes all tools, whether worn or roughout (Table 7), and one for worn tools only (Table 8).

Table 7. Classification of all stone ard points

Cross-section	No.	Aver L	Aver W	Hd	St	A	B	C	Bkn
Round	57	195	69	48	3	2	4	31	19
Wide	123	213	84	105	13	3	8	47	65
Interm.	3	224	71	3	0	0	2	1	0
Other	4	-	-	3	1	0	0	0	4

Table 8. Classification of worn stone ard points

Cross-section	No.	Aver L	Aver W	Hd	St	A	B	C	Bkn	D	E
Round	32	193	68	32	1	2	3	19	7	97	6.3
Wide	39	224	81	33	6	2	5	16	17	103	26.2
Interm	3	224	71	3	0	0	2	1	3	108	27.3
Other	3	-	-	3	-	-	-	-	-	-	-

Key to Tables 7 and 8:
Aver. average; L length (mm); W width (mm); Hd hard sandstone; St soft sandstone; A double pointed tool; B tapered tool; C squared tool; Bkn broken; D Average length of wear (mm); E average angle of side wear (degrees); Interm intermediate in type.

Of the total ard points 77 were worn, the other 110 having been abandoned at various stages of manufacture. Through the examination of the latter, the stages in and the method of manufacture of the ard points may be appreciated: the preliminary shaping of an appropriate length of sandstone; the fashioning of the upper and lower faces, butt end and pointed tip (288, Fig 31); the fashioning of the sides to achieve the correct cross-section, either round or oval-shaped – the tip often a shaped to produce the correct upper and lower faces, as well as an asymmetry at the sides of the tip (1035a, Fig 31); the pecking of the sides and lower face (1044, Fig 31) to produce a roughened surface, presumably for the better grip of the stone in a wooden mortise; and finally the fashioning of the unworn but complete ard point (641, Fig 31).

Stone ard points may be divided into two fairly distinctive groups: those with round, and those with oval cross-sections. Tools with both types of cross-section were found at Sumburgh Airport. 120 tools with oval section and 57 with round section were found in the excavations but when the worn tools alone are taken into account the proportion (39 oval versus 32 round) is far more equally balanced. The examination of all the known ard points suggests that the difference in cross-section type would normally appear to be contingent upon the quality of the sandstone. The general rule seems to be that points with oval sections tend to be made of softer sandstone, while those with round cross-sections tend to be made of harder sandstone. As may be seen from the tables the great majority of the points of both cross-sections from Sumburgh are of relatively hard sandstone, which is an interesting exception to the norm (but see below). The stone points can then be further divided into categories dependent on the non-working or butt end. Tools may be double-pointed (650, Fig 31), tapering (934, Fig 31) or squared (385, Fig 31). All three types may be either oval or round in cross-section, a fact which, if not shown directly by Tables 7 and 8 because of the high proportion of broken points, has been shown by a wider study of the tools. The shape of the butt end is assumed to have some bearing on the technique of attachment of the point to the main body of the ard. The double-pointed shares were reversible, and some tools have been found with wear marks on both tips.

The worn tools all show the characteristic wear marks expected on shares of a bow ard (Hansen 1969, Fig 24), namely longitudinal striations on the upper face (or the face which was uppermost when the share was in use) for an average of 102 mm; a U-shaped wear pattern on the lower face at the tip, the pattern often displaying a heavier wear on one side than the other; and diagonally slanting wear on the sides, again often stronger on one side than on the other. Measurement of the angle of side wear to the horizontal (or the line running between the tip and a point midway through the thickness of the share at the point of greatest thickness) indicates the angle at which the point penetrates the soil; the average on the tools was 26.6 degrees (853, Fig 31). The asymmetry often shown by the ard points at the tip is usually explained by the fact that the ard was tilted when in use so that one side of the share became more worn than the other; this tilting of the ard is known to be practised with present-day ards to compensate for the lack of a mouldboard, as the tilting helps turn the soil. The heavier wear on one side of the ard point than on the other implies that the ard was usually tilted in the same direction. This is no more than inference, however, and it can probably be taken too far.

Only a small number of ard points from Sumburgh Airport showed obvious asymmetric wear: nine showed that the point had been tilted mainly to the left-hand side, and five to the right. Perhaps only this small number was worn sufficiently for the asymmetric wear to be visible, or possibly the ard was not normally used in one direction only, except on these few where it happened that the tilting had been deliberate and systematic. Further, it was clear that during the manufacturing stage some points received an asymmetric fashioning; this could either have been deliberate to predetermine the direction of tilt of the point during manufacture or it could have been accidental. This question has some importance as it affects our understanding of the functioning of the ard. If the ard was used primarily for the preparation of a seed bed and for covering seed, one might well expect a systematically asymmetric wear pattern on the point. If it was used as a general purpose tool to level a field, for instance, or to break up clods, a more random pattern might be expected. The study of the ard marks in the ground at Sumburgh Airport, and their very variable and irregular angles of tilt warn against a too ready acceptance of the former hypothesis.

The inevitable blunting of the sides of the points after long periods of wear often necessitated the turning of the tools so that the upper face became the new lower face of the tool. The curious wear pattern displayed by the tools which have been turned is unmistakable (853, Fig 31). On the double-pointed tools, the blunting and consequent inefficiency of the tools could be avoided by turning the share from back to front so that the butt end became the tip. One point from Sumburgh Airport, now broken, shows wear on both ends (650, Fig 31). One or two tools displayed what seems best described as reshaping or repecking after wear; fresh, deep pecking marks overlie old wear striations, and this could be another method of resharpening the tool after much wear had blunted the tip.

The wear marks on the stone ard points suggests that they were held on a bow ard of the Donnerupland type, either as the main share or as the foreshare held onto a wooden arrow-shaped ard head, or share (Fenton 1963), such as the ard heads from Virdifield. The ards would presumably have been extremely heavy to manoeuvre. Even the relatively unspectacular lengths of the Sumburgh points average 200 mm and a few are as long as 600 mm. However, as Henshall comments (1958), the shortage of hard wood in the Northern Isles in this period appears to have been acute, and the inhabitants would have been used to working with heavy stone tools, and they would indeed have had little option but to use it for the hard-wearing working part of the ard. The large number of broken points at Sumburgh Airport shows the strain that must have been exerted on the tools during ploughing even in the relatively stone-free, by Shetland standards, soil of Sumburgh.

Additional ard points (Total = 18)
Of the 18 additional ard points at least seven bear the characteristic signs of wear described by Rees above and there are three blanks or roughouts. From the smaller number of ard points re-examined during the final stage of post-excavation work there were observed to be 20 which had patches of discrete pecking placed in the centre of one or both faces. In many cases this pecking was deep enough to develop a distinct notch. These were placed between 70 mm and 180 mm from the working end of the ard point (average about 100 mm). Three further points exhibited heavily pecked areas on either side at similar distances from the working tip. It is highly probable that these notches and hollows aided in securing the ard point to the plough and they occur on worn ard points as well as roughouts.

Rees noted some problems between the association of rock hardness and cross-section type. A study of the ard points from Kebister, Shetland, concluded that the rock type did in part determine the resulting cross-section, as those ard points made of the grey sandstone tended to have a much rounder cross-section than those of the red sandstone. In this case the red sandstone had clear bedding planes along which the rock cleaved naturally and would therefore have provided flat or tabular blanks. In contrast the grey sandstone was more homogeneous in structure, and its higher clay content meant that it was more tractable than the red sandstone (Clarke 1995). It is suggested here that the variety in cross-section is determined initially by the structure of the rock, rather than its hardness, and that the red sandstones from Sumburgh are bedded in a similar way to those from Kebister.

Cobble tools (Total = 44)
There are several different types of wear pattern on these tools. The most common form consists of areas of pecking over parts of the cobble, usually forming discrete areas on the ends, faces and sides. The pecking is usually quite light, although on two pieces a distinct notch has been formed on one side by pecking (A62, B171; not

illustrated) and on another there is heavy pecking all around the circumference (216, not illustrated). Four of these cobbles are a flat oval in shape, and the heavy pecking down the sides has altered the original outline. There are also discrete areas of heavy pecking on the faces and end. These latter pieces (1–A8, A200, A201, 189, Fig 35) are similar to a larger assemblage of such cobble tools from the broch site at Upper Scalloway, Shetland (Clarke 1998). A number of larger, elongated cobbles have been heavily flaked at one end through use (e.g. 1037, not illustrated). Only five cobbles bear signs of faceting (e.g. 91, not illustrated), three of which are small pounders/grinders. There are only three certain quern rubbers with a characteristic D-shaped section (431, Fig 35). Another three cobbles, elongated in shape, are quite distinct in form, with a flat and smooth lower face, sometimes with areas of pecking, and a domed upper face with some pecking over the surface (105 and 321, Fig 35). Finally, there is one cobble (A389; not illustrated) which is almost cylindrical in form with both ends worn to a flat facet and with two areas of heavy pecking on either side of the cobble. Two sub-spherical cobbles of pink granite (A393, B179; not illustrated) are very coarse in texture, and they do not appear to have been used.

The tasks to which cobble tools were put have left the distinctive wear traces on the exterior of the cobbles, and it is the type and location of these traces which form the basis for the classification by artefact type. Although observations can be made regarding the occurrence of specific and repeated wear traces in a cobble tool assemblage it is more difficult to determine the actual uses to which these tools were put. There is certainly a strong element of grinding wear in the assemblage as indicated by the quern rubbers, pounders/grinders and cobbles with flat ground faces. Others of the smaller faceted cobbles may be more closely associated with the flaked quartz industry where they may have been employed as hammerstones.

Skaill knives (Total = 23)
These are all simple primary flakes which have been detached from sandstone beach cobbles. Only one flake (449, not illustrated) has been retouched, and here the original edge has been altered heavily by flaking all around the inner face and part way around the cortical face. None of the flakes shows any obvious sign of edge damage which would indicate its function.

Stone discs (Total = 16)
Most of the discs are made on flat slabs of sandstone and are chipped around both faces to shape the piece. Two others are made of shale, and there is one of mica schist. They are generally subcircular in outline and their diameters range from 100 mm to 240 mm. One disc of sandstone is rather more subrectangular in plan. All of these most probably functioned as some form of pot lid, although there is no sign of burning around the edge to suggest that they were used over the fire. The smallest disc, with a diameter of 64 mm, has a small pecked area in the centre of both faces and this type is usually classified as an unfinished spindle whorl (A63, Fig 35). However, this type often occurs singly in Iron Age assemblages and appears to be a type in its own right (cf. a similar steatite piece from the site).

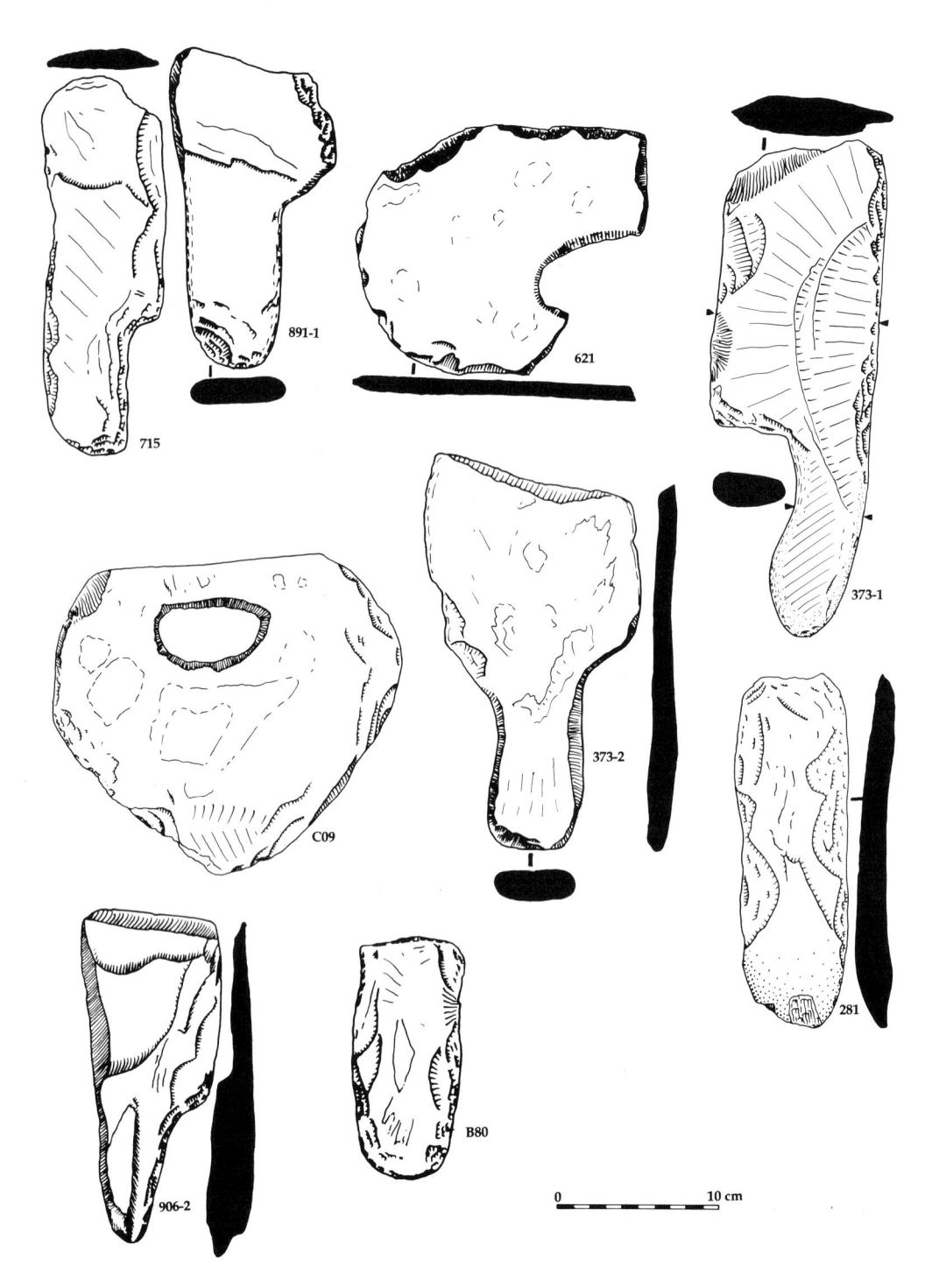

Figure 33: Coarse stone artefacts: flaked stone bars, heart-shaped pieces and cleavers.

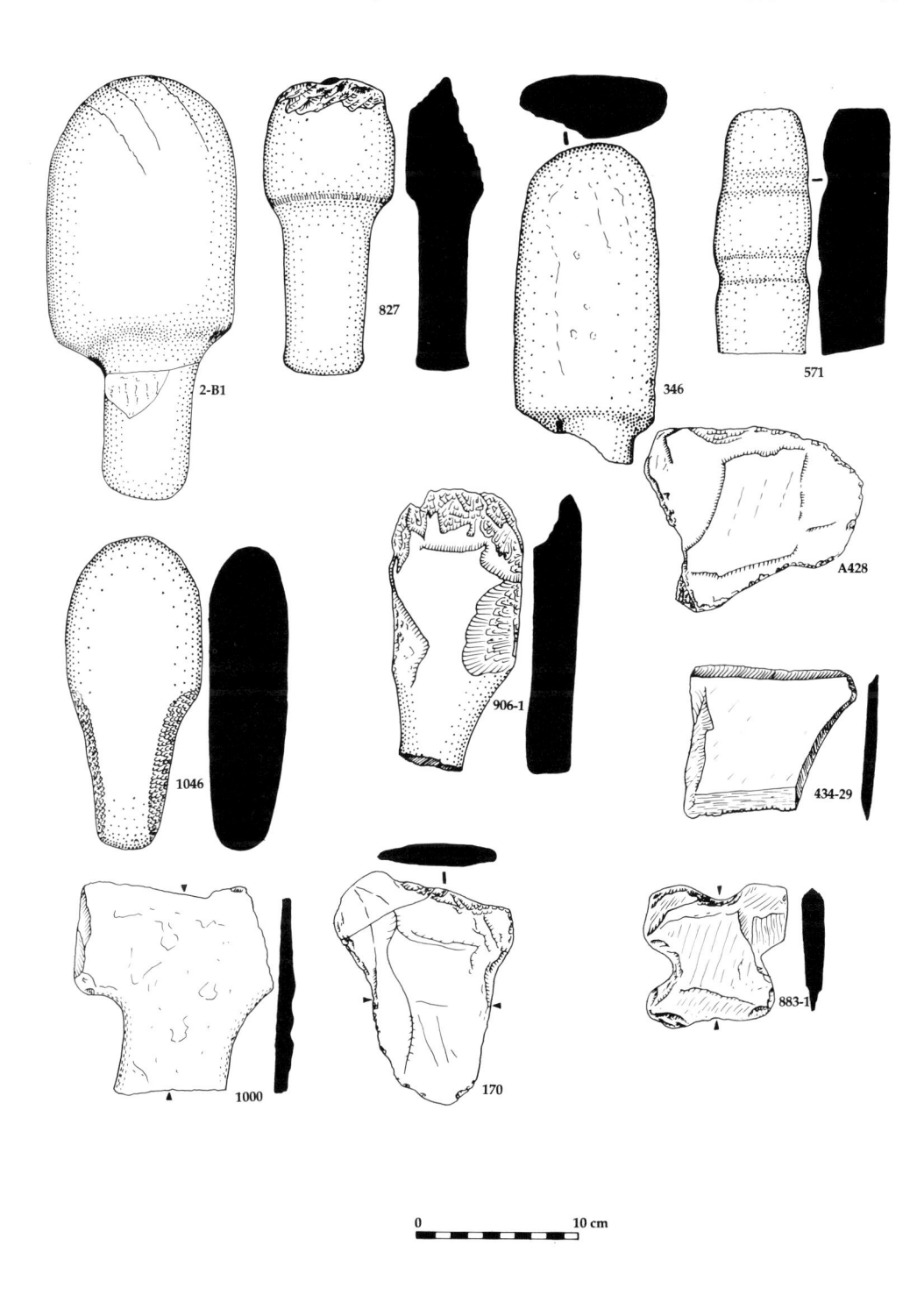

The Manufacture, Use and Deposition of Artefacts

Figure 34: Coarse stone artefacts: clubs and 'knives'.

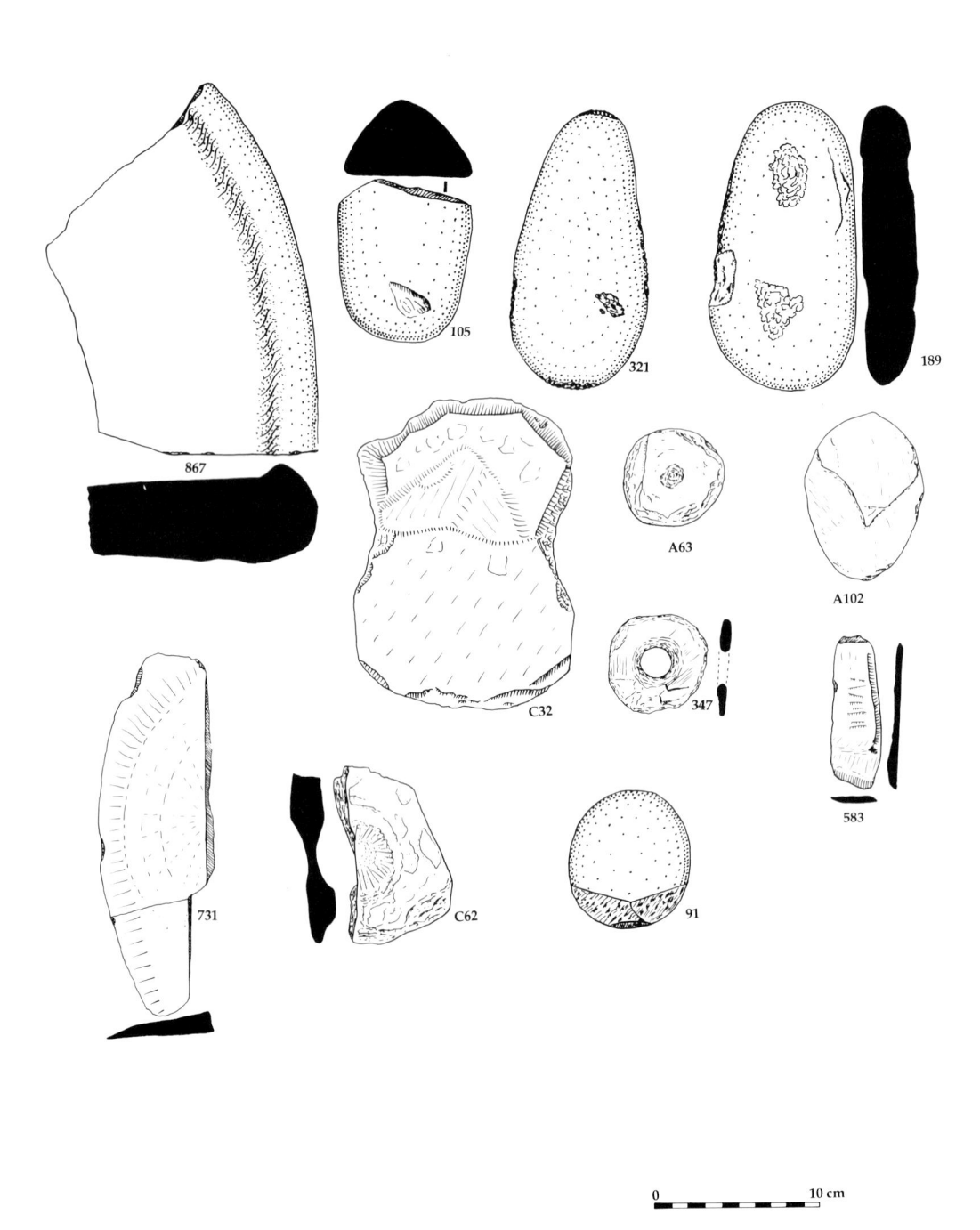

Figure 35: Coarse stone artefacts: cobble tools, perforated pieces and miscellaneous.

Clubs (Total = 40) and cleavers (Total = 17)
The handled clubs are all made of sandstone. Their common characteristic is the presence of a finely shaped handle on which a large club-like head has been formed. They appear to have been shaped from a blank by pecking and grinding. The handles are finely formed, with a round to oval cross-section; they are broadest at the head end and taper to form a rounded or pointed end (1046 and 2.B1, Fig 34), or occasionally a splayed end (827, Fig 34). The heads tend to be more varied in shape, though all may be described as subrectangular with an oval cross-section (346 and 906.1, Fig 34). The shouldering which forms the head on the handle is more often than not distinctly asymmetrical, with one side always being more abrupt than the other (2B1, 906.1 and 1046, Fig 34). Occasionally some slight asymmetrical shouldering may also be seen in profile (827, Fig 34). A huge variation does not exist in the size of these pieces, and the head/handle proportions are also similar. One piece (79, not illustrated) is possibly the beginning of the manufacture of a club. It is heavily pecked on the ends and down the sides, and it is more finely pecked towards one end where there appears to have been some attempt to shape a handle.

One surviving head is most regular in shape and symmetrical in shouldering (717, not illustrated). It bears traces of decoration around the base in the form of two parallel pecked grooves. Another possible handle fragment has two chipped grooves across one face (571, Fig 34).

There are three pieces which are flatter in section than the rest of the handled clubs (73.1, Fig 35, and 1000, Fig 34) and on the two pieces on which the handle survives there are traces of rounding and 'polish' around the handle and shoulder area (373.2, Fig 33, and 1000, Fig 34).

The function of these pieces is still not known. The heads are often very damaged by breakage or from removal of flakes. The handled club also appears to be very vulnerable across the junction of the head and handle as much breakage occurs here. The function of the 'handle' is questionable: it forms only about a third of the total length of the piece and would not function well as a handle owing to its tapering shape and short length. Nevertheless, the careful shaping of this end, the intentional asymmetry of the shouldering, and the lack of damage here suggests that the handle was in fact made to support some form of hafting.

The cleavers tend to be made of shale, though there is one of tabular sandstone (891.1, Fig 33). They have been chipped around the edge to shape a head with a handle formed down one side (373.1 and 906.2, Fig 33). The heads have a curved or straight edge and on one piece (715, not illustrated) light striations running down the length of both faces most probably indicate a type of use wear. A few pieces show edge rounding and a 'gloss' around the handle and the lower part of the head.

Shaped slate (Total = 14)
Five of these pieces may be considered as 'knives' as they have been shaped with a small curving 'handle' which is formed into a wider 'blade' with a curved edge. None is very similar to any other, but they average about 200 mm in length. A

further five pieces are narrow rectangular fragments and may be broken handles. The remaining shaped slate pieces include a finely serrated piece (434.29, Fig 34), a object with four lobes formed by chipping (883.1, Fig 34), and two pieces shaped into a slight handle with a broad flat head (170 and A428, Fig 34).

Heart-shaped pieces (Total = 14)
These are characterised by having a roughly triangular shape with a large perforation made in the centre of the piece, often towards the broad end. This broad end may be shaped either by a neat break or sometimes by chipping to form a slightly in-curving edge (C.09 and 621, Fig 33). The perforation is often quite large and shaped to a sub-oval form which tends to flatten at the side nearest the broad end.

Hamilton has referred to these pieces as shovels (Hamilton 1968, 31) with the perforation presumably being used to hold the piece. There is however, little left of a useful shovel end once the perforation has been made through the piece. There is also no evidence for any wear traces on the edge or faces which presumably would have been present had these pieces been used in such a way. The lack of wear traces together with the fact that many are liable to breakage across the perforation suggest that these objects were not used as tools but instead served a more passive role. If the perforation was designed to hold a certain thickness of rope then the piece could have been held in place or rested against something by the careful shaping of the broad end. It is suggested here that these heart-shaped pieces may have been used for tethering stock to protect the neck of the animal from being rubbed by the tethering rope. The nature of the contexts of these pieces may support this proposition (see discussion below).

Perforated pieces (Total = 3)
These pieces are all small, irregular fragments of sandstone or shale, with a perforation made by pecking from both faces and subsequently truncated by breakage. There is not enough evidence from any of the pieces as to their original function.

Miscellaneous (Total = 11)
A number of artefacts were recovered which do not fit into the previous categories. The most interesting is a bevelled and partly polished stone (743, Fig 29) of green riebeckia-felsite from Northmavine (Ritchie 1968 128–33). Apart from the bevelled end there is no other attempt to shape the piece. This could not really be called an axe, although the pecked areas towards the unshaped end on either face and the fact that the polish or gloss is present on only the upper half of the piece suggests that this was hafted in some way. The angle of the edge is quite thick. There is a similar artefact from Jarlshof (Curle 1935). This type is quite different from other axes in Shetland as it does not appear to have been flaked to shape and instead is more similar to the Orcadian axes in the grinding of a suitably small cobble to shape.

A small countersunk tabular shale pebble (C62, Fig 35) and a fragment of a flat stone dish with rounded rim (867, Fig 35) are the other pieces of note. The remaining artefacts include three apparently ground slabs of sandstone, a sandstone slab chipped to form a waist (C32, Fig 35) and several larger fragments of worked sandstone whose use is unknown.

Additional artefacts
A number of coarse stone artefacts were not examined during the last phase of post-excavation work. Comments by A. Clarke follow, based on cataloguing by R. Lamb.

Forty-two artefacts are described as slate tools of which most are probably flaked stone bars or fragments of such. Very few of these appear to be shaped shale pieces; 583 and 731 (Fig 35) may be parts of knives whilst A72 and A105 (not illustrated) may be handled pieces and one (A102, Fig 35) is described as an oval knife of polished slate. Nine of the sandstone implements are most probably flaked stone bars; Skaill knives, referred to as split pebbles (total = 6), stone discs (total = 6), handled clubs (total = 2) and a heart-shaped piece are also present. The large number of cobble tools (total = 52) cannot be placed into specific wear categories from their description. There are four perforated pieces, one of which may be a cobble weight (B65, not illustrated) and another (B223, not illustrated), which is referred to as an oblong pendant, may actually be a perforated whetstone, though there is no description of wear traces. There is also a shale ring (347, Fig 34) some 60 mm in diameter with a hole of 20 mm diameter.

Six querns were recovered from the 1974 excavation. All are described as trough querns, and two (992 and 993, not illustrated) have a perforation in the base. One of the querns (925, not illustrated) appears to have been reused as a tether stone.

Context of the coarse stone artefacts
From the summary above it is clear that several of the stone artefact types have a selective distribution throughout the stratigraphic phases, particularly from the interior contexts. However, the most numerous artefacts (the flaked stone bars and ard points) are found almost everywhere, as they occur, often together, in almost all types of context and they are clearly present throughout the entire use of the site. Given their long use, it is of interest that there appears to be no morphological development of these tools through time; within the large assemblage of shale flaked stone bars there is no discernible chronological or at least contextual difference by shape, size, and the presence of hafting and wear traces. Only the presence of a few oval forms of shale flaked stone bars in Phases 9 and 10 can be noted. Neither does Rees note any possibility of a chronological development of form of the ard points within her provisional phasing. By context there are a few clear patterns. Most notably the largest numbers of both tool types are associated with walls, either as tumble, or deriving from external contexts against the walls. A higher proportion of the ard points are present in the South House, mainly Phase 9, than in the North House and two thirds of those from Phase 9 are worn tools, in contrast to the roughouts which are more common in the earlier phases. Roughouts,

those ard points which were discarded or deposited at the preliminary stage of manufacture before the final shaping of the tools, are also more common in external wall contexts than elsewhere. Phase 9 deposits in the North House, both internally and in the walls, have a high proportion of the shale flaked stone bars, the majority of which are unworn tools. Worn tools are more common before Phase 9 in the North House. In all phases of the South House and passages the unworn shale flaked stone bars are more common. In contrast the shale flaked stone bars from the external wall deposits have more or less equal numbers of worn and unworn tools. The flaked stone bars made on sandstone are far fewer than those of shale and they have a more limited phasing distribution. With the exception of one from Phase 3 the rest occur in Phase 7 or later and are found particularly within the houses and passages. It is assumed that the ard points, certainly, and the majority of the flaked stone bars, probably, are tools of cultivation, but it is very common for these tools to appear both inside and outside prehistoric structures, where they are reused in structural contexts such as drains or walls, or perhaps as paving. There is a significant number of both tool types in the 'rubble' deposits of Phases 7 and 9 inside the houses and passages, and although they might have been deposited through primary use, as the rest of the tools most probably were, in the case of Phase 7, it is also possible that they were brought in with the rubble which was used to build up the base of the secondary floor. The Phase 9 deposits will be discussed in further detail below but it is possible that many of the flaked stone bars from the North House derive from the manufacturing area of these tools to the north-east.

The differential deposition of stone artefacts between the houses before Phase 9 most likely indicates that the South House and the North House were used for different purposes. As so few artefacts are present before Phase 7 in both houses, it is likely that there was a certain degree of clearance during rebuilding. However, the artefacts that are present in the walls of these phases, as well as externally, are similar to those from the houses, and this suggests that there was a more limited range of stone tools in use during this period than in later phases. In the North House, its walls, and external contexts, this limited range in fact continues throughout Phases 7 and 8. The only observation of note is the continuing presence of handled clubs from contexts in or around the North House, whereas only one club is found in the South House before Phase 9. The function of these handled clubs is at present unknown though it is likely that they were somehow hafted for use. The change appears in Phase 7 of the South House which has a larger range of artefact types, and this is carried on through Phase 8 of the South House with more of the same artefact types as well as the introduction of Skaill knives. The use of heart-shaped pieces in both these phases of the South House is of interest, since if they were indeed associated with the tethering of animals, then this suggests the use of the South House as a byre. Stone discs and Skaill knives here indicate particular processing and storage activities, for which there is no evidence in the North House.

External deposits of Phase 8.1 include the area of shale working which is present in two soil contexts associated with the walls to the external central-east and external north-east (see Fig 30 for area locations). Both of these deposits have large numbers of flaked stone bars and associated working debris, whilst large numbers of flaked stone bars, but a lesser amount of working debris, are also found in soil contexts by the north-west wall. It is probable that shale working was confined to the area to the external central-east and external north-east, as a paved area and clay working floors were noticed during excavation, and that the products of manufacture were then dispersed around the site.

A profusion of shale chips and worked and unworked fragments marks an episode, or episodes, of manufacturing the shale flaked stone bars. This waste is concentrated to the north-east and is accompanied by a large proportion of the flaked stone bars themselves. These are marked as Phase 10 deposits on the concordance (Table 5), although the shale-working corridor is described as Phase 8.1.

The interpretation of the Phase 9 and 10 assemblages is complex, as there are problems in determining whether these deposits accumulated through use *in situ* or whether they were redeposited from elsewhere. Difficulties in interpretation are also compounded by problems in phasing the external activities.

The assemblages from the Phase 9 deposits inside both the South House and North House and passages are very similar to each other, as artefact types, that were present in the South House before Phase 9 continue to be used here. They are now also present in the North House. Furthermore, both houses and the passages between show a marked increase in the use of cobble tools. This suggests that the assemblages from both of the houses were deposited in a similar way and that cobble tools of varying types, Skaill knives and stone discs were in commonest use. The main differences between the houses, aside from the possibility that particular cobble tool types are deposited selectively, are in the varying proportions of ard points and flaked stone bars which are present. There is, in fact, an interesting correlation between their presence in the houses and the external activities immediately around the houses: the North House, with its external area of shale working has large numbers of flaked stone bars, whilst the South House, around which there were episodes of ploughing, has a larger number of ard points.

External contexts away from the walls most often include only a few artefacts in each context. Here ard points and flaked stone bars are the most common types, and though the full range of artefact types is present, they occur in far fewer numbers than in the external wall deposits. Many of the artefacts appear to be in secondary contexts and have been re-used in paving, drains and walls.

The deposits outside the houses can therefore be split into two: those immediately beside the walls and those further away. The former deposits could be interpreted as wall heaps which were formed by the accumulation of rubble as well as of tools which were in use in the houses. The presence of the shale working area recorded in the external central-east and external north-east deposits suggests that some of the wall heap construction may not be easy to identify and separate from other external activities. The excavated external area around the South House was not as extensive as that around the North, so it is not possible to draw comparisons between the material from the wall fill and external areas of the two.

The question remains of whether the deposits from Phase 9 within the houses (particularly the North House) were formed *in situ* or whether they were redeposited. Since these are the latest deposits on the site, and therefore not subject to clearance before further rebuilding, it is perhaps unsurprising that there is such an accumulation. All sites in the Northern Isles exhibit this final phase of 'rubble' accumulation to some extent and, especially in the case of stone tools, it is usually accompanied by the greater proportion of the artefactual assemblage. One interpretative problem arising from the present archaeological record of the site is that possibility that the rubble and artefacts did not, after all, form a single deposit. This certainly could be the case where artefacts which were used in earlier wall fill are then found in the final collapse of the structures. At Sumburgh Airport this could account for many of the artefacts found internally. However, the great increase in the use of cobble tools in this phase and the fact that such tools are not commonly found in wall fills suggest that there was a degree of later activity in the houses. The use of these cobble tools cannot be separated from the presence of other tool types in this phase, because the Phase 9 deposits were, more or less, excavated as one context, and there is no way of knowing whether the cobble tools were more likely to come from the base, and presumed occupation level, of this rubble deposit, or whether they were mixed up with it. If the cobble tools, which appear to represent the latest use of the site, were redeposited from elsewhere to form a dump in the houses, then one would expect to have found other types of 'later' artefacts mixed with the latest deposits; but though a few possible later types are present (see below), these do not seem enough to represent a non-specific dumping area. Without having seen all of the cobble tools it is not possible to be conclusive, but it may be that since the house assemblages differ both in quantity of cobble tools, and possibly by particular types of tool, and since certain types only appear in external deposits, the cobble tools were deposited selectively and that these represent episodes of use inside and outside the structures.

Chipped Stone Assemblage by B. Finlayson

An assemblage of 340 pieces of chipped stone was recovered from the site, of which the majority was quartz, with three pieces of flint and one piece of quartzite. A significant part of the assemblage is likely to represent waste material, including fragmentary pieces and a few quartz blocks that appear to have been tested and then abandoned as unworkable. Thus this represents a fairly small collection of pieces. The presence of unworkable pieces suggests that collection of quartz is likely to have been fairly representative, at least for reasonably large pieces. The three flint artefacts are missing from the collection, and no description appears in the archived catalogue; however, an illustration of the tools has been examined.

Sources of the materials used

In the absence of a good flint source, Shetland lithic assemblages are dominated by quartz. Although quartz is frequently dismissed as an intractable material, it represents a major resource in Scotland, in areas with no flint, chert or volcanic alternatives. It is, however, relatively rare to not recover any flint from a mostly quartz assemblage. Unfortunately, although the use of quartz is now known to have been extensive, both the nature of the raw material and the tendency for excavators to follow less systematic collecting policies with quartz than with flint have hampered its study. There are two chief problems with the raw material. The first is the fact that quartz tends to splinter and a good conchoidal fracture is not always obtained. This means that it can often be hard to distinguish deliberate knapping from accidental breakage and also that the control exercised by knappers is severely limited. The second problems is that quartz is a very variable material, and its knapping properties are affected by the nature of the source. There are crystal quartzes, which tend to have fairly good conchoidal fracture, and very granular quartzes that tend to dissolve into sugar crystal-like grains when struck. The size of the raw material blocks also has an effect. Small beach pebbles are generally seen (in all materials) to be a problematic material, both because of the small size of the blocks and because the curved exterior makes initial blows more prone to glance off the pebble. The material worked at Sumburgh Airport appears to have been predominantly small, rounded pebbles.

The presence of three retouched flint tools in the absence of any flint debitage is interesting. The flint was presumably imported to Shetland, and it is possible that it was transported in its finished form, which explains the absence of any flint debitage. It appears likely that throughout the Neolithic and Bronze Age flint artefacts were transported in a complete state (see Finlayson, in press). However, most examples of complete flint artefacts are objects of noticeably good quality material and manufacture, normally involving extensive pressure flaking and not necessarily intended for a mundane function. The artefacts from Sumburgh Airport illustrated do not fall into that category. The closest parallel is with artefacts from Lairg, where the small collection of flint artefacts retrieved from a predominantly quartz assemblage appears to have been worked down and reused (Finlayson 1992). It is possible that a similar process has occurred here, with the flint being valued as a useful material and therefore being reduced to an artefact type that is part of the normal tool kit.

Method and location of manufacture

Two reduction techniques have been used to work the quartz, direct hard-hammer percussion and the bipolar technique (Callahan 1987; Hayden 1980; Knight 1991; Wickham-Jones 1990).

One solution to the problems inherent in quartz is to employ a bipolar knapping technique, and there is evidence that this was extensively employed here. This technique generally appears to be appropriate for small pebbles, as the initial preparation required by other techniques often leaves too little material for the block to be productive, and the opposed forces involved at least partly resolve the problem posed by the curved surface. In addition because bipolar working relies on

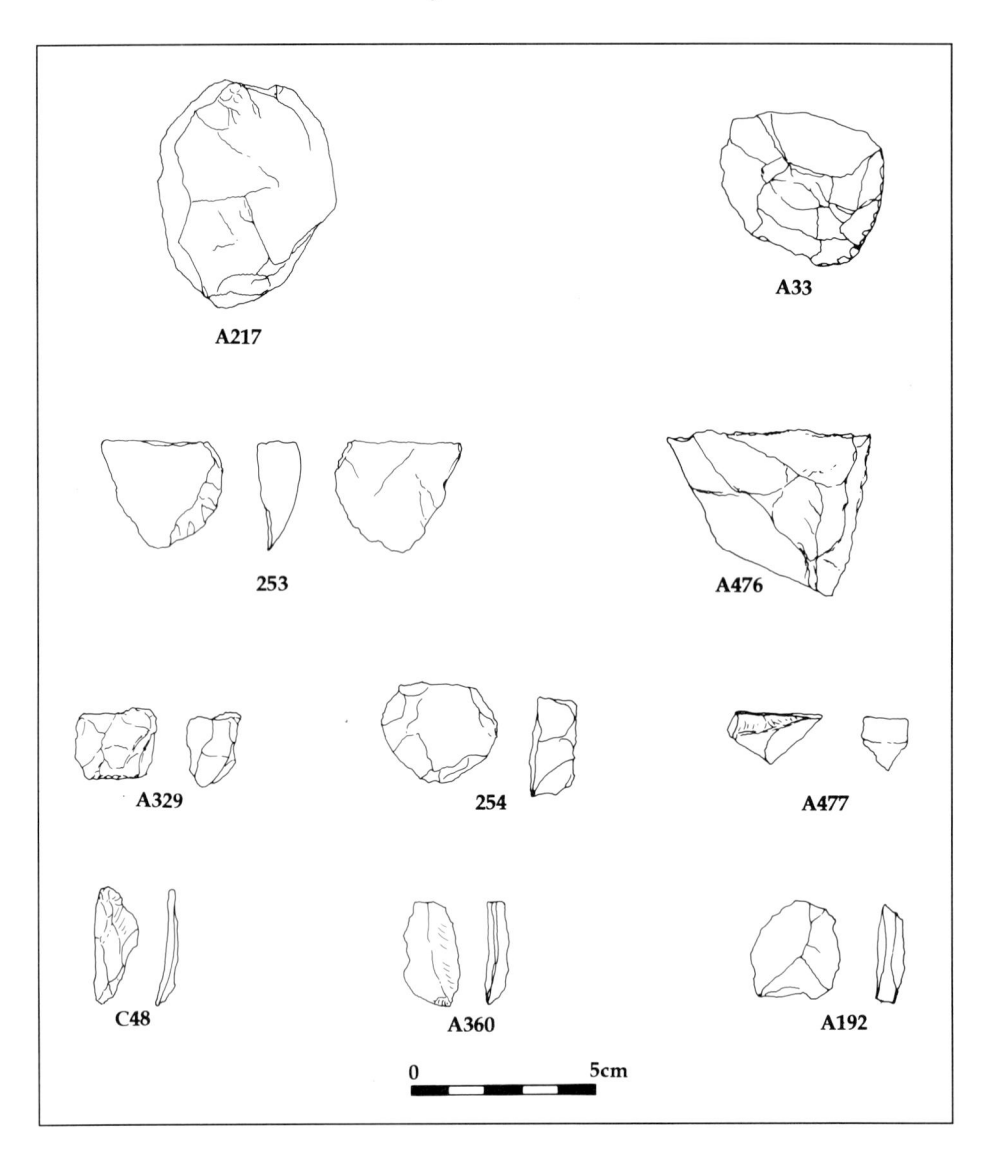

Figure 36: Quartz atefacts.

sheering rather than conchoidal fracture, it is possibly a more controlled method than flint knapping when working some quartzes.

Bipolar working appears to have been commonly employed at Tofts Ness in the late Neolithic/early Bronze Age where a similar type of material was employed (Finlayson 1991) and was used to knap the small pebble part of the quartz assemblage in the Bronze Age at Lairg.

Of the seven pieces classified as cores, two are bipolar cores (A217, Fig 36), three are fragments of bipolar cores and one is an unidentifiable fragment. The remaining piece is a platform core (A476, Fig 36). The use of the bipolar technique is further documented by the presence of numbers of flakes with clear traces of bipolar working and orange segment-shaped pieces, which can be produced during bipolar working.

That primary flaking was possibly being conducted on site is indicated by the presence of a number of pieces, such as battered quartz blocks, that have not been successfully opened, by split pebbles that have not been worked, or by pieces that have been opened and then probably abandoned as unworkable. A few other shattered pieces may be the product of burning, probably accidental, as there is no indication that the knapping properties of quartz improve on heating.

In terms of technology the Sumburgh Airport material appears typical of the later Neolithic and Bronze Age quartz assemblages in the Northern Isles. The high proportion of retouched tools is, however, unusual. The almost complete absence of flint may have encouraged a higher rate of formal tool manufacture on the quartz, but even assuming this, the percentage of retouched tools remains high, suggesting that the assemblage does not represent all the material from knapping quartz and could have been selected from an initial knapping floor and brought into the structures. This contradicts the evidence of unworkable blocks, battered pieces, cores and split pebbles that are also present. However, quartz knapping is generally a very wasteful process, with large numbers of waste flakes and blocks being produced, and through the small quantities of such material present at Sumburgh it appears that little knapping was undertaken within the houses. The assemblage appears to represent a small amount of primary material, as well as chipped stone brought into the houses, most of which has been incorporated into the structural elements of the buildings and is therefore residual. It has already been observed that there is no evidence for flint knapping, but given the type of flint artefacts recovered it appears reasonable to suggest that flint knapping was undertaken off site, possibly with the quartz knapping.

Table 9 shows the overall breakdown of the assemblage. The pattern of debitage shows a proportion of chunks (A477, Fig 36) that is, if anything, lower than often found in assemblages of relatively intractable material such as quartz. The proportions of flakes (C48 and A360, Fig 36) and splinter flakes indicate a fairly high success in knapping the quartz into usable pieces. For comparison with non-flint assemblages, both flakes and splinter flakes can probably be combined as a single class in terms of knapping intention. This is at least partly a result of the fine-grained quartz worked, which represents a material more suitable for knapping than some of the more coarse-grained quartzes sometimes employed. This impression is supported by the fact that most of the quartz flakes are relatively thin, and not blocky in form.

There are 33 formal retouched quartz tools. This represents almost 10 % of the assemblage, which appears to be a very high proportion, particularly were all the pieces representing the initial stages of knapping discounted. With one exception they are scrapers of one form or another. The one exception is a piece that appears

Table 9. Range and use of chipped stone

Blades	2	1%
Flakes, inner irregular	67	
Flakes, inner regular	33	
Flakes, secondary	38	
Flakes, primary	2	
Flake total	140	42%
Splinter flakes, inner irregular	43	
Splinter flakes, inner regular	8	
Splinter flakes, secondary	45	
Splinter flakes, primary	5	
Splinter flake total	101	30%
Chunks	65	19%
Cores	7	2%
Pebbles	10	3%
Split pebbles	12	4%
Shattered pieces	0	0%
Total	337	

to have shallow retouch along one edge. Although the piece may be broken, it appears that it is a quartz version of the edge-retouched flakes typical of the later Neolithic and Bronze Age in Orkney.

The scrapers have been classified according to a method developed for material on Orkney, where the prevalence of bipolar working meant that division of scraper types into end-scraper and side-scraper varieties was not helpful. A simple morphological system was developed (Finlayson 1991). Following that system, twelve of the Sumburgh Airport scrapers (A33, 253, A329 and 254, Fig 36) are short, thick, convex scrapers, two having flared working edges, leaving a narrow end probably designed for hafting. One has minimal retouch, but was a thick-edged quartz piece lightly formed into a scraper. Six scrapers are short, convex scrapers, one of which is flared. Four are thick, convex scrapers, three of which are flared. One is a simple convex scraper. One scraper has a denticulate retouched edge, and one has a straight retouched edge. Finally, there are six very irregular scrapers, some of which may not have been deliberately modified, but which have been scarred along the edge to produce a sort of pseudo-retouch. The refraction of light from the quartz can make the examination of retouch scars difficult.

The three known flint artefacts all appear to be short, thick, convex scrapers, and therefore replicate the type of tool that is being successfully manufactured in quartz.

Context of the chipped stone artefacts

Little of the material comes from good contexts for spatial analysis. One hundred and thirty-one pieces of quartz come from the exterior of the buildings, 35 from the walls and tumble, 36 are unstratified. Thirty-eight pieces come from the passages, but of these 24 are from unknown phases or from Phases 9 or 10. Of the 96 pieces from the house interiors, 57 are from Phases 9, 10 or unknown phases. Only one of the flint scrapers comes from an occupation context in a structure, and this is from a the secondary floor layer in the South House, which also contained five quartz pieces. All of the other chipped stone material in the South House is either from the rubble immediately below the secondary paved floor (Phase 7, 12 pieces), or just above the secondary floor level (Phase 8.1, one piece) (Figs 38 and 39).

There is a suggestion that much of the material in the North House may have been associated with hearths, with 16 pieces coming from either hearth contexts, or with deposits that appear to have been derived from hearths, perhaps not surprisingly suggesting craft work being conducted around the fire inside the North House (Figs 38 and 39). Only five pieces come from 'non-hearth' contexts; these all come from groove and post-hole contexts and may not be associated with occupation but with residual material incorporated during construction. The distribution of both artefact types and knapping techniques does not appear to vary at all between the material from late or residual contexts and the house interiors.

PUMICE

The pumice assemblage consists of 103 separate pieces, 34 of which have no immediate signs of wear on them, while the remaining 69 pieces have indications of use in one way or another. All of the pumice has a typical water-worn, rounded shape.

Source of the material by C. Barrowman

The majority of beach-deposited pumice in Britain and Ireland is derived from Iceland. Mercer (1970) states that pumice from various volcanoes on Iceland could reach the British coast by circumnavigating the northernmost reaches of the Atlantic in an anti-clockwise fashion. This may be the source for the Sumburgh Airport assemblage.

Use of pumice by C. Barrowman

The most prominent signs of function and use are indicated by smooth, flat areas which either extend over the whole length of the piece (Fig 37, B16/1 and B158/2),

110 J. DOWNES

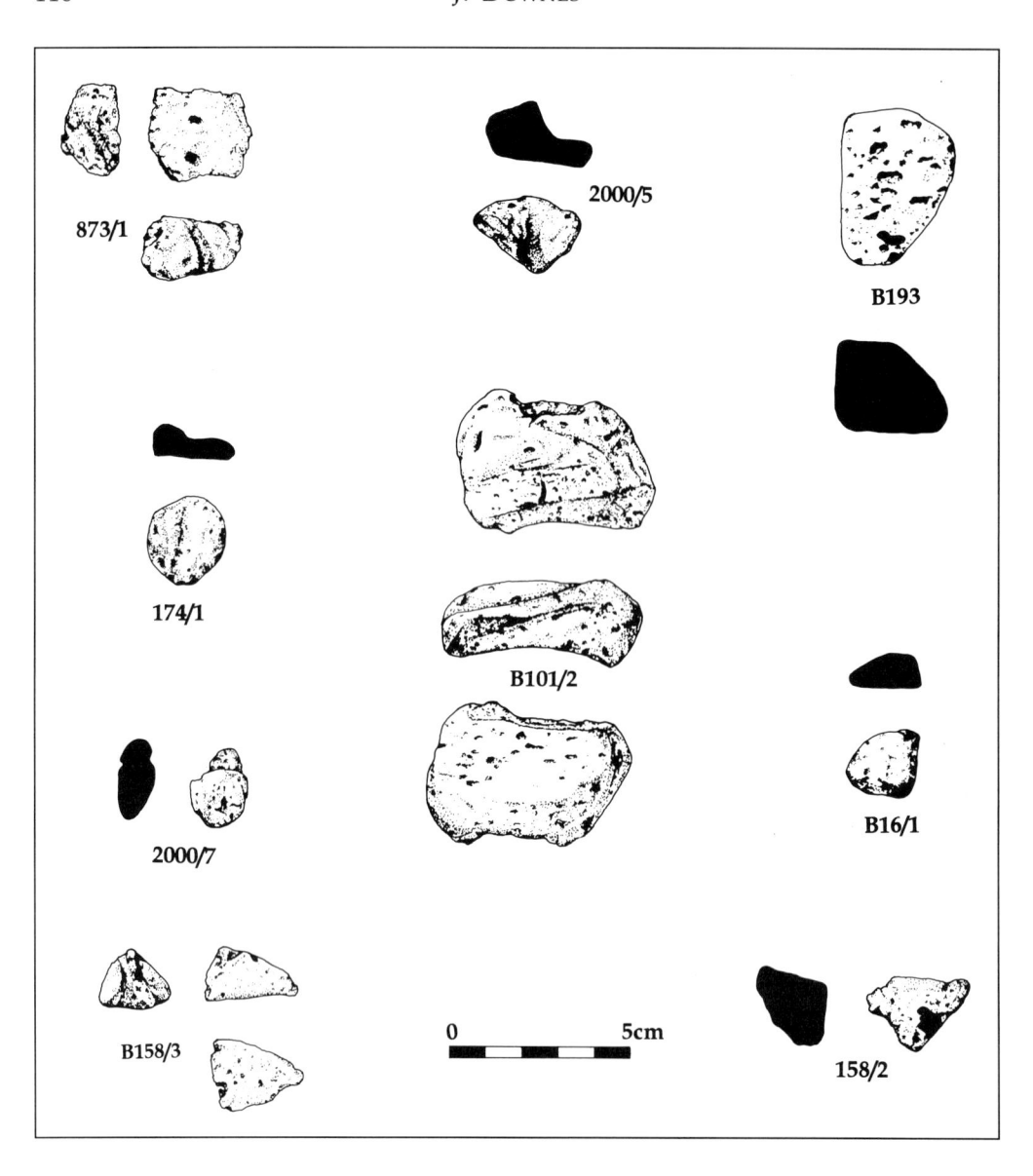

Figure 37: Pumice.

or which are on a smaller area of one side (Fig 37, 873/1). This wear is presumably formed by the pumice being used for smoothing a large area of material such as bone, wood, skin or steatite. Some pieces also have very smooth areas which are not flat, but convex or concave (Fig 37, 174/1, and B158/3). These may also have been used for working large areas of similar material which have a curved surface rather than a flat one, such as the walls of a bowl or sides of a similar curved vessel.

The most obvious signs of use can be seen on pieces such as B101/2 (Fig 37) and 2000/7 where grooves are present, perhaps formed from the working of bone or wood points. Pieces 2000/2 (not illustrated) and 2000/5 (not illustrated) display a sharp-angled concave working surface which could indicate the use of pumice for smoothing the rim of a steatite vessel, or bone.

The pumice can be split into different types by the size of the vesicles and colour variations. Vesicular (or pore) sizes range from fine to medium through to large, and the colour ranges through different shades of grey to black. It is possible to infer that the finer-pored pieces of pumice were used to create a smoother surface finish on certain materials such as bone, wood or pottery, whereas the coarser pumice with larger vesicles may have been used for a more intense smoothing on larger or tougher materials, such as steatite (B193, Fig 37). Certainly the majority of the grooved pieces have a finer porosity with smaller vesicles.

The pumice may have been used in a similar fashion to that found on other sites around Britain and Ireland, mainly for shaping and working bone, wood, pottery and skins. Its frequent occurrence on certain sites suggests that it fulfilled a versatile role. Scott describes the pumice found at Eilean An Tighe as a pottery-shaping implement, where 'pumice objects were uncovered which were similarly rounded and sometimes concave surfaces and grooves were present due to artifactual abrasion' (Scott 1950–51, 37), and he suggests that the 'grooves in these tools are caused by rubbing down rims' (ibid., 12). Pumice found at the Broch of Burrian in North Ronaldsay showed similar signs of wear, and MacGregor (1972) suggests that worked bone on the site may have been shaped by this method .

Context of pumice artefacts by J. Downes

There were no finds of pumice from the earliest phases of the site; Phase 7 was the first group of contexts where pumice was located. All the pumice derived from the interior of the South House, with none from the North. Twenty pieces were found in the interior of the building, to the west and south-west of the hearth, and no more than 1.5 m from the hearth. This distribution of finds may indicate the site of activities being conducted at the hearth side. From Phases 8 and 9 there were eight finds from the similar, central part of the South House, and 18 pieces from the North House (Fig 39), all deriving from the west cubicle and western part of the interior adjacent to this cubicle. There were also five pieces from the central passage and two from the east passage. The pumice from Phase 10 all derived from the external contexts around the North House.

If at least some of the pieces of pumice remained *in situ* close to the place where they were used, it could be said that there is no evidence that pumice was used in the early Bronze Age at Sumburgh Airport. During the later Bronze Age earlier occupation of the stone buildings, activities involving the use of pumice as a smoother or polisher were being carried out in close proximity to the hearth in the South House, and during the later occupation pumice was perhaps being used in particular places within both houses.

Origins of Materials and Artefacts by J. Downes

The range of materials from which the artefacts at Sumburgh Airport were made were all obtainable in Shetland except perhaps the flint artefacts (Finlayson, above). Pumice could have been collected from the beach and used without modification. The quartz could likewise have been picked up on the beach, and knapped at the settlement, but outside, not within the houses. The stone from which the stone tools derived was obtainable from outcrops or as beach cobbles. It may be surmised that people from the settlement quarried the outcrops and brought back roughouts. The working of the shale, and possibly other types of stone, took place just outside the houses during the later phases (early Iron Age) at least.

Although the majority of the steatite could not be attributed to a source, it was possible to determine that some came from Catpund 16.5 km to the north of Sumburgh and that the remainder is likely to have come from smaller Shetland islands at least 90 km away (Sharman, above). The steatite artefacts from Sumburgh Airport have not elucidated the issue of the organisation of the exploitation of steatite and the manufacture of artefacts. Although it appears from the lack of manufacturing debris at Sumburgh Airport that artefacts were not made within the settlement, some of the pumice has wear grooves consistent with the smoothing of the rim of a vessel.

There is a limit to what can be said about community interaction and wider-flung contacts through the consideration of the range and sources of materials and artefacts from Sumburgh Airport. Evidence for a greater range of crafts and materials came from Jarlshof, where a small circular chamber adjacent to late Bronze Age Village I Dwelling III was interpreted as a 'potter's workshop' (Hamilton 1956, 22). Bronze working and probably ironworking were being carried out at Jarlshof during the later Bronze Age and early Iron Age and the production of textiles during the early Iron Age is evidenced by the occurrence of spindle whorls. Some of these activities may have been carried out at Sumburgh Airport, but not within the excavated structures. Regardless of whether they were or not, we can too easily assume close contact between Sumburgh, Jarlshof and other settlements, and fall into the trap of marginalising these sites if we do not also assume full consciousness of, and interaction with, the wider world of later prehistoric settlement, including movements of people and goods in Shetland and its archipelago.

Artefact Context and Distribution by J. Downes

Although it is accepted that the final resting place of an artefact is not a direct reflection of its place of use, the formation processes have been clarified through the stratigraphic and artefactual analysis to the point where an interpretation of the distribution of finds can be made. For anything meaningful to be said about how the houses were built and occupied, the context of artefacts has to be considered carefully and made an integral part of artefact studies.

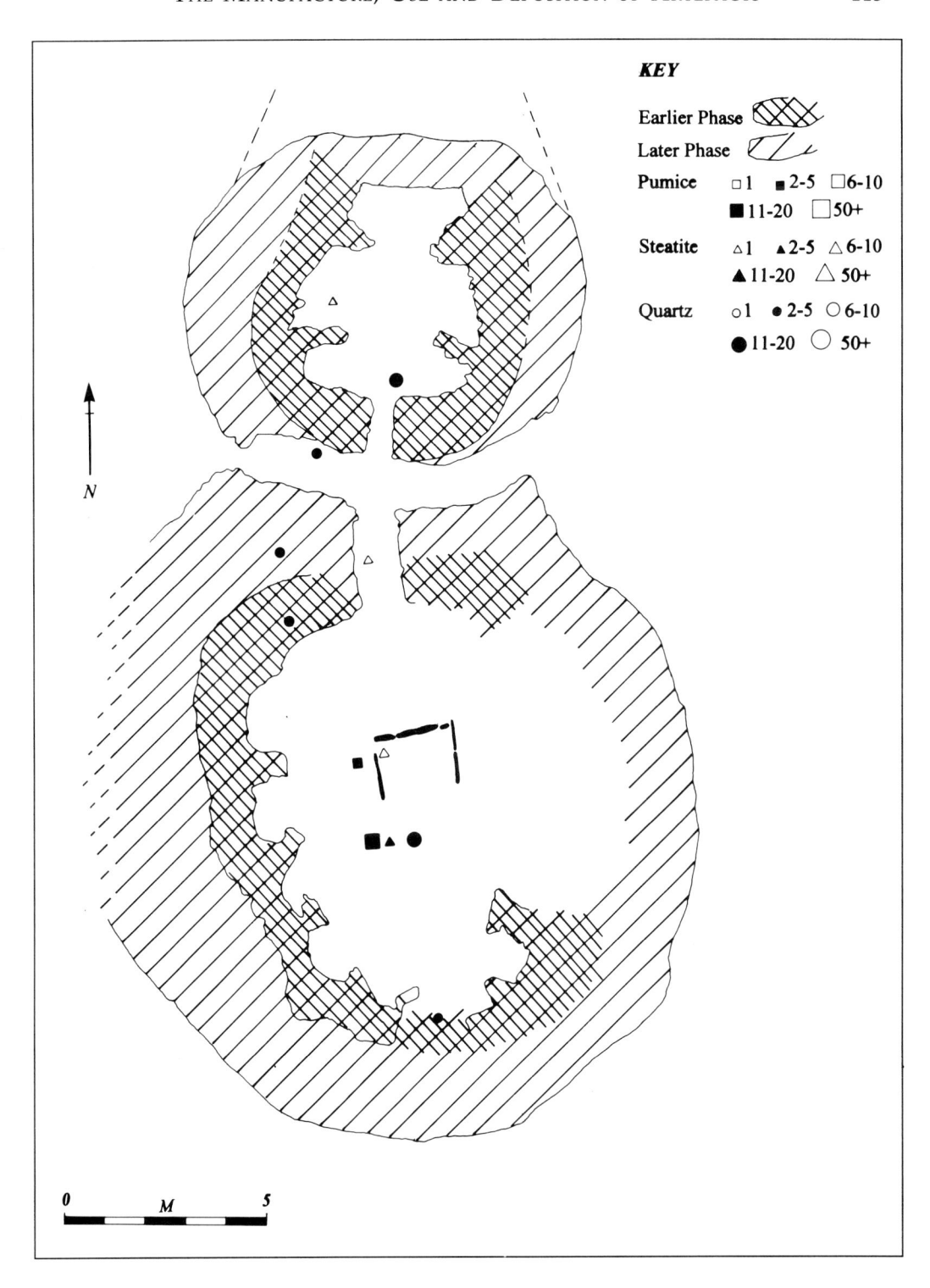

THE MANUFACTURE, USE AND DEPOSITION OF ARTEFACTS 113

Figure 38: Plan showing distribution of pumice, steatite and quartz from Bronze Age phases (Phases 2–7).

114   J. DOWNES

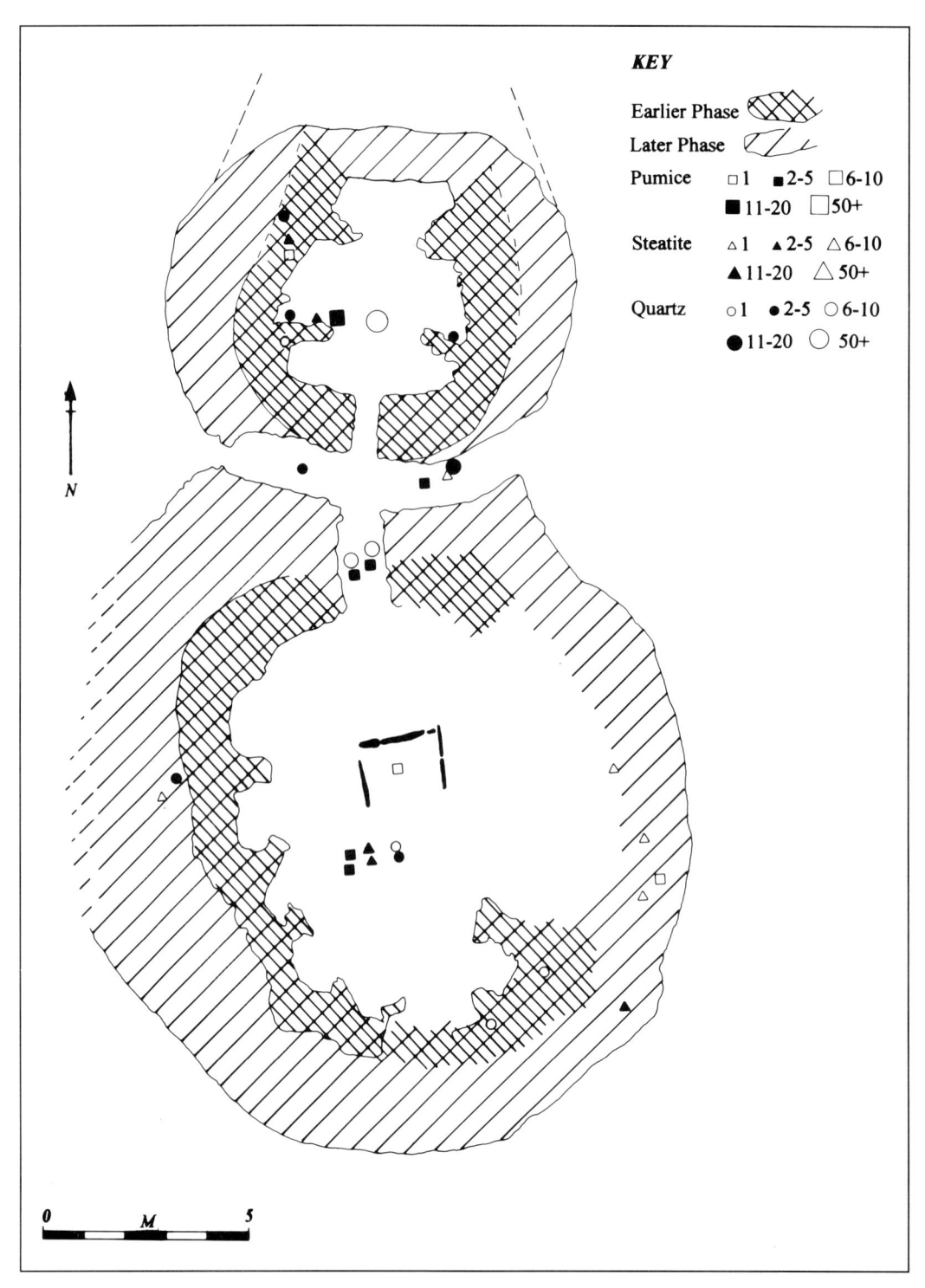

Figure 39: Plan showing distribution of pumice, staetite and quartz from early Iron Age phases (Phases 8–9).

It was not possible during the later post-excavation work to undertake analysis of the sherd size and condition of the whole of the pottery assemblage, but nevertheless it has been this class of artefact which has been most instructive in terms of formation processes. It appears that the interior of the houses was kept clean, and that the debris removed from the interiors was either dumped against the walls, or kept in midden heaps. There were, however, substantial amounts of artefacts recovered from within the houses, and this material has been interpreted in two ways according to phase. The material covered by the early Iron Age secondary paving appears to contain artefacts which were left *in situ*, with the addition perhaps of intrusive material brought in from the walls as they were levelled for the rebuilding. Primary residual refuse accumulated again in the early Iron Age North and South Houses until the North House seems to have gone into disuse and to have served as a place to put refuse. Upon the abandonment of the South House, certain artefacts may have been left *in situ*, as evidenced by the complete vessel (2–96, Fig 15) which had broken where it stood in the south end of the South House. Taking these complicated taphonomic factors into account, as well as the type of residue they are likely to leave, it can be asserted that the distribution of finds from some phases indicates the location of activities.

The distribution plans (Figs 38 and 39) show the location of quartz, steatite and pumice in the earlier and later phases. While the quartz pieces from the southernmost part of the North House in the earlier phases may indicate working of some sort, there is a clear focus of artefacts to the south-west of the hearth in the South House.

In the later phases pieces of quartz were found in the east and west cubicles of the North House which can be attributed to Phase 8. A substantial amount of pumice (18 pieces), quartz (52 pieces) and steatite was found within and in the central part of the North House, immediately outside the west cubicle. It can be said that there is a concentration of materials used for smoothing and working artefacts in the west part of the North House, which is an indication that people were working around the fire.

It is perhaps unsurprising that activities which had been taking place around the hearth in the South House then are carried out in the North House when hearths are placed within this building. However, steatite, pumice and quartz are also concentrated around the south-west part of the South House during Phases 8 and 9, which is where the hearth had been before it was paved over. While in part this distribution could be related to the baulk left in place within this part of the house, this cannot account for all the finds, and it appears that activities involving the use of these materials continued to be undertaken in the South House.

There is a predominance of fragments of large steatite-tempered jars (fabric F3) from the South House during the later phases of occupation, whereas from the North House many sherds of gritty pots (fabric F4) were found, a great number of which were soot-encrusted. The steatite sherds were not soot encrusted, and it is suggested that the gritty pots were used for cooking in the North House, whereas the large steatite jars were used for storage in the South House.

Three heart-shaped stone artefacts derived from Phase 7, and five from the early

Iron Age occupation; these artefacts do not occur in the North House. The artefacts have been interpreted (see above) as objects hung around the necks of animals, probably cattle. The tether posts to the south of the hearth, and that adjoining the north-east corner of the hearth (although this could have been part of the hearth furniture) appear to have been contemporary with this phase of occupation and to have continued in use after the secondary paving was put in place. It appears that animals (cattle) were stalled (overwintered) within the South House throughout its use and were situated in the southern part of the house and, less certainly, the north-east corner.

Through these aspects of the material culture it is possible to provide an interpretation of aspects of life inside and outside the houses. A consideration of where materials were coming from allows an account of the level of knowledge of the area/world and its make up, and of contact and interaction with other communities. The location and method of manufacture of the artefacts indicates the range of activities undertaken within and without the house, and the role different types of material culture played in daily life. The organisation of space and changes in the architectural form of the houses will be explored in the following section.

5. ARCHITECTURE, SPATIAL ORGANISATION AND MATERIAL CULTURE

J. Downes

Introduction

The relationship between the individual, the community, and architecture and material is undeniably complex. It is a subject of different forms of analysis from within different disciplines, many of which have now been applied to archaeological evidence. In all cases the aim is to enable an interpretation of how people lived or inhabited the world around them. It is not apposite to detail these approaches here, but the research into the patterning of artefacts and the cosmological referents incorporated within the architecture and the location of activities should be explored.

This section describes the changing architecture, use of space and materials at Sumburgh Airport. The type of dwelling that emerges is discussed in the context of other later prehistoric Shetland houses. These houses have attracted much comment in the past but in the absence of adequate records for most, they have been interpreted variously; the evidence from Sumburgh Airport permits a more informed assessment.

The use of space in the Sumburgh Airport houses

The preceding chapters represent layers of interpretation, through analysis of stratigraphy, materials and formation processes. The distribution of artefacts has been described, but it will now be interpreted in terms of the activities and the changes in spatial organisation which they may signal. This account will focus on the later Bronze Age and early Iron Age houses at Sumburgh Airport, for the early Bronze Age remains were too truncated to effect such analysis.

The use of space within the bipartite later Bronze Age North House, before the courtyard or South House were added, is hard to determine, as the inner part was quite disturbed. The trilobate inner part of the North House contained a hearth in the west recess. This is the only part of the building that housed fire, for the circular, paved, outer area covered a drainage network which incorporated a tank. It is possible that the inner recessed part of the North House functioned as the cooking and living area, and the circular, paved outer area as a work area and a place where animals were stalled. The evidence for a work place is indicated by the quartz pieces which lay in the south-east of this part of the building (Fig 38). The inference for the presence of animals is drawn from comparisons with the late Bronze Age I occupation at Jarlshof, where Curle (1934) interpreted the presence of dished paving within the innermost chamber of Dwelling II (northernmost of Jarlshof houses, Fig 40) as the surface of a cattle stall. Their effluent seems to have been channelled into a tank in the central part of the dwelling by means of this concave paving. We should also note the whale-bone tether in the wall of the south west recess of Dwelling II at Jarlshof. Furthermore, Curle (1934, 100) notes that the majority of the heart-shaped stone pieces found came from the far ends of the inner part of this building. These stone artefacts have been interpreted as protective devices worn around the necks of tethered animals (see above). At Sumburgh Airport the evidence is less convincing; the function of the tank is not clear, and there is a marked absence of heart-shaped pieces from the North House.

The addition of the courtyard (South House) to the North House had the effect of creating deep space, for entry to the North House would probably have been through the South House and the long, narrow joining passage. The establishment of the well built central hearth in the South House could have coincided with the blocking off of the recessed, inner part of the North House. The presence of soot-encrusted pottery, as an indication of cooking being carried out within the South House, has been noted above. The clustering of particular artefacts around the south-west of the hearth (Fig 38) suggests that the making or repairing of artefacts and clothing took place to the west, rather than the east side of the house. The presence of a line of thin stone uprights running from the north-west corner of the hearth towards the west wall (Fig 12, v) demonstrates the presence of a divider which enclosed an area to the south of better laid paving on the side of the house where cooking and crafts were more likely to have been undertaken. The stone divider would have prevented passage through the house on the west side indicating that the east side would have been the thoroughfare to the North House.

The presence of tether posts, particularly in the southern part of the house (Fig 12), and heart-shaped pieces within the later Bronze Age phases of the South House attest to the keeping of animals within this building, possibly cattle during winter. The holes pierced through the low orthostats at the northern side of the hearth (Fig 12, ak), and through one of the stones of the stone partition (Fig 12, v), functioned perhaps as tether points for smaller animals such as young livestock or dogs.

The function of the circular part of the North House remains ambiguous during these phases, as it housed neither hearth nor tank, and few artefacts were recovered from it. The North House is therefore interpreted as ancillary to the South House.

The most significant change apparent in the remodelling of the North and South Houses in the early Iron Age is the increase in access to the central areas. This is achieved by creating a circular floor plan which was entered by means of a shorter passageway. At Sumburgh Airport the subcircular interior of the North House was divided by radial piers during the early Iron Age. This interior was made much more accessible with the insertion of the east-west passageway, whereas in the later

Bronze Age phases the interior could only be entered through the South House. The hearth was no longer the dominant central feature: the hearth of the South House was paved over, and all hearths were situated in one or more of the bays formed in the North House by the insertion of piers. This would have had the effect of making the hearth accessible to fewer people, although it is possible that more than one hearth was used at one time. Despite the paving over of the hearth in the South House, the same craft activities seem to have continued to be undertaken in this part of the South House, but are also carried out in the North House (Figs 38 and 39). From the evidence of the pottery analysis it is clear that cooking activities shifted to the North House, and the South House was used for storage. The continued existence of the tether posts in the southern end of the South House and the finds of heart-shaped pieces of stone suggest that cattle or livestock were once again stalled here.

From the later Bronze Age phases of the stone-built houses at Sumburgh Airport onwards it can be seen that each house was not a single unit of space within which all activities took place, but that two or more spatially distinct parts can be recognised. Specific activities took place in each, the location of which changed through time. These changes indicate a fluidity in the nature of the settlement which reflects the dynamics of social practices and the recursive relationship between these practices, the architecture and the material culture. The use of two discrete spatial units as one dwelling can be likened to the paired houses in southern Britain, which appear to have originated in the middle Bronze Age. The nature of the organisation of space in settlements in southern Britain such as Black Patch and Itford Hill was emphasised by Ellison's re-analysis of the settlement evidence from Thorny Down (1987), where she identified settlement units comprising a large round house which functioned as living quarters (where food was consumed and certain crafts undertaken), associated with a smaller structure (or structures) which appeared to be ancillary (within which food was stored, prepared and cooked). The two-house unit continued into the early Iron Age of southern Britain. A well known example is Winnall Down (Parker Pearson 1996).

THE SHETLAND HOUSE: TERMINOLOGY AND CHRONOLOGY

Having identified the structural remains at Sumburgh Airport as a particular building type – a two-house unit – other settlement evidence from Shetland can now be characterised and evaluated. It is not the aim of this discussion either to refute existing typologies of later prehistoric houses in Shetland nor to create a new typology, but rather to set the Sumburgh Airport houses within a Shetland context. To this end it is necessary briefly to review and describe the later prehistoric houses.

Calder (1958) promoted the term 'oval house' in his description of his excavation and survey results of the houses at Ness of Gruting, Gruting School and Stanydale, amongst others. The term described the basic form of these buildings which are longer than they are wide (Fig 40). Hamilton (1956) referred to the late Bronze Age houses at Jarlshof as 'courtyard houses', which in reality they are, as each house has

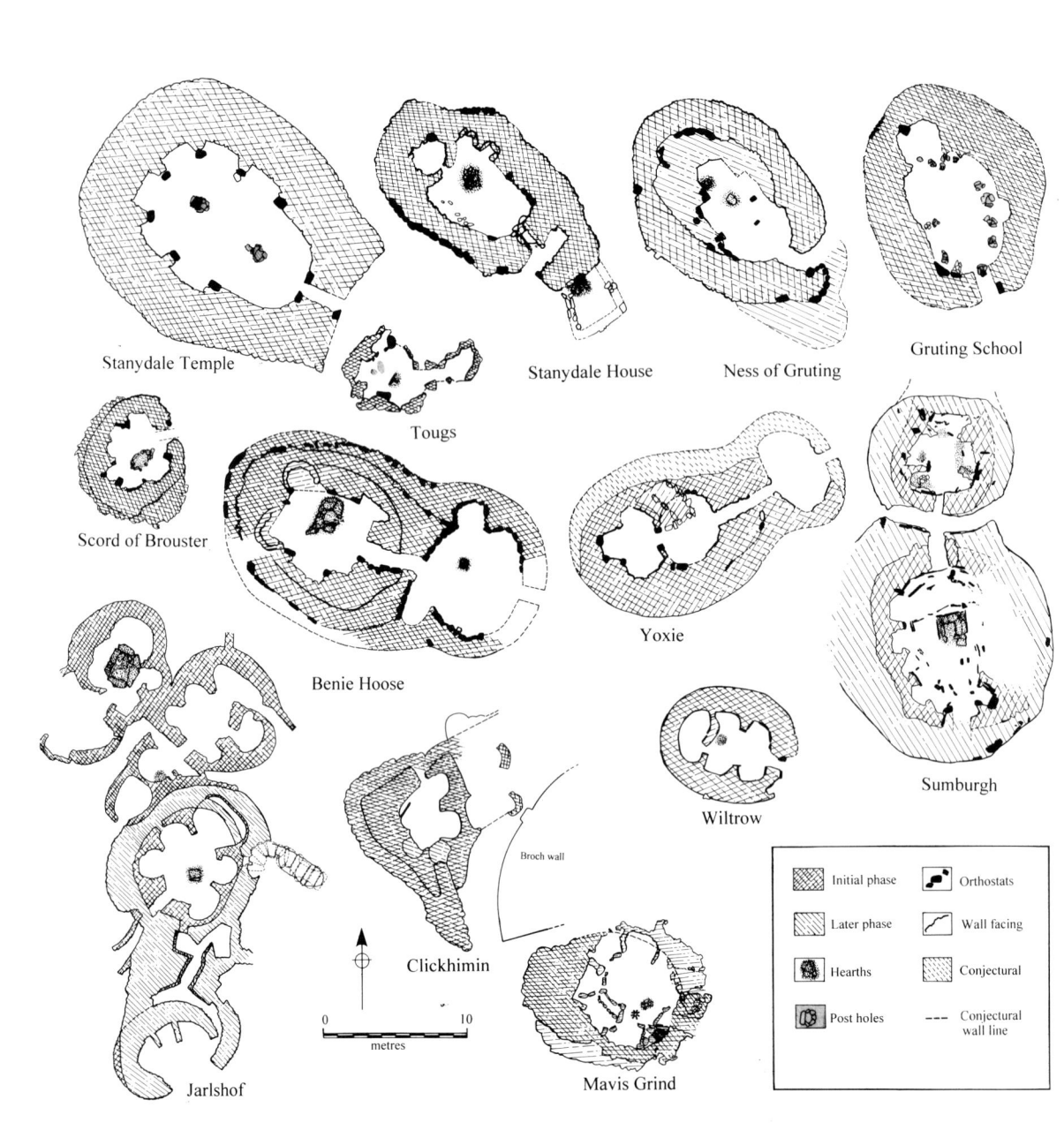

Figure 40: Plans of later prehistoric houses in Shetland.

an outer courtyard added. The term 'courtyard house' could equally well describe the Benie Hoose and the Standing Stones of Yoxie on Whalsay, as well as at Sumburgh Airport. But these could also be termed 'paired houses'. All these structures, along with those at Jarlshof, exhibit the characteristics of the two-house unit found at Sumburgh Airport. Henshall (1963b, 151) amongst others (see J. Hedges 1986) asserts that the term 'courtyard house' is a misnomer, preferring examples to be termed 'oval houses', which she contrasts with the 'round houses' of the Iron Age. Although we are primarily concerned with the creation and use of space within the buildings, rather than with the final form in plan, the terms 'oval', 'courtyard' and 'round' house are employed as they not only refer to this previous work, but signal broad differences in the architectural forms.

The form of the Shetland houses has been much discussed, as they represent a comparatively large amount of well preserved later prehistoric structures. Figure 40 shows structures excavated in Shetland which have been attributed to the Neolithic, Bronze Age and early Iron Age. Not all of the structures produced datable artefacts, and few have been dated by radiocarbon, with the exception of Ness of Gruting, Scord of Brouster, Tougs and Mavis Grind. As was mentioned earlier, there is no later prehistoric ceramic sequence for Shetland. Stanydale Temple, Ness of Gruting, Gruting School, Scord of Brouster House 3 and the Benie Hoose have all been cited and illustrated as examples of Neolithic houses and buildings (see Barclay 1996; Megaw and Simpson 1979; Ritchie 1995), although it is more likely that most, if not all, are Bronze Age (see J. Hedges 1986). House 3 at the Scord of Brouster is the latest of the three houses excavated at this site, with calibrated radiocarbon dates of 1750–1450 BC to two sigma (CAR-477 3315±60 bp) and 1910–1520 BC to two sigma (CAR-479 3420±70 bp) (Bronk Ramsay 1995, Whittle 1986). Charred barley from Ness of Gruting was dated to 2290–1970 BC to two sigma (Gr N-6168 3710±50 bp) and 2200–1500 BC to two sigma (BM-441 3514±120 bp) (ibid.). These structures date to the earlier Bronze Age, with Ness of Gruting being roughly contemporary with the early Bronze Age occupation at Sumburgh Airport. The Stanydale house and Gruting School house share enough similarities in layout and construction technique to indicate their contemporaneity with Ness of Gruting.

The early Bronze Age occupation at Sumburgh Airport, comprised one or more timber structures, possibly of sub-oval form (see above). There is a significant difference in the use of building materials between the occupation at Sumburgh and that at Stanydale, Ness of Gruting and Gruting School, although in the example of Gruting School large timbers, as well as stone, do appear to have been employed (Calder 1958). The closest parallel to the postholes from Sumburgh Airport is in Structure 1 at Kebister. This building comprised a subrectangular double post-ring surrounding a large central hearth and two large cooking pits for which an early Bronze Age date is suggested (Lowe and Owen forthcoming). The structure at Kebister is interpreted as a burnt mound site on the basis of the aforementioned internal features and drain system, although there were no burnt stones (ibid.). One of the early Bronze Age features at Sumburgh Airport (255, Fig 4) appears to have been a cooking pit, but the features in general were too truncated to assign a function to the structural remains. What the postholes and features from Sumburgh

Airport and Kebister demonstrate is that during the early Bronze Age buildings were being constructed either from timber, stone, or a combination of the two. The remains of the timber buildings are, however, more vulnerable to truncation and are less visible than the stone footings, and in both instances these structures have only been discovered because they underlie later stone buildings.

The lack of visibility of middle Bronze Age settlement remains in Shetland has been mentioned above, and a hiatus in the occupation at Sumburgh Airport appears to accord with this apparent gap in the settlement record. The only structure attributable to this period is the small recessed house at Tougs (Fig 40), dated by radiocarbon analysis to the middle Bronze Age (J. Hedges 1986, 12).

Earlier Bronze Age artefacts were discovered at the Benie Hoose, Yoxie and Sumburgh Airport, as was later Bronze Age material (Calder 1958, Henshall 1958). Although a hiatus has been identified at Sumburgh Airport, in the case of the Whalsay sites the lack of contextual information makes a sequence difficult to establish. It is probable that certain structural elements of the Benie and Yoxie have their origins in the earlier Bronze Age, but whether there is continuity in the occupation or not, the finished form of these buildings (particularly Benie Hoose) is more properly attributable to the later Bronze Age. There are close parallels to be drawn between these two buildings and the later Bronze Age phases at Sumburgh Airport. It is suggested that, in its earliest stone-built from, the houses at Sumburgh Airport closely resembled the Yoxie house, the South House at Sumburgh Airport acting as a forecourt to the bipartite North House (northernmost part ruinous; Fig 5). The passages linking the inner parts of the buildings to the forecourts are of almost identical length. The Benie Hoose is also similar in that it has an inner part and later forecourt, although it does not appear to have had an innermost chamber.

Although the later Bronze Age paired houses at Skaill (Buteux 1997) are located in Orkney rather than Shetland, they must be mentioned here as they present the closest parallel for the houses at Sumburgh Airport. In their final form these two stone-built houses are aligned north-south and their entrances are linked by a paved passage which is accessed from corridors running between the houses from the east and west. The method of construction and internal layout of these houses bear close similarities to the Sumburgh houses. The sequence of development suggested for the structures (ibid., 28–30) is that the northernmost structure, Structure 1, was the first element, with Structure 2 being added at a later date. A further similarity between the site at Skaill and that at Sumburgh Airport was the discovery that the later Bronze Age buildings overlay features such as postholes and shallow pits which may represent the remains of an earlier, timber structure.

The structural form of these later Bronze Age houses can be characterised as an inner part with an elongated passage leading to a courtyard or enclosed structure. The courtyard in all cases is a later addition and is paralleled at Jarlshof, most notably in Dwelling II, the second earliest and northernmost of the illustrated structures. However, it is a feature of all the Late Bronze Age Village I structures which Hamilton (1956) refers to as 'courtyard houses'. Of significance both to this discussion and to a consideration of social transformation in Britain, is the discernible change from 'the Bronze Age' to 'the Iron Age' at Jarlshof. At Jarlshof the change from recessed courtyard houses to larger circular houses occurs at Dwelling IV, where a recessed house (Phase a) is overlain by a larger circular two-phase house (Phases b and c), both of which have souterrains. A layer of wind-blown sand lay between Phases a and b. This may not be indicative of a hiatus in occupation (Hamilton 1956, 33), but it was one of many such events which necessitated periodic modification or reconstruction of buildings both at Jarlshof and at similar locales, such as Sumburgh Airport. Despite a sharp disjuncture in the architectural form, bronze working (which had been undertaken in the neighbouring courtyard house Dwelling III) took place in Dwelling IV during Phase b. Dwelling IVc again followed closely after IVb, but while it appears the house could have continued to be used as a 'workshop', this time it was not used for bronze working, but possibly for the smelting of iron, evidenced by the presence of a furnace, and iron slag from a bloomery found within the souterrain. There was a significant change at this point in most aspects of the material culture, with carinated vessels now dominating the pottery assemblage, and a marked increase in the occurrence of cobble tools which replace the other types of coarse stone tools. Furthermore, moulds for bronze working and scrapers are completely lacking, and artefacts such as spindle whorls and steatite armlets are found for the first time (Hamilton 1956, 33–8). At Jarlshof therefore, the change in architectural tradition from the recessed, courtyard houses to the more open-area circular houses, a radical change in house plan, can be seen to have *preceded* the change to the material culture by which we identify the Iron Age in the Northern Isles. At Sumburgh, although the change in material culture is more blurred, the same sequence can be ascertained. This finding is most significant with respect to the dynamics of culture change

Characteristics of the Shetland House

Recesses

The innermost recessed chambers encountered at the rear of the Sumburgh Airport and Yoxie houses appear in plan to be a maintenance of the feature of the small innermost chamber present in the Stanydale, Ness of Gruting and Gruting School houses (Fig 40). Here the depth of space was created by the elongated oval form of the houses, and enhanced by the lengthening and elaboration of the entrance passages. The enlarged rear recess is also prominent in the houses at Jarlshof and Wiltrow.

Recesses are a dominant feature of the Shetland architectural tradition, and can be seen to feature prominently in earlier buildings such as Stanydale Temple through to later Bronze Age houses at Jarlshof, Clickhimin and Sumburgh Airport. The similarity between the tombs and house forms in both Shetland and Orkney has been pointed out by Hamilton (1956, 1968), and more recently by Richards (in Parker Pearson and Richards 1994), who accounts for this phenomenon as the architectural expression of the ordering of world according to a particular cosmological scheme. It is possible that, in the case of the later Neolithic and earlier

Bronze Age houses, the rear recess is the most sacred space; in Shetland this may be an enlarged version of the Orcadian rear dresser recess. Whether the recesses retained the same meaning or function throughout the Bronze Age or not, they continued to be built into houses. Although the number and form varied, they are common to both the oval houses, the courtyard houses, and the smaller single houses. Recesses break down space into secluded areas offering privacy, a place to sleep or keep objects or animals. The change from this ordering of space to the more open, circular space, evident at Sumburgh Airport in the early Iron Age phases of occupation, which is also a defining characteristic of later brochs and wheel houses, is worthy of further comment.

The replacement of recesses with radial piers as space dividers is interesting, as at Sumburgh Airport the radial piers in the North House have been interpreted as secondary to the floor and wall of the structure, and they were insubstantial, as they were not bedded into the floor. It is likely that they did not stand very high; the highest of the orthostats which stood at the end of each pier was 1.05 m. Such was the case at Mavis Grind where the seven radial piers added during a secondary rebuilding stood to maximum height of 0.69 m (Cracknell and Smith 1983, 18). They would therefore have served to demarcate space, rather than enclose it as the deep recesses in the Bronze Age houses would have done.

Heel shaped facades

It was during the rebuilding of the Sumburgh Airport houses at the end of the Bronze Age that the outer part of the South House entrance is marked by a heel-shaped facade. As Raymond Lamb has pointed out (1985, 36), although the contemporaneity between Stanydale Temple and the Neolithic tombs has been assumed on the basis of this peculiar feature, this need not be the case, as the buildings at Sumburgh Airport are certainly a great deal later than the tombs. More recently, excavations at Kebister have provided another example of a heel-shaped facade which is probably late Bronze Age (Lowe and Owen forthcoming). The entrance way to the inner and earlier part of the Benie Hoose is also marked by a heel-shaped facade (Fig 40). It is apparent that concave stone walling to either side of an entrance passage was a feature that endured for millennia, and was used in various contexts, only some of which were funerary.

At both Sumburgh and the Benie Hoose, the concave entrance was made more impressive through being faced with massive orthostats. However, at Sumburgh Airport, the person encountering the facade would not have been able to view it from any distance, as it acted as one side of the east-west passage way. The heel shape, in this instance, cannot be said to define an arena or activity area (as it has been interpreted in the case of the tombs); instead its significance lay in demarcating and, moreover, accentuating the entrance to the South House.

Building with midden

A notable feature is the organic development of the houses at Sumburgh Airport. The fabric of the core of the walls of the later buildings is a product of the process of the earlier phases of occupation, and the walls increase in size through the longevity of that occupation. This is a characteristic of other Shetland houses, and although records of some excavations make it difficult to interpret the construction of the walls, the technique can be seen quite clearly at the Benie Hoose and Yoxie, and Ness of Gruting (see Fig 40). Hedges notes the addition of material to walls through time, and how this changes the form of the building (J. Hedges 1986, 23). It is probable that only some of the debris from within the houses was dumped against the walls, and that other debris was piled in free-standing middens or spread on the fields as fertiliser, or both. Although it appears that ash and all types of debris were dumped around the walls, material in each midden may have been selectively stored (see Simpson *et al* 1998, for the results of analysis of buried anthropogenic soils around Scatness Broch; Bronze Age soils have been amended by the application of domestic waste with a high ash content, Iron Age soils are characterised by the application of animal manures).

Parker Pearson et al. (1996, 63) discuss the use of midden at Dun Vulan, South Uist in the context of large middens at sites such as Jarlshof, and at Skara Brae, and Pool on Sanday, and they suggest that midden material was imbued with symbolic value associated with fertility and status among other things. In some instances of later prehistoric houses in the Northern and Western Isles, houses were built on, or cut into, pre-existing middens, as opposed to the midden material being heaped against the walls. This would have created an effect similar to the house being surrounded by midden. This appears to have been the case at Skara Brae, where the later Neolithic houses were built upon earlier midden, and the walls of the buildings then surrounded by huge deposits of midden which presumably derived from the occupation of the settlement. Childe evocatively described the settlement of Skara Brae as an organism, within which "the ... midden stands to the huts and passages in the relation as the flesh to the organs and veins of a living body" (1931, 24). At Cladh Hallan on South Uist an early Iron Age house has been cut into a late Bronze Age midden, where the earlier midden is employed as construction material by cutting the house floor down into the midden and revetting the lower parts with stone (Atkinson, et al. 1996).

During the interval that midden accumulates around the houses at Sumburgh Airport, the midden deposits are revetted with stone, as can be seen in places around the South House (Fig 7). The stone revetting of midden wall material is also apparent at the Benie Hoose and Yoxie, and it is visible in plan as stone lines within the wall make-up (Fig 40). At roughly the same time as the rebuilding of the stone structures at Sumburgh Airport, during the early Iron Age, the outer edge of the midden-and-earth wall was revetted with substantial boulders, and subsequently no material was added. Although it is not known where the midden was placed after this, the maintenance of a defined wall for the early Iron Age phases of the houses at Sumburgh Airport was a concept different from that of a dwelling which grew outwards through the addition of residues created by living within it.

Ard points and mattocks

The particular and peculiar context of ard points and mattocks in the northern isles is interesting and worthy of further mention. The presence of large quantities of these artefacts as part of the latest deposit within Bronze Age houses is a phenomenon that has been regularly encountered (see above). This phenomenon is hard to account for as these artefacts were not manufactured or used within the houses. These artefacts were also incorporated into the fabric of the buildings by being built into the walls.

Whittle suggests that the implements were dumped on the roofs of the houses while they were occupied, or kept in lofts or on the rafters (1986, 134). Alternatively it could be suggested that upon abandonment a ruined structure would have broken ard points and mattocks cast upon it as the fields were worked. Certain factors mitigate against these interpretations. First, the sheer quantity of these artefacts that are recovered, and second, their condition, which in many cases is unworn. Third, ard points and mattocks were found between successive floor levels at Sumburgh Airport and Jarlshof in instances where there had been no period of abandonment.

That these artefacts have symbolic significance has been recognised in recent years following the discovery that they are consistently located upon, or built into, the stone kerbs surrounding Bronze Age burial mounds in Orkney (M. Hedges 1979, Downes forthcoming). It is suggested that the introduction of these implements into the house prior to remodelling or abandonment of the house could be interpreted as a closing deposit. The symbolic qualities of tools which are used to break the ground and till the soil are perhaps associated with regeneration and fertility.

SPATIAL ORGANISATION AND ORIENTATION

To approach an interpretation of the experience of living in the Sumburgh Airport houses, we could start with the premise that every person and every community has an understanding of its place within the world (*ontology*) and a way of classifying that world in order to understand and affirm that place (*cosmology*). These classificatory systems, created and maintained by social practice, can be embodied within architecture and spatial organisation. As described above, materials and artefacts can also be used symbolically to express these concepts.

In southern Britain, from the late Bronze Age through the Iron Age, it appears that the majority of entrances to round houses were orientated to the east, in contrast to the houses of the middle Bronze Age which tend to be oriented to the south and south-south-east (Parker Pearson and Richards 1994). Within the Iron Age round houses, a consistency in the distribution of artefacts within the buildings has been recognised, wherein the majority of artefacts derive from the area around the porch and along the south-west side of the house (Fitzpatrick 1994; Giles and Parker Pearson, forthcoming; Parker Pearson 1996; Parker Pearson and Richards 1994).

This distribution of the artefacts has been interpreted as indicating that the right side of the houses (as one looks out from within) was a living area, and the left the sleeping area, while the threshold stands as the liminal place between outside and in (Fitzpatrick 1994). In these houses the hearth becomes a less permanent feature. The division of space within the house is seen as a manifestation of a classificatory system employing binary oppositions whereby the orientation toward the sunrise allows such distinctions as a light side and dark side to the house to be drawn. This and other oppositions have been interpreted as a microcosm of the ordering of the world (Fitzpatrick 1994; Parker Pearson and Richards 1994). Evidence from the Western Isles and southern Britain has been interpreted as showing that the house articulates both the succession of tasks – throughout the day, every day – and the annual activities undertaken outside the house (Giles and Parker Pearson, forthcoming).

These studies are important because, in exploring the role of architecture as a manifestation of order and classification, it is possible to infer meaning and describe social practices from the material residues (Parker Pearson and Richards 1994, 40). Portable artefacts are also used to assert order (Rapoport 1994), and the reflexive relationship between these and architecture has to be considered. The houses from Sumburgh Airport will be examined with reference to this framework of analysis, as Sumburgh Airport and other settlement evidence in Shetland should be more adequately placed within the context of British archaeology.

In the later Bronze Age phases at Sumburgh the entrances to both North and South Houses faced south. The distribution of artefacts certainly suggests craft activities and cooking were located in the south-west part of the South House. This spatial distinction is also discernible in both the North and South Houses in the early Iron Age phases. When the North House was rebuilt and the east-west passageway added, entry directly into the North House continued to be gained from the south, but entry to the South House was from the north. However, the addition of the east-west corridor had the effect that access from the *outside* was gained either from the east or the west.

It may be said that the paving over of the great central hearth within the South House, and the subsequent use of ill-formed hearths within the recesses of the North House demonstrates that the hearth was no longer a permanent and central feature of the house (although the same cannot be said for the evidence from Jarlshof). The aggrandisement of the northern entrance to the South House with its heel-shaped facade is perhaps evidence of an increased emphasis on the threshold or doorway as the pivotal feature of the house.

It is therefore possible to identify certain aspects of the orientation and spatial patterning observed in other parts of Britain, but there are significant differences. This is not to say that the evidence from Sumburgh Airport and Shetland as a whole should not be regarded in a wider context, but rather that ordering principles are not imposed from elsewhere and remain immutable. The principles are created through actions and are subject to reinterpretation and change.

The emphasis in terms of the experience of living within these long paired or courtyard houses would have been one of routinely negotiating a great depth of domestic space. Even if the courtyard was unroofed, the length of the passage to the inner part would have created a very dark interior.

In terms of orientation and access, the length of passage ways, the depth of deposits around the houses and the close proximity of one house to another, means that any orientation to the sunrise must have been notional, for the sun may never have penetrated the buildings. At Sumburgh Airport the separation of activities with a right/left division between working and sleeping areas, respectively, is not apparent, for in the later Bronze Age South House the right side is a through-passage. In the early Iron Age North House hearths occur in recesses at the rear and at the right and left of the house, making it hard to distinguish a binary opposition within daily activities.

There is evidence both from Sumburgh Airport and Jarlshof that animals spent some time within the houses, the most clear evidence being for cattle being stalled with the houses. This aspect is not one which has been adequately considered in studies of spatial organisation within later prehistoric houses, presumably because it is not thought that it was necessary to overwinter cattle indoors during the winter in most parts of Britain. Animals would have formed part of a classificatory system, and their place within the house would indicate how they were regarded.

Sites such as Sumburgh Airport, Jarlshof, Skara Brae were vulnerable to blown sand which could have devastating consequences, causing disruption within the houses and affecting the availability of land for cultivation and pasture. Sandblows and midden formed substantial deposits around the houses, with the result that deep space was encountered on two axes: not only were the Sumburgh Airport houses long in plan, but also one entered by going down into them from the surrounding raised platforms. Evidence from these platforms indicates that there was a correct place to undertake certain activities: coarse stone working and knapping quartz took place outside the house. These practices serve to remind us that "activities occur not only in buildings, but also in outdoor areas, settlements and beyond – in the whole cultural landscape" (Rapoport 1994, 462).

The change in architectural form from courtyard to round houses was a deliberate and sudden transformation of the use of space, and it is rare in Britain to define the 'transition' from the Bronze Age to the Iron Age with such clarity. The remodelling of the houses was not a response to accommodate a new range of technologies and crafts, for these were not introduced until after the form of the house had already changed. Although the relationship between people, architecture, and material culture is recursive, there is a point where a new order is imposed consciously by the community.

Through the analysis of the architecture and spatial organisation at Sumburgh Airport it has been possible to identify certain cosmological referents. However the incomparable quantity and quality of structural and artefactual remains in Shetland offer new dimensions and challenges to interpretation.

BIBLIOGRAPHY

Allen, R. O., Luckenbach, A. H. and Holland, C. G. 1975 'The application of instrumental neutron activation analysis to a study of prehistoric steatite artefacts and source materials', *Archaeometry* 17 (1975), 69–83.

Atkinson, S., Mulville, J. and Parker Pearson, M. 1996 *The Late Bronze Age and Early Iron Age settlement at Cladh Hallan, South Uist: excavations in 1996*. Desktop publication.

Barclay, G. J. 1996 'Neolithic Buildings in Scotland', *in* T. Darvill and J. Thomas (eds.) *Neolithic buildings in Northwest Europe and beyond*. Oxford: Oxbow Monograph 57, 61–75.

Batey, C. E. 1988 'Catalogue of finds from the Sands of Breckon, Yell, Shetland 59–84', unpublished report for AOC/Historic Scotland.

Bigelow, G. F. 1985 'Sandwick, Unst and Late Norse Shetland economy', *in* B. Smith (ed.) *Shetland archaeology*. Lerwick: Shetland Times, 95–127.

Binns, R. E. 1971 *The distribution and origin of pumice on postglacial strandlines in Northern Europe and the Western Arctic*.

Binns, R. E. 1972 'Pumice on postglacial strandlines and in prehistoric sites in the British Isles', *Scott J Geol* 8, 105–114.

Bray, I. S. J. 1994 'Geochemical methods for the provenancing studies of steatite', PhD thesis, University of Glasgow.

Bronk Ramsay C. 1995 'Radiocarbon calibration and analysis of stratigraphy. The OxCal programme' *Radiocarbon* 37 (2), 425–430.

Buteux, S. 1997 *Settlements at Skaill, Deerness, Orkney* Oxford: Brit Arch Rep British Series 260.

Buttler, S. J. 1984 'The steatite industry in Norse Shetland', PhD thesis, University of Liverpool.

Buttler, S. J. 1989 'Steatite in Norse Shetland', *Hikuin* 15, 193–206.

Buttler, S. J. in prep. 'Excavations at Clibberswick: a report on rescue work at a Norse quarry in Unst, Shetland, July-August 1983', *in* V. Turner (ed.) *Shetland steatite*. Monograph.

Calder, C. S. T. 1958 'Report on the discovery of numerous Stone Age house-sites in Shetland', *Proc Soc Antiq Scot* 89 (1955–56), 340–97.

Calder, C. S. T. 1963 'Excavations in Whalsay, Shetland, 1954–5', *Proc Soc Antiq Scot* 94, (1960–61) 28–45.

Callahan, E. 1987 'An evaluation of the lithic technology of Middle Sweden during the Mesolithic and Neolithic', *AUN* 8. Uppsala.

Childe, V. G. 1931 *Skara Brae: a Pictish village in Orkney*. London: Kegan Paul, Trench, Tubner.

Clarke, A. 1995 'Observations of Social Change in Prehistoric Orkney and Shetland based on a study of the Types and Context of Coarse Stone Artefacts', unpublished MLitt thesis, University of Glasgow.

Clarke, A. 1998 'The coarse stone' in Sharples N., 1998 *Scalloway: A broch, late Iron Age settlement and Medieval cemetery in Shetland* Oxbow Monograph 82

Clarke, D. V., Cowie, T. G. and Foxon, A. 1985 *Symbols of power at the time of Stonehenge.* Edinburgh: National Museum of Antiquities of Scotland.

Corrie, J. M. 1932 'Notes on a two-storeyed grave at Little Asta, Shetland', *Proc Soc Antiq Scot* 66, 69–75.

Cracknell, S. and Smith, B. 1983 'Archaeological investigations at Mavis Grind, Shetland', *Archaeol J* 10, 13–39.

Cunliffe, B. 1984 *Danebury: an Iron Age hill fort in Hampshire. Volume 2, the excavations, 1969–1978: the finds.* London: CBA Res Rep 52.

Curle, A. O. 1935 'An account of the excavation of another prehistoric dwelling (no. V) at Jarlshof, Sumburgh, Shetland, in the summer of 1934', *Proc Soc Antiq Scot* 69, 85–107.

Curle A. O. 1936 'Account of the excavation of a hut-circle with an associated earth-house at Jarlshof, Sumburgh, Shetland, conducted on behalf of H.M. Office of Works in 1935', *Proc Soc Antiq Scot* 70, 237–250.

Dalrymple, C. E. 1884 'Notes of the excavation of the stone circle at Crichie, Aberdeenshire', *Proc Soc Antiq Scot* 18, 319–25.

Downes J. forthcoming *Archaeological investigation of a middle Bronze Age cemetery at Linga Fiold, Sandwick, Orkney*

Ellison, A. 1987 'The Bronze Age settlement at Thorney Down: pots, post-holes and patterning', *Proc Preh Soc* 53: 385–92.

Fenton, A. 1963 'Early and traditional cultivating implements in Scotland', *Proc Soc Antiq Scot* 96, 264–317.

Finlayson, B. 1991 'Flint reports', *in* J. Hunter and S. Dockrill (eds.) *Pool and Tofts Ness, Sanday, Orkney*, unpublished ms. for AOC/Historic Scotland.

Finlayson, B. 1992 'Lithic report on the flint and quartz from Lairg', unpublished report for AOC/Historic Scotland.

Finlayson, B., Finlay, N. and Mithen, S. 1996 'Mesolithic chipped stone assemblages: descriptive and analytical procedures used by the Southern Hebrides Project', *in* T. Pollard and A. Morrison (eds.) *The Early Prehistory of Scotland*. Edinburgh: Edinburgh University Press, 252–66

Finlayson, B. in press. 'A contribution', *in* D. Johnston (ed.) *Biggar Common 1988–92: an early prehistoric ritual, mortuary and domestic landscape in Clydesdale.*

Fitzpatrick, A. P. 1994 'Outside in: the structure of an early Iron Age house at Dunston Park, Thatcham, Berkshire', in A. P. Fitzpatrick and E. L. Morris (eds.) *The Iron Age in Wessex: recent work*. Salisbury: Association Française d'Étude de l'Âge du Fer/Trust for Wessex Archaeology, 68–72.

Fojut, N. 1993 *A guide to prehistoric and Viking Shetland*. Lerwick: Shetland Times.

Giles, M. and Parker Pearson, M. forthcoming. 'Learning to live in the Iron Age: dwelling and praxis', *in* W. Bevan (ed.) *Northern Exposure: interpretive evolution and the Iron Age in Britain.*

Gordon, G. and Mitchell, A. 1877 'Notice of incised sculpturings at Feideland, the extreme north of the mainland of Shetland', *Proc Soc Antiq Scot* 11, 202–5.

Gordon, K. 1990 'Norse Viking Age grave from Cruach Mhor, Islay', *Proc Soc Antiq Soc* 120, 151–160.

Hamilton, J. R. C. 1956 *Excavations at Jarlshof, Shetland*. Edinburgh: Ministry of Public Works Archaeol Rep 1.

Hamilton, J. R. C. 1959 'Food vessel cist at Doune, Perthshire', *Proc Soc Antiq Scot* 90, 231–34.
Hamilton, J. R. C. 1968 *Excavations at Clickhimin, Shetland*. Edinburgh: Ministry of Public Works Archaeol Rep 6.
Hamilton, J. 1991 'Excavation of a cairn at Wind Hamars, Outnabreck Hill, Scalloway, Shetland', *Proc Soc Antiq Scot* 121, 45–50.
Hansen, H. 1969 'Experimental ploughing with a Dostrup Ard replica', *Tools and Tillage* 1: 2, 67–92.
Hayden, B. 1980 'Confusion in the bipolar world: bashed pebbles and splintered pieces', *Lithic Technology* 9 (1): 2–6.
Hedges, J. W. 1986 'Bronze Age structures at Tougs, Burra Isle, Shetland', *Glasgow Archaeol J* 13 1–43.
Hedges, J. W. and Parry, G. W. 1980 A Neolithic multiple burial at Sumburgh Airport, Shetland', *Glasgow Archaeol. J.* 9, 15–26.
Hedges, M. E. 1979 'The excavation of the Knowes of Quoyscottie, Orkney', *Proc Soc Antiq Scot* 108 (1976–7), 130–55.
Henshall, A. S. 1958 'Appendix II: pottery and stone implements from Ness of Gruting', *in* Calder 1958, 381–97.
Henshall, A. S. 1963a 'Appendix: the finds', *in* Calder 1963, 40–45.
Henshall, A. S. 1963b *The chambered tombs of Scotland 1*. Edinburgh: Edinburgh Univ.y Press.
Hunter, J. R. 1986 *Rescue excavations on the Brough of Birsay 1974–82*. Edinburgh: Soc Antiq Scot Monograph Series 4.
Knight, J. 1991 'Technological analysis of the anvil (bipolar) technique', *Lithics* 12, 57–73
Lamb, R. G. 1985 'Sumburgh: Prehistory under sand', *in* B. Smith (ed.) *Shetland archaeology*. Lerwick: Shetland Times, 27-46.
Lowe C. and Owen O. in press *Kebister: The four thousand year old story of one Shetland township* Soc Antiq Scot monograph
MacGregor, A. 1972 'The Broch of Burrian, North Ronaldsay, Orkney', *Proc Soc Aniq Scot* 105, 63–118.
Marwick, H. 1951 'Notes of archaeological remains found in Orkney', *Proc Soc Antiq Scot* 83, 236–40.
McCrie, G. M. 1881 'Notice of the discovery of an urn of steatite in one of the five tumuli excavated at Corquoy, in the island of Rousay, Orkney', *Proc Soc Antiq Scot* 15, 71–3.
Megaw, J. V. S. and Simpson, D. D. A. (eds.) 1979 *Introduction to British prehistory*. Leicester: Leicester University Press.
Mercer, J. 1970 'A regression-time stone-workers' camp, 33 ft OD, Lussa River, Isle of Jura', *Proc Soc Antiq Scot* 103, 1–32.
MacSween A. and Dalland M. *The coarse pottery* in Lowe and Owen in press.
Moffat, D. and Buttler, S. J. 1986 'Rare earth element distribution patterns in Shetland steatite – consequences for artefact provenancing studies', *Archaeometry* 28(1), 101-15.
Mykura, W. 1976 *British regional geology: Orkney and Shetland*. Edinburgh: HMSO.
Nicholson R. A. and Dockrill S. J. 1998 *Old Scatness Broch, Shetland: Retrospect and Prospect* Bradford Archaeological Sciences Research 5 NABO Monograph No 2
Parker Pearson, M. 1996 'Food, fertility and front doors in the first millenium B.C.', *in* Champion, T. C. and Collis, J. R. (eds.) *The Iron Age in Britain and Ireland: recent trends*. Sheffield: J.R. Collis Publications, 117–32.
Parker Pearson, M. and Richards, C. 1994 'Architecture and order: spatial representation and archaeology', *in* M. Parker Pearson and C. Richards (eds.) *Architecture and order: approaches to social space*. London: Routledge, 38-72.

Parker Pearson, M., Sharples, N. and Mulville, J. 1996 'Brochs and Iron Age society: a reappraisal', *Antiquity* 70, 57–67

PCRG 1995 *Prehistoric Ceramics Research Group guidelines for the studies of later prehistoric pottery.* Oxford: Prehistoric Ceramics Research Group.

Pilø, L. 1990 'Early soapstone vessels in Norway from the Late Bronze Age to the Early Roman Iron Age', *Acta Archaeologica* 60, 87–100.

Rapoport, A. 1994 'Spatial organization and the built environment', *in* T. Ingold (ed.) *Companion encyclopedia of anthropology.* London: Routledge, 460–502.

Rees, S. E. 1979 *Agricultural implements in prehistoric and Roman Britain.* Oxford: Brit Arch Rep British Series 69.

Rees, S. E. 'Stone implements and artefacts' in Whittle (ed.) 1986, 75–92.

Resi, H. G. 1979 'Die Specksteinfunde aus Haithabu', *in* K. Schietzel (ed.) *Berichte über die Ausgrabungen in Haithabu* 14. Neumünster: Wachholtz.

Ritchie, P. R. 1968 'The stone implement trade in third millennium Scotland', *in* J. M. Coles, and D. D. A. Simpson (eds.) *Studies in ancient Europe: essays presented to Stuart Piggott.* Leicester: Leicester University Press, 128–33.

Ritchie, P. R. 1984 'Soapstone quarrying in Viking lands', *in* A. Fenton and H. Palsson (eds.) *The northern and western isles in the Viking world: survival, continuity and change.* Edinburgh: Donald, 59–84.

Ritchie, A. 1995 *Prehistoric Orkney.* London: Batsford/Historic Scotland.

Roe, F. E. S. 1966 'The battle-axe series in Britain', *Proc Prehist Soc* 32, 199–245.

Rogers, M., Allen, R., Nagle, C. and Fitzhugh, W. 1983 'The utilization of rare earth element concentrations for the characterization of soapstone quarries', *Archaeometry* 25(2), 186–95.

Schiffer M. B. 1987 *Formation processes of the archaeological record* Albuquerque: University of New Mexico Press.

Scott, W. L. 1950–51 'Eilean an Tighe: a pottery workshop of second millenium BC', *Proc Soc Anitq Scot* 85, 1–37.

Sharman, P. M. 1990 'The Tuquoy steatite report', unpublished report for AOC/Historic Scotland.

Sharman, P. M. 1989 'The steatite' in Lowe and Owen in press.

Sharman, P. M. in prep. 'Catpund, Cunningsburgh, Shetland: excavations 1988 and 1990. Report on Area D finds and all other steatite', *in* V. Turner (ed.) *Shetland steatite.* Monograph.

Simpson, I. A., Dockrill S. J. and Lancaster S. J. 'Making arable soils: anthropogenic soil formation in a multi-period landscape' in Nicholson and Dockrill 1998, 111–126.

Small, A. 1967 'Excavations at Underhoull, Unst, Shetland', *Proc Soc Antiq Scot* 98, 225–48.

Smith, A. N. forthcoming. 'The steatite vessel fragments from Tofts Ness, Sanday, Orkney', *in* Hunter, J. R., Dockrill, S. J., Bond, J. M. and Smith, A. N. (eds.) *Archaeological investigations on Sanday*, Soc Ant Scot Monograph.

Stevenson, R. B. K. 1939 'Report on the pottery in Calder, CST excavations of Iron Age dwellings on the Calf of Eday in Orkney', *Proc Soc Antiq Scot* 73, 167–85.

Turnbaugh, W. A., Turnbaugh, S. P. and Keifer, T. H. 1984 'Characterization of selected soapstone sources in southern New England', *in* J. P. Ericson and B. A. Purdy (eds.) *Prehistoric quarries and lithic production.* Cambridge, 129–38.

Whittle, A. W. R. (ed.) 1986 *Scord of Brouster: an early agricultural settlement on Shetland. Excavations 1977–79.* Oxford: Oxford Univ Cttee Archaeol Monograph 9.

Wickham-Jones, C. 1990 *Rhum: Mesolithic and later sites at Kinloch: excavations 1984–86*, Soc Ant Scot Monograph Series 7.